T0283272

Joyce Carol Oates
Letters to a Biographer

selected and edited by
Greg Johnson

BROOKLYN, NEW YORK

Published by Akashic Books
©2024 The Ontario Review Inc.

ISBN: 978-1-63614-116-9
Library of Congress Control Number: 2023946350

All rights reserved
First printing

Akashic Books
Brooklyn, New York
Instagram, X, Facebook: AkashicBooks
info@akashicbooks.com
www.akashicbooks.com

To the memory of Frederic and Carolina Oates
—Greg Johnson

To Greg, without whom there
would be no book of letters at all
—Joyce Carol Oates

Think where man's glory most begins and ends,
and say my glory was I had such friends.
—W.B. Yeats

Contents

Preface

My correspondence with Joyce Carol Oates began in 1975 and has continued for almost half a century. When it began, Oates was already one of the most famous writers in America—winner of the National Book Award in 1970 (for *them*) and several O. Henry awards, and her stories were also included in multiple *Best American Short Stories* volumes. She was also a prolific literary and cultural critic, her essays often serving as a reflection, or a kind of gloss, on her plentiful and powerful fictions. Taken together, all her novels, stories, and essays revealed a dynamic mind at work, and a vision of America—for that matter, of human existence—that presumably comported with those of her many readers.

An undergraduate at the time I first read her, I found her work enthralling, especially in depicting the effects of a chaotic modern world upon the solitary, often flailing psyches of her characters. She wrote superbly well about girls and women—her tale of a young girl in peril, "Where Are You Going, Where Have You Been?", is one of the most celebrated short stories of the twentieth century—but equally well about men, as in her sprawling and masterly 1971 novel

Wonderland. Her forceful prose style—driving, daring, relentless—was as distinctive as her individual works were aesthetically unique as works of art. Each was different, and yet unmistakably her own.

My first letter to Oates in 1975 concerned a professor of mine who had committed suicide, and the letter inspired a prompt, empathetic response. Over the next few years, I wrote to her occasionally, usually about a new book she had written, and was always gratified that she responded so swiftly. She was then teaching at the University of Windsor in Ontario, while I was graduate student at Southern Methodist University in Dallas, Texas. By virtue of gender, upbringing, location, and station in life, we could not have been more different, yet we saw much in both art and life the same way, and as the years passed our letters increased in their length and frequency. We corresponded not only about her books, but as I began to write and publish, about my own; more broadly, we wrote about other authors and about literature in general.

As we came to be friends, occasionally meeting in Atlanta, Princeton, and New York, our frame of reference grew. Because of her success, she had come to know many famous people, and these letters contain vignettes about such diverse luminaries as John Updike, Philip Roth, Toni Morrison, Jacqueline Kennedy Onassis, and Steve Martin. There are, further, brief cameos by Joan Didion, Susan Sontag, Norman Mailer, Cynthia Ozick, Stephen King, and many others of note. After deciding to research and write Oates's authorized biography, which was published in 1998, I also came in contact with many of her friends in Princeton and elsewhere.

As the letters proceed through the late 1970s, the 1980s, the 1990s, and beyond, they also encompass personal matters, not least among them our relationships with our beloved animals—her cats, my dachshunds. When she traveled around the world giving talks, lectures, and readings, I often received postcards from exotic locations in Europe and elsewhere. With her second husband, the renowned and peripatetic Princeton neuroscientist Charlie Gross, she visited South America as well. In recent years, Oates began sending me new works of hers before they were published, and I would comment on these to the best of my ability. We often exchanged cards and gifts for birthdays and at Christmas. In all, through occasional visits but especially through our thousands of letters, faxes, emails, and cards, a friendship evolved that was close and meaningful to us both.

The following selection of letters shows Oates at her most relaxed; she is often serious in her concerns, but at other times wickedly funny. (Her sense of humor has been somewhat undervalued by literary critics over the years.) The letters form a kind of narrative, especially of the books we wrote but also of the people most important to us. Oates's parents, Frederic and Carolina Oates, are major characters in this narrative, and I am deeply grateful that I was able to know and revere them during the last years of their lives.

Unfortunately, many letters have been excluded or shortened; a full collection would run to more than a thousand pages. In this edited sampling, however, I have tried to show the essential Oates: witty, humane, and splendidly articulate. One of her friends (and critics), John Updike, once called her America's "foremost" woman of letters, and the following collection should only confirm that assessment.

Greg Johnson
January 2024

Introduction

Nothing is so unnerving as glancing into the past, seeing again as in a fever dream snatches of an old, lost life, now irretrievable; hearing again old, once-familiar names, recalling old, once-fresh incidents now faded like Polaroids. The task of confronting the past is overwhelming to some (of us), whose lives are attuned to a total immersion in the present: the writer, like any artist, lives most intensely in the present tense, and dares to look back, into the rearview mirror, at her own risk.

Greg Johnson has gathered together a remarkable collection of prolonged glances into the past, bathed in a sort of warm convivial glow. Our long friendship, essentially though not totally epistolary, began when Greg was *very* young; indeed, so was I, relatively speaking.

(It's a stunning fact, evidently, that at the age of thirty-seven, I had only given two previous public readings in my life; this I would doubt, except that I am sure Greg is correct. I do remember the visit to Miami University in Ohio, where I'd met Greg for the first time; but details of the visit commingle with subsequent visits to Ohio University in Athens where, for a brief spell, for some reason now unclear, my husband Ray and I had actually considered moving, from the University of Windsor.)

Through my life I have never really expected anything like a continuum of the kind that constitutes a narrative—that is, a continuum of a kind of which individual incidents are linked together by thematic necessity, not mere chance. When my first book of stories, *By the North Gate,* was accepted for publication by Vanguard Press in 1961, I did not seriously think—I could not have dared even to hope—that there would be a second book, let alone a third or a fourth; such a fantastic fluke of luck, it seemed to me at the time, would not likely be repeated. I am not exaggerating when I say that if I'd been told in 1963, when *By the North Gate,* with its handsome cloth cover, was finally published, that a long succession of book titles would follow this first, modest title, stretching through decades into the sci-fi domain of the twenty-first century, I would have laughed incredulously; I would have been literally incapable of believing it; perhaps, I would not even have wished to believe it.

As I'd explained to Margaret Atwood, who is of my generation, and shares much history with me from my years in Canada, I've always been a dreamy adolescent: my essential age has never really matured beyond fourteen. Entering a library, one of the sacrosanct places of my life, I found myself entranced like Alice in Wonderland, as a child; shelves of books, so many books, so many authors, and all of them *published.* I could not have imagined that my own name would be among them one day, a row of books on a shelf. Even now, such a sight seems like a violation of reality, common sense. How can I, Joyce, see my name on published books, when I am still fourteen, still dreamy and yearning? How is this possible?

(I avoid library shelves containing my books, my eye simply shrinks away. I have learned a strategy for approaching *Nabokov, V.* and *O'Connor, F.* in a kind of slant-eyed manner, managing to avoid *Oates.*)

So it is, these lovingly assembled letters present a conundrum to me. I am drawn by curiosity to read them even as I feel a strong urge to shrink away, shut my eyes. Hurtling nearly fifty years into the past is—vertiginous. I can certainly recognize the voice of the letters, which has hardly changed, I can usually recall the circumstances, but I find the very existence of the letters somewhat painful to confront: the young, naïve self, unknowing of what is to come, nearly always so enthusiastic, optimistic; and so energetic!

Reading these letters in chronological order is to experience my life flashing before my eyes. Without this jolt to my memory I would not have recalled that in 1988, in our house on Honey Brook Drive, Princeton, Ray and I threw a party to which Maureen Howard, Richard Ford, and Barry Hannah all came, along with more likely writer friends like Russell Banks and Dan Halpern; that Richard would apologize for his friend Barry who no longer had anything interesting to say, since he'd stopped drinking. I would not have recalled that a play titled *The Murder of Joyce Carol Oates* had once been performed in Los Angeles (!). I do recall with much pleasure my collaboration with the great filmmaker Martin Scorsese, on an adaptation of my novel *You Must Remember This* (which was never made); my dear, brilliant, and beloved editor at Dutton, William (Billy) Abrahams, a legend in publishing circles in his time; my association with the lively, inspiring, generously funded Louisville Humana Festival of New American Plays, where several plays of mine premiered, and my similarly rewarding association with L.A. Theatre Works through the 1990s.

There are fleeting glimpses here of my working life: my

completion of *Blonde,* at a staggering 1,400 pages (which I then cut to a more navigable 900), in 1999; my collaboration on a screenplay adapted from *American Appetites,* with a famous Hollywood actor (whose name I don't reveal in the letter; it was Dustin Hoffman); my relief that three novel manuscripts which had been purchased by Dutton could be withdrawn by me, to be replaced by three novels which I believed to be much better. (The withdrawn manuscripts, whose titles I won't list, are preserved in Syracuse University's Special Collections Research Center, where I hope no one ever discovers them.) It merits a pained smile to note, in passing, that my entering salary at the University of Detroit was $4,900! (I loved teaching there, whatever the salary.)

Very funny to recall that my novel *Foxfire* was once banned in a school in a Toronto suburb, described by an excited Christian parent as an "imported sex manual." (There are no erotic scenes in the novel at all.) Very funny to recall Margaret Atwood, invited to Princeton, asked in the aftermath of her presentation a question that made everyone cringe: "Do you think you will ever write about anything other than Canada?" (This, a near-perfect analog with the question Toni Morrison was once asked after a Princeton reading: "Do you think you will ever write about anything other than race?") Very funny to recall sharing a stage with Kurt Vonnegut in February 2006 under the auspices of the Connecticut Forum, during which Kurt regaled the audience of 2,500 persons, many of them from high school classes, with his bleak, seriocomic pessimism:

> . . . *intoning like a Buddha/tortoise, "Humankind is a disease. We're like syphilis, we should be stamped out." The high school students stared & took notes. No one seemed to think that Vonnegut might not be*

entirely serious . . . At the evening's event in an enor-
mous theater in Hartford, he continued in this vein,
oracular even when silly. Asked what was the mean-
ing of the universe, Kurt said, "The meaning of the
universe? Why ask me? I'm full of baloney."

Funny, also, to learn that at one point I'd thought that
We Were the Mulvaneys would be the last "ambitious" novel
I would write; then I'd thought that *Blonde* would be the last
"ambitious" novel I would write; subsequently I'd thought
that *The Gravedigger's Daughter* would be the final "ambitious" novel of my life. But sad that I'd had so little faith in
Missing Mom, my attempt to write a "women's novel," that
I'd doubted it should be published at Ecco or even under
my own name. (Eventually, I came around to reevaluating
Missing Mom, and now find it one of my novels closest to my
heart, as it is a fairly realistic portrait of my mother; though
the man to whom the mother is married in the novel is not
my father.)

Many thanks to Greg Johnson for saving these letters,
and those many, many more not included in this volume. In-
advertently, unwittingly, through the years Greg and I seem
to have composed a kind of double portrait that, at the outset, in 1975, neither of us could possibly have imagined; nor
could I have imagined that Greg would be my primary correspondent through most of my adult life. How ideal to have
a friend who is a prompt, warmly engaging, and always-
interesting correspondent, not unlike those legendary letter
writers of old, when letter writing was an integral part of
our emotional lives.

Joyce Carol Oates
January 2024

Part One

1975–1990

In the summer of 1975, when I was a newly minted MA graduate at Southern Methodist University, I received my first substantial letter from Joyce Carol Oates. What prompted this first letter?

A few weeks earlier, I had written her about an undergraduate creative writing professor of mine who had recently committed suicide by throwing himself from an overpass into Dallas expressway traffic. I was naturally dismayed and upset; the situation reminded me of an Oates short story. And I suppose I felt that she would commiserate, since I knew from a 1972 Newsweek *cover story on her career that she had enjoyed a fulfilling student-teacher relationship with her own undergraduate professor of creative writing, Donald Dike. I had also taken the opportunity to write of my admiration for her most recent collection of short stories,* The Poisoned Kiss *(1975), and to describe my current circumstances, since after my graduation from SMU, I was interested in pursuing a PhD so I could teach at the university level.*

At this time, Joyce was living in Windsor, Ontario, and teaching at the University of Windsor. Her 1969 novel, them, *had won the National Book Award in 1970. She had already published more than a dozen books and was famous for both the quality and quantity of her work. In a 1972 essay in the* Atlantic, *the literary journalist Joe David Bellamy had called her "the Dark Lady of American Letters." I don't remember what kind of answer to my letter I might have expected, if any, but was gratified by her warm and gracious response.*

6 August 1975

Dear Greg Johnson:

I have read and contemplated your very interesting, and very moving, letter of July 14. It's difficult for me to make any comment on your former professor (whose work I don't know, unfortunately) and what happened to him; such events remain mysteries, and similar experiences in my own life have never really seemed clear to me . . . not even after many years. The suicide acts, perhaps, according to an inner pattern or life-story which no one else can comprehend. Nor can we judge others, though it is always a temptation.

In the end, we each do what we wish, what we *will*. The exterior world cannot understand.

Thank you for your comments on my work. What you say about *Poisoned Kiss* is interesting; I still feel, years later, that the entire experience of the "Fernandes" personality was an unsettling one, which I would not care to repeat, but I'm grateful to have had it.

You must be a very perceptive and stimulating teacher, judging from your letter. I wish you luck for the future, and I hope you enjoy many lively, productive years. There is nothing quite like teaching, in my opinion.

Sincerely,
Joyce Carol Oates

In January 1976, I moved from Dallas, Texas, to Atlanta, Georgia, where I had been accepted into the doctoral program at Emory University. In April, having become steeped in Joyce's work, I traveled to Miami University in Oxford, Ohio, to attend a reading she gave to a packed audience. Until then, Joyce had been considered a relatively reclusive figure; though she was thirty-seven, this was only the third public lecture she had given. I was extremely impressed not only by the work she read but by her casual, pleasant manner and her deadpan sense of humor.

This was our first meeting in person. Shortly before then, I had begun writing short stories, and a few months later I submitted a deliberately Kafkaesque piece to Joyce and her husband, Raymond J. Smith, who edited and published the literary magazine Ontario Review *from their home in Windsor. I had published only two stories previously, so I was naturally very pleased when Joyce and Ray accepted the manuscript.*

By June 1978, the couple had moved to Princeton, New Jersey, where in the fall of 1978 Joyce had begun a supposedly temporary teaching job at Princeton University. But she loved the university, its surroundings, and her stimulating colleagues, and she would remain at Princeton until the present day.

In the following letter, she speaks of her linked short story collection All the Good People I've Left Behind *(1979), about which I had written her shortly after the book came out. She also mentions her "next novel,"* Unholy Loves, *an academic satire published in 1979, and speaks of "a more recent novel set in New York (around NYU)." But this latter novel, entitled* Jigsaw, *was never published, becoming a victim of the increasingly crowded "logjam" (as she often termed it) of her unpublished manuscripts. By now, Joyce was moving somewhat away from her trademark psychological realism (I had mentioned this in a letter to her) into the "magical realism" of the next five novels she would write, a "quintet" of long works, beginning with* Bellefleur *(1980), which explored, as she put it, "America as viewed through the prismatic lens of its most popular genres."*

June 18, 1979

Dear Greg:

It was delightful to hear from you.

Yes, we plan tentatively to remain in Princeton another

year. Everything has worked out well—despite some initial difficulties with the magazine (our printer is in British Columbia).

I'm not exactly aware of a change of tone or voice in my writing, but that's probably as it should be . . . Different subjects require different voices; content demands its own particular form; or so I *think* . . . I find it significant that you chose to work on Emily Dickinson [for my dissertation], unquestionably one of the finest (and most enigmatic) poets of all time. How different she and Whitman are, yet both completely "American." There has certainly been a great deal of biographical nonsense published about her. I wonder what you think of the Sewall biography—its exceptional length, its astonishing details—!

The *Paris Review* interview went very well, primarily because an old friend, Bob Phillips, interviewed me. So there weren't any silly or irrelevant questions. It's my most personal and accurate statement about myself, and I am hoping it will make future interviews unnecessary; the process is not only a time-consuming one, it's absurdly self-conscious. I liked the Joan Didion interview very much (strangely, she was interviewed by Linda Kuehl, who was the first literary journalist to interview me, many years ago; I was shocked to hear that she had committed suicide). Margaret Drabble, an old (but now rather distant) friend, said some fascinating things too.

I did like Annie Quirt of *All the Good People* . . . and am pleased that you responded to her. My next novel might interest you because it is set on a university campus (not Cornell, not Bennington, but near Lake Champlain in upstate New York, a prestigious university not quite on the level of Harvard/Princeton/Yale) and deals, in part, with the problem of an intellectual class deprived, by economic circumstances, of employment, and power . . . but this is only a kind of subtheme in the novel. I've treated the theme at greater length in a more recent novel set in New York (around NYU) but I'm not certain whether I want that novel published next, or another. This problem—of a highly educated and disenfranchised intellectual elite, an entire generation (or more)—is one of our most serious problems. The other week I received an offer from a university, a very high salary, only one course to teach, and I responded by saying—why not hire two or even three young PhDs for that salary, and forget about "JCO"? But no response.

. . . If you'd like a recommendation for a college or university position, I would be happy to write one for you. (I have not seen the review of *Son of the Morning* yet. I agree about organized religion—it's difficult not to become rather depressed, or wildly amused, by some of its manifestations.)

All good wishes,
Joyce

・・

In the spring of 1983, I sent Joyce a photo of myself and my closest friend, Ernest White, who had died in December at age 31 of complications from HIV/AIDS. She sent me the following letter of consolation in response.

6/17/83

Dear Greg:

Thank you for writing, and for the photograph. I'm haunted by it—the warmth and obvious happiness represented in it, and the extraordinary pain and suffering that followed. Please accept my sincere condolences. I'm really very, very sorry to hear of your friend's death. Judging from the picture he really did radiate something special. It's a pity—a senseless loss—that he had to die so young.

These extraordinary events force us to realize that we don't at all control our own lives, let alone our "destinies." The diseases we suppose to be curable are only curable because of some little-understood chemistry in our bodies which, if it gives out, leaves us totally defenseless. "Medicine" and "science" are finally quite inadequate . . .

We hope you will keep in touch, and that we can publish something of yours before long. Our primary problem—one I gather is shared by numerous editors right now—is that we have a considerable backlog of good material, and are usually very reluctant to accept more.

Ray joins me in sending our warmest regards and sympathy.

All best wishes,
Joyce

The next substantial letter from Joyce came the following summer, and alludes to her friend Kay Smith, who died unexpectedly at a relatively young age. Kay was a troubled but vibrant woman in Joyce's circle of female friends in the Detroit area, during the years Joyce taught at the University of Windsor. Of all her friends during those years, Kay was probably the closest.

Joyce also alludes here to a review I published of the correspondence between Austin Dickinson, Emily Dickinson's brother, and Mabel Loomis Todd, a younger woman with whom he conducted a passionate love affair in the 1880s. An ongoing feature of my correspondence with Joyce was a back-and-forth discussion of books we had read (and often reviewed).

7/4/84

Dear Greg:

It was good to hear from you. Your letters are always extremely interesting, and welcome.

What you say about your bereavement reminds me of Hemingway's description of his own "death" when he was wounded as a young man. His soul, he said, seemed to come out of his body like a silk handkerchief pulled out of a pocket. It flew around, then came back again, and he was "alive." The image always haunted me powerfully. I'm sure Hemingway was telling the truth—and *he* was never the same person again.

I've only glanced at the new *Georgia Review* but I did read your review of the Austin/Mabel letters. It seems the most balanced of all the reviews of the book I've come across: the eerie self-inflation of Mabel, the genuine interest of the affair itself as illuminating a curious corner of history. I recently read the massive Virginia Woolf/Vita Sackville-West collection of letters, which might be of interest to you too, at least in part. I found it quite a memorable experience, and though the book is long (600 pages) it somehow isn't long enough. Virginia's death comes so abruptly.

It may be that you can never write directly about your loss, but you are probably writing about it, all the same. I did experience something comparable—though the person was not so close to me—an old friend who had always seemed healthy in all senses, happy, energetic, content—who died in a manner not quite natural yet not technically suicide either. Her name was Kay Smith; we were extremely close when I lived in Detroit and Windsor. Whenever things are discouraging for me (and they frequently are: I seem to be the butt of all sorts of stray ill humors and downright malice, as if the mere fact of my writing and publishing angers some people) my thoughts drift onto Kay, and I think of the utter mystery of her death, which means her life as well; all our lives, probably; that we don't really know each other—apart from the cliché it happens to be true. And that *is* depressing.

People who try to cheer one another up always seem to me misguided. However well-intentioned . . . It's like telling someone not to mind, his broken leg will mend in a few months. But it hurts while it hurts. And afterward the memory itself hurts.

I hope your summer is enjoyable. I don't have any readings planned until October, in California. Ray says hello too—

Joyce

⤸

The following January, I sent Joyce and Ray a new short story I had written called "Distant Friends" as a submission to Ontario Review. *It would become the title story of a collection of stories, my first book of fiction, which the couple would publish in 1990. They had recently started a small publishing house, Ontario Review Press, whose primary mission was discovering and promoting new writers. Before* Distant Friends *appeared, however, I had published my first book of nonfiction, a critical study of Emily Dickinson's poetry, a copy of which I sent to Joyce. She responded via the following postcard.*

12/7/85

Dear Greg:

Thanks so much for your superb *Emily Dickinson: Perception and the Poet's Quest.* I had not wanted to read it until I completed a long essay I was commissioned to do on Dickinson (for the 1986 E.D. Conference at the U. of North Carolina—will you be attending?) for fear—justly, as it turned out—of being unduly influenced by it. It's very well done: my congratulations! (As to E.D.—she *is* inexhaustible, isn't she?) I hope you are well. Things are fine here, pleasantly busy as usual. (Have you ever applied to Princeton for a position?)

Best wishes,
Joyce

꙳

In the following letter, enclosed in a Christmas card, Joyce refers to a recommendation she had sent on my behalf to the University of Georgia. "Charles" is Charles Willingham, a friend of mine she met during her visit to Emory, and "Freddie" was my dog, a miniature dachshund.

12/18/86

Dear Greg:

Ray and I are sorry to be returning this extremely interesting and well-written story, but we are seriously logjammed with material and seem to be accepting only about 1 submission out of 80 to 100 these days. It is an impossible situation, and I'm afraid it will get worse. Please don't be discouraged from trying us again sometime, particularly with a shorter story. We do look forward to publishing you again.

This card is to wish you Season's Greetings. I received a very nice note from the chairman at Georgia, thanking me for my recommendation and telling me how impressed they were with you. So we'll keep our fingers crossed . . .

All is well here, though the holiday season seems to be busier than usual. I will be participating in a special session—as it's called—of the MLA on the 28th, on the new formalism in poetry. Three weeks ago Ray and I flew to Las Vegas (!) courtesy of *Life* magazine, which talked me into doing a feature story on Mike Tyson, the 20-year-old heavyweight title holder. (I suspect you don't approve of boxing—but to me it's a multifaceted thing, a phenomenon of our culture; not a sport in the usual sense of the word. Not a sport, really, at all.) Apart from these excursions we plan to stay close to home for months.

We hope you're well, and will have a happy Christmas. Please remember us to Charles. And give Freddie a special hug.

Warm regards,
Joyce

In the winter of 1987, I was working on my first book-length critical study of Joyce's work, to be published in the fall. Entitled Understanding Joyce Carol Oates, *it was an overview of Joyce's fiction from 1963–1986. I was having trouble getting permission to quote from her work, and had asked if she would intercede. Also in this letter she refers to what she calls her "pseudonymous adventure"—i.e., her decision to publish a book under the pen name of Rosamond Smith, a name she thought, perhaps naïvely, might shield her from critical presuppositions that attended each new book published by "Oates." (Her cover was blown in a newspaper article by the late gossip columnist Liz Smith.)*

In the last paragraph of this letter, she included a startling bit of information that had me watching my mailbox for days afterward. Jacqueline Kennedy Onassis, an editor at Doubleday, did write to me about my fiction, and subsequently my agent at that time, Diane Cleaver, sent her a manuscript of short stories; but Mrs. Onassis could not get enough support from her publishing colleagues to make an offer on the book—the collection was simply not "commercial" enough. Though this response was not unexpected, it was a major disappointment in my writing life.

2/22/87

Dear Greg:

I wish you had written to me sooner if you are having trouble with permissions . . . For one thing, many of my Vanguard titles are now out of print, and Vanguard does not hold copyright anyway. And I believe I could intercede for you easily at Dutton.

Why not, then, simply go forward with your use of quotes? You may say that I have given you permission. I don't believe that critical books are really obliged to pay fees for reprinting brief passages from books; I've published several [volumes of criticism], and this has never been an issue. So—why not go ahead? I can assure you that nothing will come of it.

Yes, the pseudonymous adventure proved dispiriting in the end. I had truly wanted a new identity—a minor, even modest, undetectable one, far from the associations I now seem to carry with me everywhere, like Kafka's Gregor Samsa the various objects of his doom (embedded in his beetle-back)! I am being rather extreme, and don't, I suppose, really mean it—since, after all, at least the majority of the associations are "good"—but, still, the metaphor has some poetic validity.

You may be hearing from an unlikely correspondent

soon: a former First Lady of such renown and notoriety she, or her image, appears often in that most populist of popular publications, the *National Enquirer*. Don't be surprised! ...

Warm regards,
Joyce

⊸◐

Our correspondence through the rest of 1987 mostly concerned her positive reaction to my book Understanding Joyce Carol Oates, *a copy of which she'd sent to her parents, by whom it was, she wrote in November, "if possible, even more appreciated! My mother and father remain my most enthusiastic and happily uncritical readers"; and with my search for a university teaching position. In December I interviewed for a tenure-track position in American literature and creative writing at the University of Mississippi, and was offered the job in January.*

2 February 1988

Dear Greg:

Your news about the Mississippi appointment is absolutely splendid—both Ray and I are delighted. It's as welcome a bit of information as any we've received in many months—and I should say that we seem to have received a goodly number of pleasant bits of news lately, ranging from Press/career things to the fact that, the other day, our beautiful calico Christabel, missing for over 24 hours, and more or less given up on, suddenly reappeared—perfectly healthy, but saying not a word about where she'd been. We also had a 5-day visit to San Francisco last week every moment of which was idyllic: we had a lovely dinner with Alice Adams (with whom you've corresponded?—poor Alice, the nicest of women, has just gone through a ghastly and protracted breakup with a man with whom she had been living for years), Diane Johnson (whom I had not met previously—her friends call her "Dinny" and she too is exceedingly nice), and my editor William Abrahams (newly off crutches from a knee operation and flushed with happiness regarding the wholly deserved success of his newest book, Thomas Flanagan's *The Tenants of Time*—which Ray and I are eager to read). Having hauled 400 pp. of galleys for my collection of essays (*(Woman) Writer: Occasions and Opportunities*) to be published in June, I was relieved to hand them over to Billy. I assume you know San Francisco, at least to a degree? We walked and walked and walked; jogged in Golden Gate Park (a sort of tradition of ours), where it was already spring; saw *The Dead* (very good) and *The Last Emperor* (so good it is actually off the scale—if you have not seen it you *must*); met with Werner Erhard, whose reputation seems to lag behind, or misrepresent the man—he is hosting an adult education seminar in which I participated (as the "creative artist" evidently) with a live audience of about 400 people and a television audience of about 6,000—this went quite smoothly, in fact very well indeed, and I liked Erhard (his friends call him "Werner") very much. (Someone told me a bit cattily that Werner was born "Joe Rosenbaum" and that the elegantly Teutonic name is self-styled.) We also met Lily Tomlin, surely one of the funniest women alive; surprisingly warm and unpretentious, however. We quite like San Francisco, particularly Chinatown, the water, the hills (in moderation) . . .

I have received numerous good comments re. your *Understanding JCO*. And I suppose I am prejudiced in your favor a bit, myself.

Have been reading Oliver Sacks's intriguing but slightly

truncated *The Man Who Mistook His Wife for a Hat* (we met Dr. Sacks briefly in SF) and, for review, David Roberts's rather depressing *Jean Stafford: A Biography*. The advantage of the assignment is that it sends me back to Stafford, whom I intend to reread virtually in her entirety. Another book I've liked—of a very different species—is the Abrams *Alice Neel*. And the magisterial *Oscar Wilde* by (the late) Richard Ellmann.

Greg, congratulations again on the appointment! We are *truly overjoyed*. Were you closer, we could have a celebration w/champagne, cats and Freddie not excluded.

We laughed heartily over your description of Rowan Oak, and Barry Hannah. Our mutual friend Richard Ford brought Barry (unsolicited) to a party of ours about two years ago, during one of his drying-off periods. I was puzzled by his slow, even lethargic manner, and a sort of countrified ingenuousness . . . in other words, Hannah seemed frankly stupid. (He'd never heard of Maureen Howard, also at the party.) Afterward Richard, an old friend of his, apologized—"He's the boringest person in the world when he isn't drunk."

Stay well—
Joyce (& Ray)

❀

Early in the summer of 1988, I contracted to write a book on Joyce's short fiction for a series published by G.K. Hall. (The book would be published in 1994.) I had written to Joyce that Jacqueline Kennedy Onassis had taken a long time to consider my book of stories, though it turned out that, according to my agent, the fault lay with her Doubleday colleagues, not with her. Joyce and Ray had recently had lunch with Mrs. Onassis in New York, at her request.

7/1/88

Dear Greg:

... How frustrating Jacqueline Onassis must be! Did I mention, we had lunch together a few weeks back? She is utterly charming (of course), but seemed unable or unwilling to talk about professional publishing matters, talking instead about art, the theater, horses. When I asked her a question about her writers at Doubleday she sidestepped it. If you think that her assistant's advice is good, perhaps it will be helpful in the long run. Publishing is so whimsical these days, who knows? I do hope you won't be wasting your time with them, however.

Yes, I'm sure I can provide some material for the G.K. Hall book. This *is* good news. This is blessedly in the future, so let me know when a deadline is approaching. We could choose a story between us, perhaps, and I could provide some "journal" background for it if there is anything suitable. I am interested in stories right now that turn upon small—very small!—moments of grace of a kind, as in "Death Valley," where a good deal of the story's meaning falls upon the final comma, and the throwaway word "much." (This would sound like sheer madness to a nonwriter, but I know that you know what I mean.)

We think it's great that you are going to be living about 100 yards from Faulkner's former house. Amazing.

I don't know quite how to respond to [Richard] Gilman's attack on Updike. It was so relentless, it left me rather chilled. Some of what he says might be true but perhaps there is much more of significance that hasn't been said? I doubt that it will make any difference to Updike's reputation, however, which is surely one of the most secure of our time. I too am sometimes troubled, however, by a mysterious absence in

Updike's fiction of the kind of acute critical intelligence he displays with such seeming effortlessness in his reviews and essays. Though his prose is nearly always brilliant, the characters he lavishes life upon don't seem worthy of the prose, or of him. In a way he seems to no longer have a subject. But the short stories continue to be very fine.

If it's in the mid-90s in New Jersey, it must be even hotter there! Keep Freddie inside where it's air-conditioned.

Best wishes,
Joyce

⁂

In the fall of 1988, Joyce visited Atlanta to give a lecture at Agnes Scott College. Most of the following letter, however, deals with the writer we are calling "A.K." who had been a colleague of Joyce's at the University of Detroit many years earlier.

12 September 1988

Dear Greg:

I'd love to visit with you and Charles but, unfortunately, we're leaving Saturday morning—for St. Louis. (I'm going to be awarded something called the Saint Louis Literary Award, of which I had not previously heard; but it sounds like a fine group, and we'll enjoy seeing St. Louis.) I hope in the interstices of busyness that evening we'll at least have time for some talk.

Ray and I were acquainted with "A.K." ... in Detroit, but have not seen him since 1972. Yes, he is mentally unstable, has had psychotherapy (I think), but is harmless (I think!). You should reply saying thank you, but there will probably not be another edition of the book. All he seems to want (I should mention that he writes to everyone who writes about me sooner or later) is to be noticed.

My mistake with A.K. was *not* replying to one of his letters, and I do regret it. I had introduced him to my agent, helped him get his first novel accepted (by Putnam's, ages ago—I don't think he has published any novel since), and even, under pressure (I was very malleable in those days, the late 1960s), gave him and his publishers a blurb. I didn't want to do it . . . but, for some reason, I did. So my name is on the novel's jacket cover. After this, A.K. wrote me several letters asking, then more or less demanding, that I review this very novel for the *New York Times Book Review*. I was upset by his tone, and finally just didn't answer his last letter, which seems to have sent him into a permanent rage against me. Though he has threatened my life, indirectly, I don't any longer think he would go to the trouble of actually killing me . . . though I must say that when I visited San Francisco for the first time, I was worried he might appear . . . You certainly don't want to get involved with him in any pen-pal way, which is what he would probably like. He was teaching at community colleges for a while and may still be doing so. I can't imagine the man's life . . . aged 51 or thereabouts, and so fixed upon an event that happened, or failed to happen, back in 1972.

I hope you receive *The Assignation*; the books are just off the press, and I think it looks very good indeed.

Ray and I are sorry we won't have more time in Atlanta. We hope Ole Miss turns out to be enjoyable. Since you didn't mention the elusive Mrs. Onassis, I'll assume things are dormant in that sphere. (The only scene I halfway liked in Tom Wolfe's rather racist and sophomoric *The Bonfire of the Vanities* is the restaurant scene in which a man dies and is hurriedly carted out so that a dictator's wife can dine quietly. It reminded me of the lunch—in fact, quite a lovely lunch—when we were guests of Mrs. Onassis. The tremulous fawning and slavering over Celebrity!—but very, very subtly done. I probably mentioned to you, we didn't discuss books at all. But the woman *is* very nice, and I don't mean to sound critical of her in any way.)

Have you read *Paris Trout* by Pete Dexter? It is one of the National Book Award titles I truly liked.

Warm regards,
Joyce

12/21/88

Dear Greg:

Just to wish you Happy Holidays and the like ... it's kind of you to be concerned about my out-of-print titles. As Vanguard went into its slow, lengthy, inevitable decline, reprint rights were simply guarded (irrationally), not resold. Now that Random House has acquired the titles perhaps something will happen but, if not, I can't think it an extraordinary loss since there are perhaps too many books of mine available anyway.

Like you, I stand too close to my work to "see" it. I had thought *American Appetites* a dangerously cerebral, possibly overly "refined" novel, yet I see reviews that call it a "thriller." I just now read a review by the *New York Times* daily reviewer that dismisses the elegiac ending (which I'd hoped was not *too* elegiac) as unbelievable, because the hero (and the author) have decided just to forget about the death of the hero's wife.

I'd appreciate a quick listing, in fact, of stories of mine you think should be included in a selected collection ... from the early titles, I mean; not beyond *A Sentimental Education*. My imagination just blanks out, trying to gauge; it's like arranging poems in a logical sequence for book publication. Truly the hardest task I can think of.

Ray and I both admire your short fiction, and though we are somewhat overcommitted in terms of publishing for the next several years (our most recent acquisition is the "quality trade" edition of a long journal sort of piece recording the off-the-cuff conversation with a former student when Auden was about 40), we would be happy to consider it. Would you mind if Ray made some fairly hard-edged editorial/critical suggestions? I may keep out of it, except to read the stories, since in a way I feel too close to you, and to your writing, to make any objective assessment. A general impression is that at times your stories take too long to gather momentum . . . they are beautifully composed, cerebrally (!) structured, but need more obvious drama; fewer words.

I'm doing the screenplay, for Martin Scorsese, of *You Must Remember This*. A fascinating experience, converting one sort of consciousness into another. In a movie, "story" exists apart from "language"; you can't cocoon yourself in a comforting blanket of words, which is unnerving at first. But very challenging, even invigorating. Having recently finished a near-final draft of a long novel (*Songs of Innocence* [later retitled *Because It Is Bitter, and Because It Is My Heart*]): which takes me from 1956 to 1964, about the end of the "historical" period I am interested in evoking) I am ready for a change, and a considerable change. As you must know, nothing is more lacerating and exhausting than a "serious" novel you care about. I mention this because it's instructive how far fewer words we need to tell our stories than we imagine we do. I would guess that is true for your short fiction as well, though "Metamorphosis" seems to me perfectly realized, not a word too long.

Fondly,
Joyce (& Ray)

2/18/89

Dear Greg:

Ray and I are very pleased to be publishing your first story collection, and hope that you'll be agreeable to some of our suggestions. We've been reading and rereading these stories for weeks and discussing them.

My general feeling is that the stories tend to be a little slow; so that the dramatic focus is blurred. This is very easily remedied by the time-honored practice of cutting. You'd be surprised at how much of our prose is expendable, though of course there is a point at which narrative becomes too thin and quickly paced, and that isn't good either. But some fine stories of yours ("The Burning," "Summer Romance") do need rigorous cutting.

I'd like to make another suggestion: since there is a good deal of time, why not try your hand (your "voice") in another mode? I recall a powerful poem of yours about an AIDS victim, and in this poem your first-person narrator struck a tone that could be transposed into prose. Why not some short stories in that voice, about that subject? They could be very short, in fact.

Our object at the Press is to publish gifted writers in a rather handpicked way, and to work closely with them. Like all publishers we want to bring out the very best book of which the writer is capable. In your case, I feel that the collection could be a beautiful and powerful one, and I'm particularly pleased that we can be working together.

(Did I thank you for the thoughtful and perceptive commentary in *Georgia Review*, on *The Assignation*? I do love the "miniature narrative" form and have found it almost addictive.)

Warm regards,
Joyce

⌾

In the spring of 1989, I moved back to Atlanta from Oxford, Mississippi. Although I had some excellent course assignments and wonderful colleagues at the University of Mississippi, small-town life had not suited me, after many years in Atlanta. I accepted a welcome offer from Kennesaw State College (later Kennesaw State University) to teach half the year and have the other half "off" for writing. This proved to be a mutually agreeable situation, though Joyce often kidded me about now being a colleague of Newt Gingrich, who was teaching a course at the school. No sooner had I arrived at Kennesaw State than my colleagues urged me to invite Joyce to give a reading; she was unable to comply right away, though she eventually did come to the university in 1991.

4 August 1989

Dear Greg:

I called your number . . . and left a message reluctantly declining Kennesaw College's gracious invitation. But my spring calendar for 1990 is simply too crowded. Perhaps 1991 . . .

It sounds as if Kennesaw is a very interesting school. Ray and I are delighted that you're there, back in Atlanta, and apparently so happy. (Was anything in particular wrong with Oxford? Or was it simply too provincial? Frederick Karl's biography of Wm. Faulkner doesn't make Oxford sound like an attractive place, and it seems to have had an injurious effect upon Faulkner's personal life. He was in an impossible position—he needed his locale for his writing, and never wrote convincingly, let alone powerfully, of other settings; yet the existential fact of living there, in a society of "equals" like that egregious Phil Stone, was stultifying.) Atlanta is certainly an exciting city. We'll miss not seeing Freddie, as sweet a creature as my 24-pound Muffin. (Actually, Muffin has been on a rigorous diet, and may have lost as many as four pounds. He is the hero—have I mentioned this?—of my first and surely last children's book, *My Cat Muffin and How He Came to Live at Our House*. Dutton is bringing this extravaganza out sometime. Like most books for very young children it is going to be mainly all pictures.) . . .

We are very excited about *Distant Friends* . . . Ray tells me to tell you that the ideal jacket art would be vertical and in black-and-white. The Dufy is charming but not dramatic/disturbing enough to suggest your work. Maybe you underestimate its impact? . . . A woodcut too might be effective. Do keep looking at your end, and we'll keep looking at ours.

We'll be gone from Aug. 22 until Sept. 8, on a trip to England/Scotland. We're taking my parents along—their first time ever. Needless to say we are all very excited. (Maybe just a little *too* excited.)

I will have a quiet publication this fall—a book of poems, *The Time Traveler*. Poetry attracts little attention, and since I'm not considered a "poet" it should attract even less than usual. John Updike once observed wryly that he can't even get to the status of "minor poet," and I know exactly what he means. In poetry, though, the writing is the main thing—the publication very secondary.

Did you write a review of *Soul/Mate*?—I seem to remember someone mentioning having seen it, but Dutton has sent me no reviews in weeks, or is it months. Since being under the auspices of New American Library, an aggressively commercial organization, my publisher seems to be becoming ever more remote. (Though my editor Billy Abrahams is just great.)

This letter has grown far more than I'd intended. Again, thank your colleagues for having invited me; and I hope I might have a rain check for 1991. If not, I'm sure that you and Ray and I will get together before long.

Warm regards,
Joyce

⟨⸜◯⟩

The following postcard refers to the Louisville Humana Festival of New American Plays, which was about to present a new play of Joyce's. Though she claims not to look forward to "any career as a playwright," in fact she would write and have produced dozens of both short and full-length plays throughout the 1990s and beyond. She enjoyed the collaborative nature of the genre, especially since she spent so much time at home alone, working at her fiction. Also, she later refers to several screenplays of her novels that were in various stages of "development hell"; unfortunately, none of these made it to the screen.

2/15/90

Dear Greg:

We'll be in Louisville for the festival weekend (my play to be staged March 30); otherwise, I'll be there for the final rehearsals and the local opening March 3 (but not Ray). All very exciting—though I don't anticipate any career as a playwright of course . . . And so good to hear some supportive words re. *Because* [*It Is Bitter, and Because It Is My Heart*] . . . which will probably draw sharp criticism for the racial aspect alone. (Yes, I quite agree re. the "allegorical" aura.) We think you will like the new *OR* [*Ontario Review*], with your poems, and other strong work.

Best wishes—
Joyce

7/9/90

Dear Greg:

I just now discovered your very thoughtful, and very welcome, essay-review of *The Time Traveler* in *Virginia Quarterly Review.* Many thanks!

And for your lively, newsy, funny (especially the Barry Hannah passage) letter & card.

Ray and I had to be fingerprinted for identification purposes, in connection with being co-owners of a racehorse. (Pacer—cf. *Because It Is Bitter* . . .)

The Rise of Life on Earth will be published, as a novella, by New Directions, in 1991 . . .

I guess you were bemused, as we were, by Alice Adams's comment on *Distant Friends.* When we mean good, solid, rewarding, textured, non-minimalist fiction, we're in danger of saying "old-fashioned," and assuming others can translate.

The Scorsese project is, they say, advancing (i.e., seeking millionaire investors). The *American Appetites* project is on hold, awaiting the whim of a famous male actor. The *Because It Is Bitter* . . . project is only on p. 15, and going *very* slowly. (Possibly because writing this letter is more fun, and easier.)

Stay well, and write again soon.

With affection,
Joyce

⟨⟩

*On my way to the university one rainy September morning,
I was involved in a major car accident on the expressway.
I was not seriously hurt—just shaken up—and missed only
one day of classes. This collision reminded Joyce of an accident she and Ray had endured many years before.*

9/28/90

Dear Greg:

What a shock to Ray and me, to hear of your accident!
It sounds as if you've had a terribly close call. (And the other
car simply kept on going? How awful.) We hope you'll be
able to forget it—to some degree. Obviously, you'll never forget it entirely.

Once, driving on the wicked John Lodge Expressway in
Detroit, in winter, Ray hit a patch of ice, and our car—a Fiat
convertible sports car, lipstick-red in fact—went into a spin,
leisurely turning and coasting horizontally through several
lanes of awestruck traffic. Our fellow motorists, autos and
enormous trucks alike, were stunned into silence by our ma-
neuver. Finally we skidded onto a shoulder, hit a guardrail,
spun a bit more, and came to a complete dead stop. I don't
remember what came next except we just sat there for a few
minutes. What *is* there to say, or even to think, after such
experiences?

Well, though your car is "totaled," you at least are not.
That's something.

I've sent you something for the *Review* [a literary magazine published at my university]. Since I don't have much short fiction right now, perhaps you could use one or two or even all three of these monologues from my play *I Stand Before You Naked*. (This is the order in which they should appear.) The play opens in early November at the American Place Theatre, a fine off-Broadway house on West 46th St.; the first preview is October 31.

I've fallen in love with the form of the short play; better yet, the short-short play, or miniature play. (Like my miniature narratives in *The Assignation*.) If you have not written plays thus far, perhaps you will someday. The activity is quite different from writing prose fiction since the writerly cocoon of the narrative voice is stripped away, and you're left with simply dialogue, action, subtextual movement.

I've recently agreed to edit *The Oxford Book of American Short Fiction*, which will provide me with much reading, going back to Washington Irving and pushing forward, for perhaps the next year. Also, I am editing, with the able assistance of Robert Atwan, *The Best American Essays 1991*; so if any particularly compelling, eloquent essay attracts your attention, please let me know. (Not articles, nor literary pieces—just essays.)

Your courses sound as if they will be wonderful to teach, and will provoke a good deal of discussion among your students.

Ray is sending along your postcards [featuring the cover art of *Distant Friends*]—very striking, we think. We'll be using them too, of course. Though *Distant Friends* is not in fact your first book, I've been thinking of it, in a way, as the first. It has that air of freshness and discovery about it.

All warm regards,
Joyce

Part Two

1991–1992

In early 1991, Joyce was "between novels" but would soon write the novella Black Water *(1992) and begin work on one of her longest and most ambitious novels,* What I Lived For *(1994). Near the completion of that novel, I was visiting Princeton and she led me back to her study where, she said, I would see something that would "haunt [my] dreams." There, beside her typewriter, was a stack of approximately 1,000 manuscript pages. This was her longest novel to date, though a few years later she would produce her epic about Marilyn Monroe,* Blonde *(2000), whose first draft was more than 1,400 pages. She also continued to write plays, and attended as many openings around the country as she could.*

25 January 1991

Dear Greg:

. . . As I've probably told you, I have become extremely interested in theatre—(they *do* spell it that way, in the trade)—though only experimental, marginal theatre, where the stakes are not high. (We just returned from Los Angeles, Santa Monica to be specific, where the L.A. Theatre Works did a "staged reading" of two short plays of mine, that was quite an enjoyable experience. The actors, though not known to me, are highly respected and the audience loved them— Ed Asner, JoBeth Williams, Héctor Elizondo, Joyce Van Patten. Also, we had a great time in Santa Monica, right on the ocean, rising early and jogging along the beach for miles. Perhaps because it was all very unreal—fresh, clear summer days with temperatures in the mid-70s while, back here, we'd had an ice storm just before leaving—and because we knew it was a brief visit—we found it paradisical.)

Ray says to tell you that he is trying to get hold of reviews of your book, if they have appeared, in the *Washington Post* and the Chicago newspaper: the editors never send tear sheets, and he is writing them to inquire. *Distant Friends* has certainly received some very fine reviews, and we continue to hear excellent things about it. By now, our friend Rosalie Siegel (an excellent agent, incidentally—she represented "Rosamond Smith" in Rosamond's initial, somewhat naïve enterprise) has spoken with your agent about a sale to a French publisher, dependent upon your allowing them to see your novel. I told Rosalie it hardly seemed like a problem.

I did enjoy [A. S. Byatt's] *Possession* but would not care to reread it: it's a very polished, accomplished, willed, and quintessentially *British* novel—virtually nothing subterranean, brooding, startling, let alone disturbing. Yet, I think it's wonderful that so intelligent a novel has done well commercially.

I read *A Dangerous Woman* too, and seem to have liked it less than *Vanished*, which had something magical about it. I met Mary McGarry Morris at the NBA award dinner (she was nominated last year, I was one of the five judges) and liked her very much.

I may have mentioned that I am the editor for *The Best American Essays 1991*. It's a very exciting undertaking to be reading so many—*so* many—essays on such a wide variety of topics. *Harper's*, the *Georgia Review*, *Gettysburg Review* publish consistently excellent work . . .

I am also editing an even more ambitious project—*The Oxford Book of American Short Stories*. I've discovered little-known, in fact unknown, stories by people like Stephen Crane, Mark Twain, Jack London, Edith Wharton; plus a number of black writers, and, of course, "women"—Oxford University Press chose me, I'm sure, to redress old imbalances, which I'll take pleasure in doing. I have nearly a year to do this in, so I shouldn't be pressed for time. The contemporary section will give me the most difficulty—there are simply too many good writers, all sorts of excellent "emerging" minority writers, plus my old, good friends who can't *all* be included; but will not like being left out.

Yes, Toby Wolff is very good—very odd, off-beat, funny. I think you would like his "memoir"—how much is fiction, how much autobiography, his friends are doubtful—*This Boy's Life*. I've given up reading, or trying to read, Frederick Barthelme and other minimalists. But I have a very good story by Bobbie Ann Mason for the Oxford anthology.

I'll be doing the screenplay, probably, for a "Rosamond Smith" novel called *Snake Eyes*, for the producer Arnold Kopelstone, who did, among other stark, serious titles, *Platoon*. Since the intense, headachy, anxious days, and some nights, of writing *Because It Is Bitter* . . . I seem incapable of writing, or even considering, anything large, ambitious, close to the bone; so I've been doing shorter things, and find it a welcome change, so much expansiveness suddenly, and a sense of freedom, so that book reviewing assignments seem suddenly very welcome. (I've begun reviewing for the *TLS*, and have been doing some things for the *Washington Post* recently. In the past, I'd done no more than two reviews yearly for the *NYTBR*.)

Please do say hello to your friend Charles, and to Freddie. (I hope Freddie is well?)

Warm regards,
Joyce

11 May 1991

Dear Greg,

What a lovely time we had visiting you—it was a highlight of this spring, indeed. Your party—your home—your friends—not least Freddie—and the conference experience itself: everything was wonderfully orchestrated, memorable. (I'd love to have a copy of your eloquent introduction of me, if it isn't inconvenient.) The snapshots are wonderful . . . The pictures of me at the podium have a comically Beckett look to them—a head emerging out of an upended coffin? (Even Beckett didn't think of that!)

We look forward to seeing *Paris Trout* soon—thanks so much. It looks as if another actress, not Ellen Barkin, will be in *Because It Is Bitter* . . . named Geena Davis, of whom I have heard, but have never seen. But this too is tentative, as always in Hollywood. Until contracts are actually signed. The producer is happy with the screenplay I've written except for the Savage family, primarily Allan—he is too nice, too quiet, too "academic," too—too much, I guess, like the kind of men and women with whom we ordinarily associate, in such places as Princeton. So I must make him more "interesting"—!

So too with *American Appetites*. The producer acquired the rights because he "loved" the novel—the characters—the tone; now he wants "more of a thriller/suspense" plot, and the character of Ian more "interesting." Perhaps a serial killer/cannibal/academic?

It's a lovely spring day here in Princeton, and Ray and I are eager to go bicycling. We're truly sorry to have missed the magnificent Atlanta dogwood/azalea season, but it's still in full force here.

I just returned from a very nice visit to Randolph-Macon College (in Ashland, VA); next, on Monday, is the big literacy benefit at which Barbara Bush and Walter Cronkite (the true stars!) will preside. The FBI, or perhaps the Secret Service, checked out Ray and me last week to see if we were "security risks," thus ineligible to approach Mrs. Bush, but since we haven't heard otherwise I guess we have passed the test.

When I'd been invited to meet Gorbachev some time ago, our telephone was tapped, so crudely that everyone who called us was aware of something odd. This went on for about a week, with no explanation or apology. How disappointed these surveillance people must have been listening to Elaine Showalter and me discuss Princeton gossip . . .

Again, thanks for a splendid visit. You can certainly try Toni Morrison—maybe she would come, or maybe not. Some speakers, like Toni, charge very high fees to discourage invitations, since they receive so many.

I continue to work on short things—miniature narratives, one-act plays. I seem not to have the energy, or is it the spiritual audacity, to so much as plan a long novel, let alone write one. It's as if I swam across a river and almost didn't make it—though, to others' eyes, judging from a distance—it seems I *did* make it; I'm in no hurry to risk that again.

Please pet Freddie for us both. We hope to see you again before too much time goes by.

All best wishes,
Joyce

Around this time, I first broached the idea of writing a critical biography of Joyce and her work, though this soon broadened out into a full-fledged biography that would be published in 1998 by Dutton.

6/14/91

Dear Greg:

Thanks for the unusually attractive birthday card. And for the snapshots you'd sent earlier . . .

I'm happy to write to Syracuse [Joyce's archive had been placed at Syracuse University] giving you permission to peruse the manuscripts and worksheets. When you see these—the sheer quantity—you will wonder why on earth anyone wants to write; what possible madness can account for it. The drafts of some novels, like *You Must Remember This*, are staggering. Writing a novel must be like the proverbial childbirth phenomenon—you don't remember afterward how much you suffered. The proof of it being, you wind up doing it again.

[T]he journals don't go back to 1967. I believe they—it—starts on New Year's Day 1973. Also, there are no other "Eden County" stories. Nor did I keep worksheets in those days—I cheerfully threw everything out. I didn't save much correspondence, either. In fact I didn't have much correspondence. What blissful days, come to think of it!

I'd be delighted if you did a critical biography someday; the emphasis being upon, not the life, but the writing. Yet it's true that people whom I know, teachers especially, are beginning to show signs of terminal mortality. (Donald Dike, poor man, died of cancer of the throat years ago.) Nor are my parents (who are due to arrive in about an hour for a few days' visit) getting any younger.

Walter Sutton was a favorite professor of mine at Syracuse. He's retired now, but still lives in the city, I think.

I'm reviewing the Jacqueline Rose book on Sylvia Plath, for *TLS*; and the Anne Sexton [biography], for the *Washington Post*. These are serious, intelligent, well-researched books. Plath's premature death was particularly tragic. Sexton seems to have written all that she had in her, which may be one of the reasons she wanted so badly to die. But Plath—! What a loss.

Thank you for sending your new story, too, which Ray and I have both read, and want to reread.

Again, having looked through your letter, I should say that, yes, a critical biography by you would be exemplary ... We certainly had a grand time in Atlanta, thanks to you.

Much affection,
Joyce

7 July 1991

Dear Greg:

Thanks for your very nice letter. Though I feel ambivalent about any work being done on me—"me" in an abstract literary sense—I must say that I would prefer you doing it; whether criticism, critical biography, or whatever. If I were not myself, and faced with the prospect of writing about me, I would see the challenge as, simply, how to make a writer's life interesting in any narrative, dramatic sense. The writer's life—this writer's life, certainly—is so inward, secretive, and obsessive, the "surface" is largely irrelevant. Perhaps I worry about you, with whom I partly identify, toiling to make something interesting that is *not*.

Still, I've sent your (and my) snapshot to my parents, and told them that this very nice young writer might be calling them sometime. They are familiar with your work—some of it. They are wonderful people, I think, kindly, sweet, "wise" ... though their lives have not been easy, or maybe because their lives have not been easy. But they are rather shy, quiet, unemphatic. I don't truly think they would have much to say about me that would be helpful to you, but if you want to call them, their number is (716) 689 8329. Address: Carolina and Frederic Oates, 11580 Transit Rd., East Amherst, NY 14051. Bob Phillips, the new director of the creative writing program at the U. of Houston, has just moved there ... (Poor Bob, moving in July, to Texas!) Blanche Gregory is no longer my agent; she is semi-retired, and spends much of the year in Florida/Maine. My new agent is John Hawkins, but I'm afraid he scarcely knows me at all; he is enormously busy, and would not be helpful to you. The person to speak with is William Abrahams, my surpassingly brilliant, devoted, and seemingly indefatigable editor. (Billy must be about 72, may retire soon—though I hope not.) Walter Sutton at Syracuse would scarcely remember me, either. Many of these people, including my parents, *are* aging . . . I suppose if a biography, or a biographical sketch (which might be more practical), were to be done, ever, it should be started while these people are still available . . .

I feel as if I have just emerged from a sustained horror/ trauma . . . several weeks of writing a short novel [*Black Water*] suggested by—but, as it turns out, very different from— the Chappaquiddick incident. I'd written a short story, "Dark Water," about this, to appear in *Lear's* (of all places!—the magazine, for "mature" women, strives consciously for an upbeat tone), but wanted to develop it further. Actually I had wanted to write a novella about the situation since 1969, but was only roused to begin by the Kennedy/Palm Beach incident of some months ago.

There isn't much available on the subject in book form. A somewhat repetitive, not very well organized book by a man named Leo Damore was all I could find, but its focus is exclusively on the legal aspect of the case, the aftermath; nothing at all about the young woman who drowned. It's infuriating when Ted Kennedy repeatedly refers to the incident as a "tragic accident"—it was an accident that, while drunk, he drove a car into the water, but it was no accident that he allowed his passenger to drown. Imagine—he didn't report the accident for nine hours. Yet he wasn't charged with anything except leaving the scene of an accident; and he has been elected to the Senate ever since. There is a tragedy here—the tragedy of bankrupt moral leadership, for one thing. I became very passionately involved in writing the novella (as I suppose this indicates—I should stop talking about it) and so emotionally tense that I could hardly sleep, and have been preoccupied for weeks as if a part of me was trapped in a submerged car, trying to survive until help comes; and help is never going to come . . .

Weeks ago, my director (for *Because It Is Bitter* . . .) Larry Schiller telephoned, to say, excited, "I have 99% good news!" (They had seemed about to sign Geena Davis.) Luckily I took that with a grain of salt, since I have not had word from the man since.

Yes, you can use the term "authorized" biography. (I don't believe Bob McPhillips is going to do one after all. Have you ever met him? He and Bob Phillips have become friends, and what an odd couple . . . their names, I mean.) As I say, I guess I worry about you, trying to make a project "interesting" that seems to me, from my perspective, not interesting at all.

We recently saw *Jungle Fever*—found it enormously energetic, disturbing. Marvelous capacious roles for actors in Spike Lee's films.

Ray says hello, and warm regards to all. Please do send us more stories as you'd indicated you might . . .

Much affection,
Joyce

8/17/91

Dear Greg:

Just a quick note: thanks for the very nice review [of *Heat*]. (Reviewers don't seem to take note, or to be much concerned, that a story like "Family" is about our environmental tragedy; not a morbid-minded individual family, or a writer with an unusually dark imagination. It's rather like blaming Margaret Bourke-White for all those depressing photographs of WWII—and by a woman, no less.) . . .

I'm wondering how the visit to the archives went. Yes, Syracuse is a diverse, generally very attractive campus. (The campus of *Because It Is Bitter* . . . is really the one I envision.) I feel that a fellow writer would feel profoundly depressed, seeing the many, the numberless, revisions of pages, even paragraphs, I've done; thinking, Is so much effort worth it?

Yet, to have the facility of a Mozart, to toss work off without any effort at all, would not be much fun.

I don't know about Truman Capote attacking me, though people mention it now and then. [Probably while drunk, Capote had suggested Joyce was "the most loathsome creature in America" and should be "publicly beheaded in Shea Stadium."] I never wrote him a fan letter!—my God, certainly not. I've scarcely read him, in fact. Maybe he was drunk, or confusing me with another woman writer. He may have imagined me as a rivalrous younger writer in the days of his decline, as older writers do, so misguidedly, with younger writers who are reviewed often or who do reviews.

Your essay on literary feuds sounds like fun. I'll look forward to reading it.

Now, my parents are eagerly awaiting your call!

Much affection,
Joyce

(On Aug. 21, there will be a made-for-TV movie of *Lives of the Twins*—in a recent announcement, noted as *Lies of the Twins*! I don't want to automatically expect the worst, but, in any case, Rosamond Smith is to blame; yet even she did not do the screenplay. It will be on USA-cable, which we don't get.)

(Yes, Rae-Jolene ["Rae-Jolene Smith" was a pseudonym Joyce used for stories in *Yale Review* and elsewhere] was Rosamond's predecessor. But no one knew . . .)

1 September 1991

Dear Greg:

Thanks so much for *Lies of the Twins*—which we hope to see, soon. It was certainly very thoughtful of you to tape the movie for us. (I suppose I feel a bit hesitant about seeing it!)

I have just been released from jury duty: the first time I've ever been a juror, at an actual trial (a drug dealer accused of, and found guilty of, assault against a woman he believed had informed on him)—a haunting experience, overall. Have you ever been a juror? . . .

I'm touched that you have written to my parents, and hope the visit goes well. How far away July 1992 seems—!

Ray says hello, and warm regards as always.
(Your Syracuse/archive descriptions are most interesting!)
Joyce

⟿)

In the fall of 1991, I contracted to publish a second book of my short stories, A Friendly Deceit, *with Johns Hopkins University Press; the book came out in 1992. Around this time, my agent sold my first novel,* Pagan Babies, *to Dutton for publication early in 1993, and I placed a book of poems,* Aid and Comfort, *with the University Press of Florida.*

In October I visited Princeton, with my friend Charles

Willingham, to see two of Joyce's short plays that were being produced that fall at Princeton's McCarter Theatre. Joyce's interest in playwriting continued to intensify, and over the next few years she would see dozens of both short and long plays produced around the country. I had begun the spade-work on my biography of Joyce, and much of our correspondence concerned this project.

18 Sept. 1991

Dear Greg:

CONGRATULATIONS on the Johns Hopkins Press acceptance! We're very happy for you, and, since it is *OR*'s hope to "launch" new talent, we're proud, too. *Distant Friends* is one of the best-received books we've published, and the second collection should do even better.

I've spoken with Elaine Showalter . . . and she says she'll be happy to speak with you sometime. You'll be meeting Elaine—and a virtual horde of other friends and colleagues—at the reception following the plays . . . You might also speak with Edmund [Mike] Keeley, Robert Fagles, Leigh and Henry Bienen (all of Princeton U.); Daniel Halpern (Ecco Press); Russell Banks and Chase Twichell (also of Princeton—on leave now, but returning in Nov.). Ed Doctorow and Robert Stone . . . Richard Ford . . . Alice Adams . . . know more of my work than of my life.

We'll hope that you and Charles can come out to the house, perhaps on the 28th . . . Since my parents are visiting, and I'll be at rehearsals before the performance, things will be complicated but not impossible. You can see the Press's "headquarters"—Ray's rather modest (and usually very messy) study. And our cats—though, sadly, not our really beloved cat Muffin, who died yesterday. He was thirteen, and died of the most common ailment among cats (perhaps dogs, too), kidney failure. With a sense of the irony involved (one must be affluent to do such things!) we took him, in all, to four vets; one prolonged his life for an astonishing year (after the first had suggested he be put to sleep)—so we've felt we were granted some gratuitous happiness. I must say I'm still quite broken up, though "rationally" we anticipated this for weeks . . . the extraordinary thing about certain animals is that they do seem to forge a bond with us, and that bond, the very metaphysics of it (!), is, in time, the only thing that holds them in life; in a state of nature they would die unnoticed, with non-caring or not-affluent owners they would die, but, with us, they are able to live—for a while, at least. The only people who dismiss animal lovers as sentimental are people who haven't really known animals intimately, and haven't discovered that animals' personalities are as individual as ours.

Someone said—a poet?—I can't remember who—that the unarticulated animal suffering, at the hands of human beings, over the centuries, is just too terrifying to contemplate. So, we don't.

How I wince when you mention those discarded mss. of mine! I wish, now, that I'd rethought my archivist's request (he wanted everything, or nearly!), and simply thrown them out. I can't believe these old novels even exist . . . The disturbing thing is, *Jigsaw*, *Graywolf*, and *Lucien Florey* were all *bought* by Dutton!—and were going to be published. (This was at the time of my leaving Vanguard for Dutton, and Henry Robbins, arguably the most respected editor of the era—to whom I went at Joan Didion's suggestion.) In retrospect, I can see that I wrote at least two of these because I wasn't ready yet to write *Bellefleur*. But as soon as I did, I bumped the others, and finally withdrew them altogether. Thank God.

[The manuscript of] *The Wheel of Love* [1970] is lost. Vanguard, somehow, simply "misplaced" the manuscript. At the time, I didn't seem to feel a great loss.

What fun, to peruse Bob Phillips's papers. Bob is without a doubt the most literary-gregarious/generous/just plain nice guy of his generation. He has more energy than anyone I know, and he's already thriving at Houston where he's chairing the graduate writing program. If the English literary style is best represented by Kingsley Amis, a foul-mouthed sexist/racist/alcoholic (his memoir is appalling)—I'd like to think that our American style is represented by Bob Phillips . . .

Classes begin this afternoon; I teach on Wednesdays and Thursdays, two workshops of about ten students. On Friday I fly to Kansas—I am lecturing/reading on "the ethical dimension of literature"—and my [lecture] agent (Janet Cosby, in Washington) told me that I am the "main event" of the entire academic year . . . which is a bit daunting. In any case, lecturing/reading is far easier than writing, as we all know.

Ray and I look forward to seeing you on the 28th. When you arrive, on the 27th, will you give us a call?

Again, congratulations on the short stories!

As always,
Joyce

10/16/91

Dear Greg:

Thanks for the great snapshots! We all look very cheerful, which was my main recollection of the weekend. It was wonderful to see you at last in our house; and to be reacquainted with Charles.

I know my parents would be delighted to receive an enlargement of the snapshot. They were much taken with you.

(I cringe a little trying to imagine what fond memories they are recalling when they talk about me . . . But it's best, I suppose, not to interfere. Not even to try to discover what they might be saying.) (Ray and I are often correcting each other's memory. Or filling in gaps. Maybe it has to do with concentrating so much upon work, which is always in the present tense, but I've discovered whole areas of experience, admittedly minor ones, that I've forgotten, and Ray recalls. Thank God for the Other!) . . .

We're having lovely autumn days here. Just perfect for running/hiking in the country.

I thought the Nobel Prize to Nadine Gordimer was a wonderful surprise. She is a great writer, and the unofficial word was that she would never be given the award until a black African had received it. It *is* a political award, or anyway political-literary. (Most "literary" awards are.)

Yes, *Black Water* is scheduled for May. I didn't watch the Clarence Thomas/Anita Hill hearings, but everyone has commented upon the discreetly low profile Senator Kennedy kept. In my novel, the Senator is not an entirely unsympathetic figure; he isn't Kennedy, in fact has a bit of Bill Bradley about him (Bill, one of our two New Jersey Democratic senators, is the only politician with whom I'm acquainted: a wonderful, idealistic man clearly too intelligent, sensitive, and good-hearted to campaign for president)—in terms of politics, I mean! *Black Water* is really about the death of idealism in our time. The resignation of Thurgood Marshall and the recent Supreme Court decisions, not to mention the stacking of the Court, left me with a feeling of absolute estrangement and disgust, this summer. Now, things actually look worse—the political climate is so hostile to what used to be considered good liberal causes, virtually unquestioned "good" causes.

I'd be curious about Ned Rorem's response to your notice [in the *New York Times*, regarding my work on Joyce's biography]. Ned is a wonderfully gifted composer and writer, but people who've been in his diaries often say that he gets things very wrong. Interestingly wrong, at least.

Little Reynard [Joyce and Ray's new kitten] is a dynamo these days, and is winning over, by degrees, our tank-sized male Tristram. (Tristram is the late Muffin's brother. I wrote about these hefty, good-natured fellows in a story called "The Seasons.")

Congratulations again on your forthcoming publications. That's great news.

Much affection,
Joyce

28 December 1991

Dear Greg:

. . . Thank you for your comments on the *Atlantic* story ["Life After High School"]. I've received quite a few, one in particular from a gay writer who said he deeply resented the story until the end; then, he decided he liked it very much!

Did I mention how powerfully your "Metamorphosis" was received by my writing students? It made quite an impression on several of the more imaginative ones.

I'm sure you're right about the biography; I can't claim that I feel like a very "biographical" subject. I just finished a review-essay on a new, authorized biography of Muhammad Ali, for the *New York Review of Books: there* is a biographical subject, indeed. At one time, in fact for years, Ali was the most famous person in the world—better known than any president, or the pope. Amazing . . .

For some time I'd wanted to write a novel titled *Snake*

Eyes; finally, the plot came to me, and diabolical-minded Rosamond Smith executed it. More recently, I'd been intrigued by the title *Double Delight* (which refers to perhaps the most exquisitely beautiful hybrid tea rose I've ever seen); Rosamond is obsessively writing that, at the moment. Often, though, I ponder over titles for a long time; settle for something that seems adequate, and then get re-inspired again, as the novel heads into production and it's almost too late.

We've been having an idyllic holiday time—hours at a stretch of uninterrupted work (most of our Princeton friends are traveling); a few very pleasant social events. My father, whose classes at U. of Buffalo don't resume until late January, has been feeling a bit restless, so we're having them come visit next week, and we'll all attend the opening of *The Three Sisters* here, which Emily Mann (whom I think you met?—a close friend, and artistic director of the McCarter) has directed. The 1992 Humana Festival at Louisville will be doing a short play of mine on a bill with Lanford Wilson and Jane Anderson, so we'll be going there for that weekend in March, also with my parents. We love having them, and they've really grown to appreciate theater.

Are you still interested in house- and cat-and-canary-sitting for us sometime? We plan to be traveling a bit, probably May 1-12 or so. That may be too long a time for you to be away from Atlanta, so a briefer period could be worked out. There's no hurry in letting us know; our plans are still tentative.

Amazing about Margaret Doody at Vanderbilt! Everyone here knows that the heroine of *Nemesis* is based upon Elaine Showalter, who gave the "fatal" party, and whose great failing (as I'm forever teasing her) is that she is *too good*. It was Elaine from whom I learned much of the suppressed information of the case, and with whom I commiserated. (She had a terrible academic year, that year.) Margaret Doody, whom I scarcely knew, was very much on the periphery. I'm surprised that she would imagine herself as Maggie Blackburn; and, having done so, that she would be unhappy about it!

Happy 1992 from all of us, including Reynard the Fox (who has grown alarmingly long since you've seen him last) . . .

Much affection,
Joyce

᳁

In the first part of May 1992, for ten days I did "house- and cat-sit" for Joyce and Ray while they were traveling. During this interlude, I interviewed a number of Joyce's Princeton friends for my biography. The cats were rather shy of me, and their pet canary, Daisy, made sure I got to work early by beginning his loud trilling at approximately six a.m. each morning.

Shortly after Joyce and Ray returned from their trip, they were involved in a car accident, rear-ended by a teenager who was busy fiddling with her radio. No one was seriously hurt, but the wreck was written up in the Trenton Times *on May 20. Joyce sent me the article along with the following letter.*

21 May 1992

Dear Greg:

As you can see, we've quickly returned to the swing of things!

(She must have been going 50 mph. The rear of our car

collapsed like an accordion. The seat belts SAVED us: I'd have gone through the windshield.)

Thanks *so much* for the photos & journal. Fascinating entries.

Arnold Dolin, at NAL/Dutton, is also an admirer of your work. Elaine [Koster] says she likes you very much. (We had dinner recently.)

This is hardly an adequate response to your nice letter, etc. We're *terribly* busy . . .

Your comments on Princeton are very interesting. My friends simply distrust this project, I think, which is why I'd hoped they would meet you, and see who you are. Freddie looks darling in the photos!

Thanks for the wonderfully clean house & the *flowers*.

Joyce

[Added on a Post-it] Your comments on [the manuscript of] *Tales of the Grotesque* are very helpful. Maybe I will drop one or two stories, and add "The Insomniac" . . . The manuscript is still in flux.

(Right now, Reynard is "escorting" ducks around the pond. Much fun!)

16 June 1992

Dear Greg:

Many thanks for the birthday gift and letter! We've all been enjoying the cartoons.

Sorry about Leigh Bienen [who declined to be interviewed for my biography of Joyce] (who thinks she might write something of her own someday), but Henry will be happy to speak with you.

We're so pleased you've agreed to be literary executor . . .

but I hope it won't come about for awhile. Yes, we'll be doing a *Selected Stories*, possibly in 1993, or '94 . . .

Reynard misses you—and Freddie!

Much affection,
Joyce

7/8/92

Dear Greg,

. . . We're terribly sorry to hear about Freddie. She's a very sweet dog, and has quite a personality. Let's hope that, with medication, she will improve. Muffin died at 13, but the Halperns' cat, suffering from the same kidney ailment, is 22!

After stalling for months, maybe years, I've embarked upon a new "ambitious" novel. [This is the novel that would become *What I Lived For*, though her working title was *Corky's Price*.] I've been blocked for anything involving a span of years and richness of detail. This time it's my hope to get deep inside the skin of a man totally antithetical to me in personality . . .

Congratulations on your (latest) contract! Your agent must be dazzled by you these days. I should confess that I knew a bit about it, because both Elaine Koster [then president of Dutton] and Billy [Abrahams] had discussed it with me, Billy in some detail. He is *most* impressed with your prospectus or outline.

My parents are looking forward to seeing you enormously. I hope things work out.

Black Water teasingly approached, but never did get on, the *NY Times* best-seller list; its highest national rating was #12, for two or so weeks, in *Publishers Weekly*. But Dutton did an excellent job of promotion, I think. (What is your editor's name?—Audrey—? [Audrey LaFehr])

Everyone is well here. Daisy is trilling robustly this very minute.

Much affection,
Joyce

25 Aug. 1992
Dear Greg:
. . . Did my parents mislead you? We aren't going to Paris/ London until late October; and then only for a week. (No house sitter!—just a kindly young woman who also does canary-toenail-clipping, a true specialty.) . . .

So glad to hear that Freddie is better. Our menagerie continues as before, with Reynard developing into a true hunter. His specialty is frogs—he doesn't eat them, nor even kill them, but brings them up into the courtyard, mews excitedly, and Ray hurries out to return the frog to the pond. Reynard enjoys the attention and the notoriety. (How long can this routine continue, you may ask; the answer is, apparently indefinitely. The frog supply is never diminished.)

The *Pagan Babies* cover is excellent. Terrific!

My parents had a lovely time seeing you. But the visit was, from their perspective, too brief . . .

Everyone is well here, and enjoying the rapidly diminishing summer—

Best wishes,
Joyce

6 September 1992
Dear Greg:
Enclosed is a tentative list of the titles for *Where Are You Going, Where Have You Been? Selected Stories of Joyce*

Carol Oates. (As I type that out for the first time, it does seem a bit ponderous . . . But it's too late to change my name to H.D. or Ai.)

After reading your letter, and your remarks about A.K., Ray and I drifted into a truly nostalgic mood. Not so much about A.K. as about other friends of that period of our lives, now long lost. We didn't have disagreements with them—our lives simply evolved in different directions. I realize this is true—even quite natural—for everyone. But it is a poignant thing to remember friends who were close, even intimate, whom, now, we don't at all know; in many cases we don't even know where they live. (I was extremely close to a wonderful woman named Liz Graham, who lived in Birmingham, Michigan, through much of the 1960s and 1970s. She was a friend too of Kay Smith's—Kay, now dead, to whom I dedicated *Expensive People*. I don't know where Liz lives now—she never answered my last letter, written perhaps a decade ago, after we'd moved to Princeton.) One friend of that era whom you might contact is Lois Smedick (now dean of the graduate school at the University of Windsor)—I still feel extremely friendly with Lois, though I haven't seen her in ages. (She too is a poor correspondent!)

A.K. probably has not told you, if he even remembers, that, at the time of the "rift" (as you call it), we weren't seeing much of one another any longer . . . I never wanted to think that A.K. was primarily interested in me, and in Ray (we were both friends of his, we'd thought), in order to exploit me; but, who knows?—I was amazingly naïve then. I tend to be more cautious now, for obvious reasons.

Still, when I consider the hundreds (thousands???) of younger writers with whom I've been involved, there hasn't been a single other person (that I know of) who has turned against me the way A.K. did. So his example, early on, was not really representative of the cynical truism "No good deed goes unpunished."

I'm amazed that A.K. photocopied essays of mine—which I've entirely forgotten, I guess. And letters! I can't imagine what on earth those letters contain . . . Do I dare ask to see them? (I cringe and cower as I make this request.) Clearly, the relationship must have meant more to him than his subsequent behavior would suggest. And more than it meant to me, evidently . . . I didn't save any of his letters even at the time. The mystery to Ray and me still remains: why did he make so much of so little? and for so many years? . . .

The menagerie is in fine form, and asks to be remembered to you. Especially Reynard, who has perfected the art of rolling over and stretching to twice his size, with an appealing-kitten look. All the cats miss Freddie, who kept their adrenaline charged.

Much affection,
Joyce

September 20, 1992

Dear Greg:

Thanks so much for the letter—your suggestions about the selected stories, and the staggering quantity of typed prose that constitutes my correspondence with my former colleague and friend A.K. . . .

Ray and his distributor would in fact like to bring out the selected stories in hardcover; I'm feeling maybe paperback would be more appropriate, so the book would not seem to be calling attention to itself. And I doubt that we can, or should, make it very long. I feel conflicted about doing it at all, I suppose. I'll certainly take your—and Gert's—suggestions seriously. ["Gert" was Gertrude Bregman, the agent who handled Joyce's short stories at Blanche Gregory's agency.] It seems impossible that Gert sold 392 stories of mine! Can that be an accurate figure? Yet each time I write a story, or even begin taking notes for a story, it feels like the first time. The anxiety waxes and wanes, but it's always there.

My most consuming/obsessive project at the present time is my novel. I've had to take time out to breathe, and am doing the libretto for *Black Water*, collaborating with the most talented, congenial, rather wonderful man, the composer John Duffy, in his mid-60s (I think), music director at Lincoln Center. Even if nothing comes of the opera—it seems quite improbable, doesn't it?—I will have enjoyed the experience. Hearing John Duffy's music, quite apart from my words being sung to it, is already a remarkable experience. Ray is quite captivated by this process, too.

I have to confess that I was surprised, or more than surprised, by the many letters, and the *lengthy* letters, I'd written to A.K.! The chatty/newsy/improvised tone, the trivia I saw fit to record, the frequency with which I'd written—all seem out of character somehow . . . I seem always to have loved to *write*—shamelessly. But at such length! I'm taken that A.K. should have saved my half of what I had taken for granted was a wholly ephemeral, inconsequential correspondence . . . Ray and I laughed over many of the things in the letters, and shook our heads over, and marveled over, others—such as our penchant for summer school teaching *for something to do.* (The pay was minuscule. In fact, our regular salaries were minuscule. When I started at [University of Detroit], my salary was $4,900. Things improved dramatically at Windsor, but still we'd teach because we liked to teach, not for the money. Now, I haven't taught summer school since 1978 and I'm sure I never will again.)

We were marveling too over how we seemed to have so

much *time*—for all sorts of inconsequential but playful things. Lunches "three or four times a week" with our colleagues? Amazing . . .

The letters almost painfully make clear what I remember of myself from those years—how emotionally open, accessible, vulnerable I was—to friends, colleagues, students. I seemed to be perpetually available emotionally; my relationship with A.K. wasn't unique, but representative of a number of friendships of that era, with both women and men. A.K. wasn't my closest friend, even—but a good, chatty, newsy friend . . .

My "other" career [playwriting] continues, modestly: an opening of *The Secret Mirror* at Penn next week; *Friday Night* and *Greensleeves* at Cornell in early October. We'll be going to the Penn opening, but not the other.

Much affection from both—
Joyce (& Ray)

                                        17 October 1992
                              (a heartbreakingly lovely autumn
                                    day here! if only it would last)
Dear Greg:

We are off soon for London and Paris, which I anticipate with my usual ambivalence. Once we're in motion, I nearly always have a great time; beforehand, I can't see how I'll get ready in time, and I know I'll miss my work, friends, home. Especially I'm reluctant to leave my work which seems to be moving at a snail's pace. (Sometimes, in fact, it goes backward.) We're scheduled to see *Death and the Maiden* in London, among other plays. And we're looking forward to seeing the splendid museums in Paris, which won't require more than rudimentary French to enjoy . . .

Ray allowed me to see most of his replies [to questions for *Invisible Writer*]. They seem, to me, quite straightforward and accurate, and often very moving. As you must imagine, it's virtually impossible to write about anyone so close as a spouse of thirty years. Thirty years! (It seems like yesterday . . .) I've so assimilated Ray into my identity, my dreams frequently occur from the perspective of a double dreamer, some mysterious amalgam of the two of us.

Ray and I do disagree on one matter: the most reasonable attitude to take regarding biographical "memories" supplied by various friends and acquaintances. Ray thinks erroneous facts should be corrected, I think the contributor (like Madison Bell) should be allowed his or her recollections, especially if they are offered in good faith and without malice. It's certainly not an attractive prospect to be trying to censor others' memories of us. I remember trying to dissuade a Detroit friend (Kay Smith) who swore that the first glimpse she had of me I had hair long enough to sit on! Gently I said, "No, Kay, not really, I've never had hair longer than my shoulders," and gently Kay said, "Yes, yes you did, I remember clearly," and so on, and so forth, until I began to wonder if human memory is so frail and easily distorted as to be a kind of madness. And people will cling to their memories, passionately, even when they're proven wrong . . .

It sounds as if you're embarked upon a whirlwind of activities! (Far easier than staying at home writing, isn't it?) . . .

Your winter quarter course sounds wonderfully provocative. *Notes from Underground* would be ideal, too. Not to mention the supremely and elegantly diseased *Death in Venice* . . .

Thanks for your remarks on *Where Is Here?* and the Oxford anthology; the dust jackets of both are gorgeous,

I think. (I have to say, I had a strong hand in choosing the art.)

Much affection,
Joyce

13 November 1992

Dear Greg:

I was speaking with my parents last night, and they mentioned that you have been in touch with our old Millersport neighbors the Windnagles! Can this be possible? After forty years? If so, it's remarkable. I don't recall giving you these names, though possibly I did.

(Truly, I can't imagine what Jean Windnagle [a friend of Joyce's from early childhood] could recall of me after so long. To say that the Windnagles were not "bookish" people is a considerable understatement.)

(My poem "Back Country," in *Invisible Woman*, is about that family, the father, Miles, shooting the family dog, Nellie. I *do* remember that . . .)

My parents are very well, and ask to be remembered to you. They will be coming up in January for another McCarter Theatre benefit evening of two plays of mine (*Gulf War*, *Black*), on the 23rd—coincidentally, Ray's and my 32nd anniversary.

I read with much interest your essay-review in the current *Georgia Review*. Prizes!—like money, if you don't have them you think about them so the only means of not thinking about them is to acquire them but that necessitates thinking about them, and so to infinity. Even, or should I say especially, the ancient Greeks had literary prizes, not always felicitously given. (Euripides did poorly.)

I will say, though—as you do, in your piece—that an

award, even an honorable mention, at the right time in one's life, can make all the difference. My private theory is that awards are the external justification for what the writer is going to do anyway, for purely private reasons; it makes the madness seem somehow less mad.

Ray and I had a busy, at times exhausting London/Paris trip, and especially enjoyed Paris—walks along the Seine in lovely autumn weather, an evening concert in an old church on Île Saint-Louis (sacred music by Faure, and surpassingly beautiful), extraordinary art museums (especially the Musée d'Orsay with certain, to me, lesser-known impressionist paintings). We also became acquainted with the novelist-photographer François-Marie Banier, a most engaging, warm person, of about forty; very Parisian, very hospitable. (He has even invited us to spend some time at his house in Provence next summer—though I doubt that we'll get there.) I was interviewed and photographed a few too many times in both Paris and London, especially for one who doesn't take herself that seriously! . . .

All the household is well here, including Daisy (with a striking new black wrought-iron cage). We hope things are good there, too . . .

Joyce

2 December 1992

Dear Greg:

I was deeply moved by my old, long-lost friend's letter. I've begun to see that this matter of The Biography involves all sorts of unexpected revelations. Jean's reticence and concern surely have to do with the fact that her family was what is currently called "dysfunctional"; she must have traumatic memories of her abusive father, unless she hasn't much memory of him at all . . . There were certainly many very poor and "dysfunctional" families in our part of the world in that era.

(But how did you locate Jean, at all?)

I've enclosed, in no special order, a few more names for you to consider. Henry Bienen tells me he is awaiting your call. (He'll be around in January when you come visit.) . . .

We'd love to see you here in January; that would be great fun. Very likely my parents will stay through until Monday morning, so we could all go out on Sunday evening. The theatre hasn't been able to sign up anyone so famous as Ed Asner this time, unfortunately . . .

Reynolds Price was here last week and gave an extraordinarily moving reading. One of his stories dealt obliquely with AIDS. He's a warm, lovely, funny man whom I don't know at all well though after a few hours I felt I did, somehow. His semi-paralysis seems not to have made the slightest difference in his life, or I should say in his attitude toward life.

My parents, needless to say, will be delighted to meet with you. Answering your questions is a project they take very seriously. (Not that I don't, but, as you know, I feel somewhat embarrassed about it all . . .)

The proposed interviews you mention will surely work out. Should you want to observe a class of mine sometime, too, that would be fine with me . . .

Much affection,
Joyce

Part Three

1993–1995

During the next few years, I was busy researching and writing Invisible Writer, *and much of our correspondence concerned this book. As I interviewed (confidentially, in many cases) her family members and friends, Joyce was often concerned that people might have faulty memories of the past. On the whole, however, she was extremely helpful in providing names, addresses, and other information that enabled me to do as thorough and accurate a job as possible.*

Joyce continued to write plays, both short and long, but her main obsession during these years was the novel she was calling Corky's Price, *a long, richly detailed story of a New Jersey man who was, she said, as little "like myself" as she could imagine. The scope and ambition of the novel are suggested by her epigraph, from James Joyce's* Ulysses.

Another notable project during this time was her full-length "romantic comedy" The Perfectionist, *an "experiment in genre," as she called it, that premiered on October 1, 1994, at Princeton's McCarter Theatre under the direction of Joyce's friend Emily Mann. After her immersion in the long novel, Joyce continued to write plays with her usual prolificacy, and she attended as many productions as she could.*

Otherwise, life was relatively quiet and routine at 9 Honey Brook, and as always, Joyce found space in her letters to describe such domestic comedies as her cat Reynard's penchant for catching frogs.

4 Feb. 1993

Dear Greg:

It was really wonderful to see you the other weekend. I thought the visit went extremely well, and though my parents did seem uncharacteristically dour during our interview, I know they enjoyed it, and they certainly enjoyed your visit with them last summer. (It might have been that my father cautioned my mother not to remember things incorrectly. She *does* have what one might call an imaginatively active memory. This could be attributed to her age, though I must say a number of our friends have the same malady, too; most infamously, in fact, both the Bienens!)

I've told Leigh and Henry that, in your eyes, they are "engaging and effervescent." Leigh says you should observe Henry around the house . . .

Of the people you mention interviewing in Detroit, I'm astonished at the inclusion of Norman McKendrick. We didn't know each other at all well, and he seems thoroughly to have disliked me! I doubt he's ever read a word of my writing. (His sour, disturbingly ironic personality is the model for the Jesuit in my short story "The Jesuit.") I can't imagine he intends anything good to say about me . . .

On Feb. 12, at 9 p.m., NBC will show a documentary on Mike Tyson in which I'm very briefly interviewed. I'm dreading how it will turn out . . . my feelings about Tyson are unformed, inchoate. I've thought that what happened to him is a tragedy, and I've thought that what he did excludes him from being taken that seriously. But it seems likely he'll never be a great boxer now, which is a loss to the sport. (This most ambiguous of "sports"!)

Off to London tomorrow! (Please do send intelligent reviews of *Pagan Babies*. We'd love to see them.)

Much affection,
Joyce

15 March 1993

Dear Greg:

Thanks for the poems! And for your newsy letter. Chris Bigsby of the BBC is also an American literature professor at a provincial university in Norwich—wonderful person . . . In London, people do actually listen to such interviews, as, in Paris, they avidly watch author-interview programs and even discuss them afterward . . .

Thanks for the *Wonderland* paper [written by a student of mine]. The student *is* intelligent, and at times ingenious "discovering" parallels between *Alice* and this novel. I've been tempted at times to name influences and models for novels of which I know nothing and have never read, to see if close-reading literary critics will "discover" the parallels. I'm going to include an epigraph from Joyce's *Ulysses* for *Corky's Price* [*What I Lived For*], simply can't resist. There are obvious parallels, and a few less obvious, but, beyond that—?

Speaking of which, I've at last finished the first, substantial draft. If I believed in God, I'd be on my knees giving thanks. Russell Banks and I tease each other about our long novels-in-progress (his, on John Brown, keeps expanding just as mine has done) and he's a bit envious; except, when I told him the length (over 800 pages) he laughed his sadistic-sounding cackle. *His*, he's determined, won't go over 700 . . .

I reviewed, just a bit critically, though in essence very positively, Peter Taylor's new book of stories. Now I've learned Taylor is a rabid enemy to people who've crossed him. (I hope he doesn't see *TLS*!)

Much affection,
Joyce

April 4, 1993

Dear Greg:

Thanks for your letter, and for the excellent "A Barbarous Eden" [an essay on Joyce's debut collection that I published in the journal *Studies in Short Fiction*]. If I had read the essay before Ray and I compiled my collection of "early" stories, a few titles might be different. It's certainly a highly intelligent piece of writing, of interest, I think, on its own terms apart from having to do with my work. Your criticism is always first-rate, and provocative—I'm thinking of several recent *Georgia Review* pieces, and the Emily Dickinson study. (I can think of numerous academics for whom the Dickinson book alone would constitute much of a career.) . . .

I've found much in *Aid and Comfort* [my book of poems], especially the first section, to admire. Congratulations on the excellent *PW* review. Ray and I thought the *NYTBR* review of *Pagan Babies* quite good, if brief. The reviewer might have noted your strong female portraiture—Janice is a vital, lively character—and your sardonic sense of humor. But any notice, I suppose, is good . . .

Ray and a Mr. Guss of the USIA are making elaborate plans for our Spain-Italy-Portugal trip. Ray loves to travel, but I tend to feel reluctant to leave home. Now that my novel is finished, however, I should feel more enthusiastic . . . I think I've been overdosing on airports lately: recent trips to Denver, Brown University in Providence, Florida State U. in Tallahassee. The visits all went well, and I met extremely nice people, but nearly every airplane was delayed, or worse. I'm getting to know the Atlanta airport intimately, however.

The Contemporary American Theatre Festival at Shepherd College, Shepherdstown, West Virginia, will be doing a production of *Black*, July 7-Aug. 1 (in repertory with other plays). We will be there on July 17, to visit with Pinckney Benedict, too. [Benedict is a fiction writer and a former Princeton student of Joyce's.]

A new one-act play of mine, *The Rehearsal*, will be at the Ensemble Studio Theatre in New York, June 2-13. This theater is truly off-off-off-Broadway, inclined toward experimental and determinedly noncommercial work.

It's that season—Daisy is singing much of the day, especially when stimulated by our Italian language tape and/or the vacuum cleaner . . .

If you read the new *OR*, let us know what you think about the Janice Daugharty story in particular. We plan on doing a collection of hers—she's really remarkable. Jewel Mogan, too, is extremely talented, I think; but what a sad story—she'd published an early story in *Mademoiselle*, had a few rejections from magazines, and stopped writing for thirty years. It's a terrible loss, really heartrending. Someone should have prepared her for the vagaries of the writer's life.

Last night, we had dinner with Bob Stone and his wife, at the Halperns', and Bob was reminiscing of his early writing efforts, and rejections, as we all were. What prevented us from succumbing, as Jewel Mogan did, to a kind of premature despair is anybody's guess! . . .

I would prefer the title of [a new story collection] to be, simply, *Tales of the Grotesque*. But Billy, and others, seem to think that a single-word title (like *Heat*) sells books. The theory must be that shakily literate people can remember at least one word if it's a single-syllable common word. *Haunted: Tales of the Grotesque* is probably the title we'll go with. The dust jacket will probably be . . . Goya's *The Sleep of Reason Produces Monsters*. I haven't seen any designs yet. The Plume paperback of *Black Water* is very handsome . . .

We'll hope to hear from you soon. And we hope all's well there.

Much affection,
Joyce

⁓◑)

Joyce returned from her busy USIA trip with seemingly more energy than before she left. Again I "house-sat" for her and Ray while they were gone, interviewed many people including the Princeton poet-scholar Mike Keeley and her former editor at Vanguard, the then elderly Evelyn Shrifte, in New York. But Joyce's exuberance in returning to Princeton and to a stable writing schedule was dampened by the increasing ill-health of her parents Fred and Carolina, a concern she mentions in almost every letter during the coming months.

19 May 1993

Dear Greg:

We returned home to find everything in perfect condition—that's to say, what passes for perfect at 9 Honey Brook. There was even a large bouquet of flowers waiting on the front step, evidently delivered after you'd left, from Billy Abrahams, Elaine Koster, and Billy's assistant at Dutton, welcoming us home. (And saying they "love" Corky!—who isn't after all totally lovable.) The resident cats appeared one by one, and Daisy tittered a little—though, today, a shockingly gloomy, damp, cold day for spring, he's been virtually mute. (We hope he sang for *you.*) . . .

We perused your letter with much interest! How lucky you are, to have seen *Angels in America,* seemingly with so little planning and effort. (It's very difficult to get tickets.) Did you like it? Perhaps "like" is too weak a word—people have been enormously enthusiastic, including many friends of ours. Ray and I hope to go sometime this summer . . . though, at the moment, we seem not to want to leave home again, ever.

My father is unwell, and depressed; he probably won't

be able to take classes any longer—failing eyesight, hearing; other problems. He's been in the hospital for tests that are inconclusive thus far, which doesn't sound encouraging. He sounded particularly sad over the phone just now—he feels he has told you everything he can about me, and really can't come up with anything further, saying, "If I keep trying, I'll have to start making things up." I assured him that you didn't want him, or my mother, to invent anything! (They are so obliging, and are so fond of you, I'm afraid they've already confabulated a bit, particularly my mother.) My father's deterioration seems to have something to do with his thyroid and he's on massive doses of medicine that have unfortunate side effects. This is not to depress you—I hope!—but to explain that perhaps he and my mother might be of less help to you than in the past.

. . . I'm glad—though not surprised—that you liked Mike Keeley: he's terrific. And Evelyn Shrifte has always been rather like the way you describe. She would frequently call me very early in the morning—around 8 a.m.—when I was getting ready for the university (of Windsor), always beginning with, "Oh, am I calling too early?" with an air of apology. James T. Farrell was *the* writer of Vanguard Press history, so I don't wonder that Evelyn wanted to talk about him . . .

Our favorite cities of the tour were Rome, Florence, and Barcelona. We liked Granada very much, at least to look at— we were there so briefly. *Black Water*, in its various guises as *Agua Negra* (Spain), *Acqua Nera* (Italy), and *Aguas Negras* (Portugal), materialized as if by magic; so interviewers asked me—inevitably!—about Ted Kennedy. Headlines somehow had to do with "Hillary Clinton," several times—Europeans are fascinated with "Hillary," in rather negative terms, and have made her into a kind of caricature. I should say, though, that on the whole interviewers and cultural journalists generally were very well informed about my work, and about American literature; many of them spoke English. I was a bit overwhelmed by the warmth with which I was greeted, by people who seem to have read my work either in translation or in English; it's impressive how much foreign intellectuals know about our country, while most of us know so little in return.

We arrived home last night, went to bed around 9 p.m. (3 a.m. in Europe), woke promptly at 4 a.m. and got up to work—now it's 7 p.m. and the day has been *very* long, but hasn't yet wound down; there's a curious sort of momentum that carries you, at least for a while, when you travel rapidly westward from Europe. Last time, when we came back from London, I felt as if I'd been mysteriously charged with energy allowing me to wake up very early, work much of the day, and go to bed at our usual time—midnight, or later. This lasted for maybe two weeks, then the old schedule asserted itself. Not that we didn't like our tour—of course we did, at least most of it—(discounting Naples, which must have an air pollution index equal to Mexico City!)—but we were both enormously happy to get back home. I gave 13 lectures and talks in 16 days on the ground; not to mention numerous interviews, some of them lasting an hour, and all of them intense; not to mention ceremonial luncheons, dinners, and receptions "in my honor." We dined in palatial US embassy residences—in some cases, as in Rome, Madrid, Florence, actual former palaces, amid beautiful gardens. We certainly met some marvelous USIA officers, as we had in 1980, too. The foreign service includes some remarkable men and women, some of them with PhDs . . . And various writers, translators, publishers, professors, American literature students—all most interesting, and *intense*. I've had a flood of impressions, rich and combative, enough to last me for six months; though the experience, overall, was not so dramatic, nor so strained and anxious, as the 1980 tour in East Europe. And I doubt I'll be writing much about it, as I did, somewhat obsessively, after that trip. (The Berlin Wall alone was enough to inspire me for weeks!) Of the cities we saw, you would probably find Rome the most fascinating. But it needs to be *lived* in for longer than the three days we had, discounting the demands of my program.

Ray says thanks enormously for the *OR* work. [I had read submissions while Joyce and Ray were in Europe.] This is certainly very, very helpful to us. You can see how few submissions seem publishable, though many are "promising"; and virtually all have some merit. And with a publication like ours, which appears only twice yearly ...

I *do* think that John Hawkins is a very fine agent: aggressive, very tough, when required. It's Sharon Friedman with whom I work more closely; John deals with book contracts primarily. I'm sure that any agent would be less than perfect. It's true that I've been strangely indifferent to my "career" over the years—partly because I've been involved in my writing, and can only really feel anxiety about one world at a time. (Where you can't feel anxiety—for instance about money, or prestige—you can't make yourself *care* very much.) As far as sheer intelligence goes, John Hawkins is unbeatable. He's monumental, too—a big man—I do mean *big*. Next to him, Dan Halpern is a bantamweight ...

You didn't say much about Russell Banks. I hope the visit went well. Russell can be extremely dogmatic, even overbearing sometimes; he says he doesn't approve of biographies, yet, at the same time, he seems to approve of interview-articles, which are precisely the same thing except shorter. He's said repeatedly that no one is going to write a biography about *him*: he's destroying all the evidence. (With his four wives, and

other women, and his history of drinking and belligerence—
Russell has good reason to not want a biography written.
I like to tease him by assuring him that one will be written
anyway, with or without his consent.) . . .

Again, thanks so much for house-sitting for us. I hope you
managed to get some work done. Sorry for the fragmented
nature of this letter—I'm a bit distracted by thoughts of my
father (who, I seem to feel, this time, might not overcome his
health problems) and my mother (who has said guardedly on
the phone that it "isn't easy" to live with him in this state—
ordinarily, Daddy's so active).

Dan Zins's [a student of Joyce's at the University of Windsor, later a professor and scholar] essay is very well done. I
can hear his voice so distinctly in it!

Much affection!—and pet Freddie for us.
Joyce (& Ray)

28 May 1993

Dear Greg:

Thanks so much for the wonderful review [of *Black
Water*]—it was a most welcome surprise. (And the reproduction of the cover is beautiful.) I've sent it off to my parents,
who can use some cheering up right now. Your comments
are extremely interesting, as always. The final lines are most
touching. *Thanks.*

The issue of a writer's "unevenness" is intriguing. I've
wondered—whose work is "even"? Not Faulkner; not even
Emily Dickinson; nor even Shakespeare. I acquired *Sense and
Sensibility*, the only Austen novel I hadn't read, to read on
our plane flight back the other week, and was astonished at
how slow, dull, didactic, and unsparkling it was—hardly a
Jane Austen novel, at all. Trying to maintain a dutiful inter-

est in its turgid, repetitive plot and its minimally interesting characters, to get me through the hours of the flight, plus two more hours in a car from Kennedy, was quite a chore! (The suggestion that a prolific writer is "uneven" implies that other writers' work is consistently good, which can't be the case. And one would prefer a lesser work by a major writer— Lawrence's *The Lost Girl*, for instance—over the strongest work of another writer not of Lawrence's stature.)

(I realize that critics have to say *something* about a writer! In Europe, again, I was asked the usual, "Why is your writing so violent?" A few times I said jokingly that, by American standards, it *isn't*; I was known as the "Jane Austen of Detroit" for a while. Whether this was perceived as humor, I can't say. Next question!) . . .

Next week is the premiere of a one-act play of mine in a "festival" of one-acts at the Ensemble Studio Theatre, so I've been involved with that. Still distracted by my father's health. (He's had a "minor" heart attack.) It's difficult to extract from them any definite news, but we'll be going up to visit in a few weeks . . .

Again, many thanks for the review!

Give Freddie a hug for us.

Much affection,

Joyce

20 June 1993

Dear Greg:

I've sent off notes to Mr. Tanselle and Mr. Evert. (I have to confess I wasn't very strongly motivated at U. of Wisconsin [where she earned her Master's in English]—the scholarly/academic/traditional approach to literature, that's to say literary history, was very different from the exciting atmosphere of Syracuse U., where literature seemed virtually a living thing, in certain of my classes at least. And women were less encouraged, than they'd been at Syracuse; I know I was *dis*couraged from pursuing a PhD.) . . .

After this [biography], you can set up shop as a private investigator. Think how much more fun it would be if you were pursuing a real mystery, your life in danger! I don't doubt there are surprises in store for me, but they will be more along the lines of "So that's what he/she privately thought of me at the time!" than anything more significant.

The Rehearsal went very well at EST. Next is *Black* in West Virginia, and beyond that *The Perfectionist* which opens (!) Oct. 1 at McCarter. Since everything depends upon a strong actor in the title role, the play's fate will virtually be set at casting time in mid-August. Wish us luck! (It's very difficult to get "good" and "well-known" actors in the age range 40-50.)

When I attended my high school reunion (20th year? 25th?) I was struck by how my old classmates were "revising" history. Seemingly, they "knew" I was going to be a writer. I remember so very little of the people you've named, I had to think twice to realize that Dick Gregory is obviously not . . . *the* Dick Gregory. I'm sure he knew as little of me in high school, but he may invent an anecdote or two for you . . .

Next Monday is a reading in NY of the *Black Water* libretto. John Duffy continues to work on the music—he seems inspired, but the composition goes slowly . . .

The Killer [the title of an early, unpublished novel she'd mentioned in her journal] was the first version of *Expensive People*, written before I had the "voice." The other [unpublished] novels or projects are long vanished, and forgotten. (Fortunately!) . . .

Post-*Corky*, I feel almost too relaxed; I miss my headachy

stress & tension, that sense that, waking in the morning, I was sure to have a wretched time for the next several hours. Now, things seem *easy*; and even if they're not, they somehow don't seem important. At least not anxiously important . . .

Thanks for the birthday card. My birthday was very quiet . . . it's become a sheerly generic birthday now, with no numeral attached. Everyone is very diplomatic. Still, on the downside of 50, it hardly seems important any longer what one's age *is*. I'm sure I felt far more meditative turning 30.

(Considering the various casualties falling by the wayside, or seriously ill—most recently, Harold Brodkey with AIDS!—just to attain a certain age is an accomplishment.)

All the cats are well, if a bit sleepy with the heat; and Daisy, after a period of not singing, due to molting, unless he's just been taking time out, has started tentatively to sing again. Best of all are the bullfrogs, though, through the night.

Much affection,
Joyce

3 July 1993

Dear Greg:

I've sent off the letter to Syracuse, and I hope they comply. I'm astounded to hear you've unearthed my valedictory speech, which I didn't believe existed, at all. Do I dare ask to see it . . . ? I have only a vague swooning sort of memory of intense relief when it rained in great slashing pelts at the outdoor ceremony, and everything was curtailed, including my speech. I'd never addressed a large audience before and had been apprehensive for weeks. The only thing I remember about the speech itself was my faculty adviser (whom I'd only seen once, and who had a restrained interest in the project) advising me, "Remember, when you stand up to speak, they will be mainly waiting for you to sit down."

It's fascinating, too—(I should confess that your letters are the only letters I receive that I open with *extreme* interest! never guessing what might await inside)—to learn about my long-ago high school classmates. Though I've promised I will not second-guess people, and attempt to limit or censor others' memories/anecdotes, I do believe that some confabulation is imminent. I scarcely recall these people and would be hard pressed to say ten words about any of them, let alone recall/concoct "anecdotes." There were "clubs"—"sub-deb clubs"—in our high school, for girls, and I belonged to one of them; through the graces of my friend Gail Gleasner, who, like most of the girls in it, indeed like most of the students at suburban Williamsville (in contrast to rural Millersport), were solidly middle/upper-middle class. I really didn't belong to their world of expensive tartan plaid pleated skirts, matched sweater sets, "professional" fathers and "volunteer" mothers, but they were kind enough to behave toward me as if I did. I couldn't have any of them over to the house—our house was too small, rooms too cramped, and anyway we lived so far away—so for years I was a guest of others' hospitality, which I hope I appreciated at the time. We were all very good friends in this club—which must have "met" once a week?—but I can't remember a single occasion, nor can I remember, or even guess, what on earth we talked about so earnestly for years . . .

What is your novel about? Remember: the first sentence can't really be written until the last sentence is written, and you return to the beginning. So despair beforehand—though we all experience it!—is beside the point . . .

This July 4 weekend we are seeing virtually every Princetonian who has not gone away . . . Now that I am finished with *Corky* I'm in the kind of stunned/suspended/unreal mood in which, after all, it hardly matters what I do since what I do isn't of intense significance to me or others (not that, while writing a novel, we're doing what matters much to others anyway—but you know what I mean: that keen anxious/pleasurable sense of mortality)—so I can enjoy these excursions up to a point at least.

So much animated discussion about poor Harold Brodkey, and AIDS! Most of it is so critical of Harold, it's bewildering. Can there be a right way and a wrong way of dealing with a terrifying mortal illness? . . .

Ray has just hurried out to scare some deer away from a flower bed. Hearing him, Christabel, a warm furry plump weight on my lap, has stirred and growled menacingly . . .

I'm surprised, but happy, that my father wrote to you. He has serious eye problems . . . He's droll, philosophical—"I feel as if I'm being held together by pharmaceutical glue," he told me—eleven kinds of pills, some of which are to counteract the others!

Our friends Leigh and Henry are off in Bozeman, Montana, for a month—it is *very* quiet in Princeton. (I mean that literally.)

(The *Gettysburg Review* is an enormously attractive journal, isn't it? Very well edited.)

Much affection,
Joyce

15 July 1993

Dear Greg:

Thanks so much for the Kennesaw publication, and the valedictory speech. The latter was not half so awful as I'd anticipated though the youthful writer was *very* somber and rhetorical. Thank God for rain and all of us scurrying for shelter!

Your essay on the redoubtable "Oates archive" is very touching. I'm happy that my penchant for revising, and so forth, has not had the effect of dampening your enthusiasm for the writerly life. (Its motto: Nothing Gets Easier with the Passage of Time.) I think many people want to believe that writing comes easily, that "genius" expresses itself in quicksilver motion with few second guesses and revisions. (Mozart is the great exemplar—but was Mozart entirely *human*?) But I've come to be cozily content with revising; it's first drafts that are difficult . . .

When Emily Mann's father was dying last year—slowly, of cancer—I'd been starting a play more or less "for" Emily and the McCarter Theatre, a serious/"powerful" play (as I'd hoped). But I set it aside to quite deliberately write a comedy—a romantic/satiric comedy, *with a Happy Ending*. It was my first experiment with theatrical "genre"—*The Perfectionist* . . . Emily is currently casting *The Perfectionist* and has some excellent possibilities, she thinks. I'll keep my fingers crossed. Serious, good actors love live theater but need films and TV to make money, so we've lost at least one Tobias (the main character)—Richard Dreyfuss. Also, James Naughton—a Broadway actor whose name is probably unknown to you, but he starred in *City of Angels*.

The fluorescent-orange [jacket design] of *Foxfire* [1993] is certainly not what I would have chosen, but, unfortunately, no one sent me a final sketch. The general design is striking, though—I can't complain. (The Macmillan cover is absolutely pathetic. I saw it, politely rejected it, and—months later—here it is. What can one do but have a contract that stipulates jacket approval—which I thought I'd already had.) . . .

Much affection,
Joyce

4 August 1993

. . . Did I ever tell you how much I enjoyed, and was fascinated by, your "The Madness of Scholarship" [an essay on my engagement with the Oates archive]? It's a peculiar reversal—to identify more with one's biographer than with oneself!

Last night at Endicott Books, a lovely literary bookstore on the Upper West Side in New York, I read from *Foxfire* for the first time, and answered, or tried to answer, questions about it. I'd also been interviewed, somewhat awkwardly, by Charles Gibson on the *Good Morning America* TV show— the interviewer seemed not to have read the novel, and possibly the interviewee, casting about for things to say, had not, either. Without a "handle" of some meta-fictional sort, it's virtually impossible to talk about a novel. To find some external theme to discuss is the only way out, yet that violates the spirit of fiction itself.

Last night, at a sort of celebratory dinner before my reading, some NAL/Dutton people—among them Arnold Dolin, Lisa Johnson—spoke warmly of you. Your editor Audrey [LaFehr] was not present—I've never met her. There is a young editor who assists Billy now, Rosemary Ahern, who is most impressive, and may well become my editor when Billy retires (as he has been murmuring about doing lately—I certainly hope he doesn't!).

By now you should have received a copy of *Foxfire* "compliments of the author."

My play *I Stand Before You Naked* did extraordinarily well in Paris! The director sent a thick packet of reviews—all of which, he claims, are good. Since they're in French, I feel absolved from having to make my way through them . . .

We visited my parents last week briefly, and I drifted

about Lockport, seeing old sights, revisiting my grandmother Woodside's neighborhood (a fairly shabby house at 188 Grand Street—across from a factory that manufactures re-volvers!—as my father says, they don't advertise their prod-uct. But I don't believe the factory made revolvers in my day). The Erie Canal locks, the steep walls of the canal and the powerful cascading waterfalls are most mesmerizing, to me at least. I always seem to be encountering former-selves, lost-selves, in such places . . . what a mystery individuality *is*.

The Perfectionist is still not completely cast, including the main role, and rehearsals begin Aug. 27! Emily has offered the role to Bruce Davison (*Longtime Companion*) who has said he "loves" the role and wants to do it, but is awaiting a decision on a film possibility.

Tomorrow, I travel to Washington, DC, and will hope to see some museums in the interstices of interviews. Yesterday in New York, I saw a remarkable exhibit at MOMA, "Latin American Art of the 20th Century"—filled with treasures. A really stunning visual experience—one work of amazing art after another, most of them by artists unknown to me.

Ray says hello, as do Reynard, Christabel, Daisy, and Tristram . . .

Much affection,
Joyce
(I learned recently from Gert that Blanche [Gregory] is 92 years old!—)

25 August 1993

Dear Greg:

We've returned from our trip not exactly rested but in many ways refreshed. We had a lovely time on the West Coast in particular—lunch with Alice Adams, Diane Johnson, and

Billy Abrahams in San Francisco; some idyllic days in Santa Monica. *Foxfire* has surprised me considerably—not the novel, I mean, but people's reactions to it, especially women. David Selby, an excellent actor, and not Bruce Davison, will be in *The Perfectionist,* after all!

As always,
Joyce

3 September 1993

Dear Greg:

You've certainly been enormously busy! And your fall semester must be starting immediately. (Our first day, not of teaching per se but of related responsibilities, is Sept. 9.) Rehearsals have begun for *The Perfectionist*, with which I'm involved, though less intensely than Emily and the cast, who work from 11 to 6 every day except Mondays. Thus far, the actors seem extremely gifted, and fit together harmoniously. David Selby very much looks the part of the man I'd envisioned . . .

The promotional tour for *Foxfire* was, overall, a good deal of fun. One of the features of such travel is its *focus*—you simply concentrate on one thing, and do it. At home, our lives tend to be extremely fragmented—fractured. I've been working on short things exclusively since finishing *Corky* and don't believe I will ever write anything long and exhausting again! (My English agent Murray Pollinger, who has just begun to read *Corky*, said rather ominously that it was a "fearsome" read; then added hastily, as if he'd forgotten he is after all on my side, that of course there would be all the more to admire . . .)

It would be ideal to plan for dinner on Saturday, Oct. 2. I'm glad you're staying over. I think my parents will be here—barring sudden health problems . . . I'm enormously impressed with the McCarter Theatre as an ensemble—the staff is young, vigorous, imaginative and hard-working; Emily is terrific as a director—gentle but steely-willed; we have a first-rate set designer named Tom Lynch who has done many New York plays; and a composer named Lucia Hwong whose most recent work was the music for Anna Deavere Smith's *Twilight in Los Angeles* . . . As if I had not already been interviewed many times recently, a vast machine is now rolling requiring me to be interviewed by local NJ media to help with the play's publicity. Well—as I've said many times, it's much easier than writing a novel.

I'm very curious—I think!—to know what my Windsor friends and ex-colleagues had to say to you. They are not, overall, the most widely read of people—except for Lois and John Ditsky—and I can't imagine that they have actually *read* much of my writing. (Or much of contemporary fiction in general.) . . .

I began the Janet Malcolm piece, which I liked when she was being personal and/or analytic regarding the art of biography (though she seems to have a characteristically low-minded or cynical attitude toward it: what of the great biographers Leon Edel, Richard Ellmann, Joseph Frank, Justin Kaplan—are they too merely dealing in gossip and trivia?); but found it tedious and repetitive when she gets to the heart of her own research, the familiar round of names—Alvarez, Olwyn, Ted, Mrs. Plath, and so forth. Elaine, just returned from London, says that literary London is talking of nothing else—but that's because literary London is *in* the piece, more or less . . .

I'll be looking forward to your essay-review [on biographies] in *Georgia Review*. I very much enjoyed your last piece on the collections of short stories. My own theory about biography—as a genre—is that we read it fascinated to know how someone else has "done it"—gotten successfully (or even unsuccessfully) through a life. And there is always a mystery in others' lives one hopes the biographer can illuminate. I remember, not that long ago, as an adult, taking up a biography of Hemingway and actually trembling with excitement . . . of course, by the time I'd finished, Hemingway's life emerged as so miserable, his genius so betrayed by his meanness and vanity, I'd almost wished I hadn't begun. The massive Blotner biography of Faulkner is even more dispiriting. As Oscar Wilde so wittily said, "Biography lends to death a new terror" . . .

We look forward to seeing you Oct. 1. Stay well & give Freddie a hug for us.

Much affection,
Joyce

14 October 1993

Dear Greg:

It was wonderful to see you here, and to meet Dedrick. (I agree that he has a quiet, or at least unforced, sort of charisma.) . . .

The opening night of *The Perfectionist*, with my parents, friends, and Princeton acquaintances, was really a once-in-a-lifetime event. I think the actors did superbly under Emily's direction. In the short run, the play is a "success"—it surpassed its "single ticket sales goal" last Tuesday, and is surprising and delighting McCarter people (and me!). Beyond that, who knows?—it may be a purely local phenomenon, timely but time-bound. I thought of it as an experiment in genre—romantic comedy—something I'd never before attempted . . .

The Philadelphia Festival Theatre for New Plays is offering me a commission, which I think I will accept, to write a new, "serious" full-length play. I've been wanting for a very long time to write a verse drama (!) about Henry David Thoreau, but can't get started; can't get the voice. I feel very frustrated and will have to settle for characters and a setting more within my capabilities . . .

Everyone is very proud of Toni [Morrison], and happy for her. She won the Nobel Prize in the very best way, as I've told her—no rumors! It's a relief, too, to me, to know that lightning will never strike twice; media people will never again come to 185 Nassau to seek out a Nobel Prize winner. It seems increasingly ludicrous to me that my name should even be mentioned in that context. Toni is on a completely different plane of achievement and, more importantly, of significance; she *means* something beyond herself and her books . . .

I hope your various readings & visits go well. Much affection from the gang at 9 Honey Brook—

Joyce

8 November 1993

Dear Greg:

It's always a pleasure to hear from you, and usually a surprise—I mean, your letters carry unpredictable surprises. I had no idea that Kay Smith had an "Oates archive" . . . After Kay's death, her husband Joe returned to me a hefty packet of letters and postcards I'd written to Kay, and I remember the shock of opening the box and seeing my own letters— it was quite an emotional experience. Beyond that, I didn't know that Kay had anything. And how odd, it's been kept until now. Kay had indeed suggested she might write a biography, but this was a casual remark; frankly, Kay would not have had the discipline or the academic/critical sensibility for such a project . . .

I dread to think what the sales figures were for my early books at Vanguard; in fact, for most of my books at Vanguard . . . *and* at Dutton . . . (Don't tell me, please!) I deal with the brute reality of sales reports by quickly tossing away royalty printouts without looking at them . . .

I haven't read Margaret Atwood's new novel, though surely I will; I like her humor, at least in her short pieces. (As fuel for an entire novel, it might be a bit forced.) I recently reread, after many years, *Main Street*, and enjoyed it thoroughly.

The ill-fated title of my next novel is now, permanently, *What I Lived For*. This is a title I can live with, that at least doesn't misrepresent the tone of the novel. (Though in my heart it will always be macho-juvenile-cheery *Corky's Price*.)

Much affection from the household here, and a special hug for Freddie—

Joyce

⁓⑩

This next letter discusses Joyce's troubled long-ago student at the University of Detroit, Richard Wishnetsky. Mercurial, brilliant, and having formed a special attachment to Joyce, Richard was the inspiration for two of her finest short stories, "In the Region of Ice" and "Last Days." Ultimately, in a fit of psychotic rage, he murdered his local rabbi during services and then killed himself.

28 November 1993

Dear Greg:

I was very moved to receive and to reread the Wishnetsky material. Thanks for sending it. (I recall that I, too, wrote something, an essay/memoir for one of the Detroit papers . . . which of course I have not seen, nor thought of, for years.) You would have had to have known Richard W. to appreciate how keenly, how intransigently he *lived*—until his mania, or whatever chemical it surely was, overtook him. Strange to think how we are all, fundamentally, phenomena of "biochemical" balance, or imbalance; a misfiring of some crucial neuron and we become manic, or depressive, or schizoid, or, like my sister, autistic. Hard then to be "proud" of one's well-being and/or talent . . .

So you spoke with Charles Murrah! [Murrah was a colleague of Joyce's at the University of Windsor.] What an apparition out of the past . . . No one had much to say about him when we visited Windsor, and it's hard to believe that he is still drinking as compulsively as he once did. The story I wrote stimulated by a mutual student's trauma at his hands (?)—"Gay"—has never been reprinted [after appearing in *Playboy*], to my knowledge . . .

I'm relieved that *What I Lived For* is *the* title, finally. Billy was perfectly willing to stay with *Corky's Price*. But no one liked it, and I do think the advice was well-made. It has a posthumous tone that belies the novel's voice, which is a fast-paced talky/vernacular voice, but that can't be helped. What Corky lived/lives for is, I think, the sheer *livingness* of life—in him, nearly always unpremeditated when it actually occurs (though he plans a good deal, plots that invariably misfire); he's so far from being a "hero," I would not even classify him as an "antihero." It may be that, like some men, I suppose some women, too, Corky is addicted to his own adrenaline . . .

Enclosed, for your curiosity, since I don't think you've ever seen him, a photo of redoubtable John Hawkins. (Please return eventually.)

Ray says hello.

Much affection,
Joyce

✺

One of Joyce's notable preoccupations in 1994 was her becoming absorbed once again in short fiction, after the long stint of playwriting that succeeded Corky's Price. *One of her most famous, or infamous, short stories was "Zombie," published in the* New Yorker *that summer. (This was her first publication in the fabled magazine, but many more stories, essays, and poems would appear in its pages in years to come.) Based loosely on the case of Jeffrey Dahmer, "Zombie" captured her imagination so strongly that in late summer she transformed the story into a short novel, which Dutton published the following year.*

January 20, 1994

Dear Greg,

I've just marked *Greg visits class!* for April 20. I'd love to photocopy and "teach" a story of yours in that workshop . . . though perhaps that would be distracting (to you, as an invisible observer). Let me know.

I finished revising the Thoreau play—it was one of the most fascinating and haunting periods of writing I've ever experienced! I was literally (metaphorically?) transfixed for weeks . . . It's painful, however, to have to leave so much out. As it is, the play is probably too long. Inhabiting the imaginations of Thoreau and, to a lesser degree, Emerson, for a sustained period of time, was a remarkable experience.

I've been writing plays, and thinking/dreaming of plays, continuously for some time. I've stopped "thinking" in prose—or whatever it is writers do. Now it's visual scenes, oral exchanges . . .

(I haven't written a short story for so long . . . it's like losing track of an old, close friend.)

I very much admired your review-essay in *Georgia Review*. The biography of Elizabeth Bishop seemed particularly appealing, and unexpected. (Bishop's "sparing" oeuvre is the result of her drinking and ill health . . . !) Just so, the precision of the (middle-aged/older) writer's prose, the eager willingness to revise, revise, revise, is a consequence of the diminution of energy and inventiveness. My imagination was always so brimming, decades ago, I didn't want to make time for the fastidiousness I take now for granted. Was it Rousseau who copied over an entire volume, out of a desire to reinhabit its creation?—and to forestall moving on to something new and frightening? I know that feeling, almost . . .

. . . Yes, just two titles for 1994. Dutton hopes to promote *What I Lived For* as a "big" event . . . good luck to them! [The Rosamond Smith suspense novel] *You Can't Catch Me* is scheduled for 1995, and possibly a story collection, *Will You Always Love Me?* (A terrifying question, isn't it?)

As always,
Joyce

8 February 1994

Dear Greg,

We sympathize with your trauma at moving. Yet it's far

worse to move a long distance! Which is why we will *never* move from 9 Honey Brook.

(Our weather is . . . unspeakable! More snow! Sleet! We're missing a dinner with Athol Fugard, Antonia Byatt, Toni Morrison, and others!)

Frank Aronson [a man Joyce had dated before meeting Ray] called today—out of the blue! Do you have his address? He wouldn't leave a telephone number, saying he would be too hurt if I didn't call back.

Stay well—

Joyce (Do I dare see those early stories?)

6 March 1994

Dear Greg,

. . . I enjoyed your "Scene of the Crime" in the current *Southern Review*—an inspired ending.

We look forward to your Princeton visit. On Saturday, however, we must go to New York—we're meeting Marianna Torgovnick (the feminist/American studies critic—a friend who teaches at Duke), and, with Larry and Mimi Danson, seeing a matinee of *Carousel*. In fact, would you like to join us? If so, call for a ticket soon. We'll be driving in, of course. The play opens soon, and will be quite a sellout, I think. We'd tried to see it in London but there were absolutely no tickets.

. . . [My parents would be] delighted to see you. My father's radiation therapy has almost ended; that is, the intensive phase is ended, but he must have follow-up sessions for a few months. Apart from being extremely tired, he says he has suffered few side effects. My mother says he has done very well, too.

I admire my parents enormously—in the midst of the worst winter in recent memory, they've continued with their swimming! I don't think they ever miss a day . . .

Yes, Frank Aronson telephoned, and spoke with—really *at*—Ray, for about ten minutes . . . Very strange. I have only pleasant memories of Frank, yet not very many, I'm afraid. I believe he majored in biochemistry, and got a PhD from Cornell (?). We'd completely lost track of each other. Our relationship was more of a friendship than a romance, as probably others have told you . . .

After a long siege of playwriting, I'm back writing short stories. Still so relieved to be finished with *Corky*! (Not Corky the man, but the pressure of writing so long & sustained a narrative.)

Much affection,
Joyce

6 May 1994

Dear Greg,

Enclosed is a virtual grab bag of items, most of them just for fun. (Though you may find the essay on Flannery O'Connor as a racist disturbing . . . it didn't surprise me very much.) My parents are here for a busy weekend that includes Henry Bienen's birthday party (his 55th); a McCarter opening of a lavish new production of a Marivaux play (18th-century French); a modest production of six short pieces of mine at the university, including "I Got Something for You." (The elder Menendez brother in fact was a student at Princeton until expelled for cheating.)

My parents are both in good spirits, and ask to be remembered to you. I was steeled for Daddy looking gaunt and drawn but he looks *fine*! He hasn't even lost any hair from his radiation therapy. They are both busily working about the house and grounds on this sunny-gusty May morning. Thanks so much for the poem of 8-yr-old JCO. I do remember the elephant "trademark" now! (So do my parents.) Yes, I did attend Bible camp for a week; I must have been about ten. I did memorize many Bible verses, beginning with the Book of John. I believe I was considered amazing—I must have recited the verses by rote, without understanding much. (This was an example of my "religious" devotion, I suppose.) I wish I could remember the context more clearly. A Methodist Bible camp, I believe . . . We loved seeing you, all too briefly.

Joyce

27 May 1994

Dear Greg,

Maybe Ray, Freddie, Lucy & I can have bit parts in *Pagan Babies: The Movie*. It sounds like a serious prospect! (Is the name "Lucy" in any way allusive, like "Freddie"?) [The movie rights for my novel *Pagan Babies* had just been optioned by Miramax, with Julia Roberts and Ethan Hawke to star; but the movie was never made. My dog Freddie was seriously ill, so I acquired a miniature dachshund puppy named "Lucy."] We are leaving for LA (for the ABA where I'm giving a short talk—on a bill with Archbishop Desmond Tutu!) and for several days of museum visits, etc.; then renting a car to drive to Las Vegas to attend the Horror Writers Association/Antiquarian Booksellers Assoc. convention—I'm the 1994 recipient of the Bram Stoker Lifetime Achievement Award in Horror Fiction (!).

John Updike recently astounded me by indicating that he wants his letters in my archive read . . . not buried away, as I'd assumed was the proper stipulation. So, anytime you wish, these wonderful letters are open to perusal.

Much affection,
Joyce

7 June 1994

Dear Greg:

... I was indeed surprised that John Updike indicated a certain impatience with me ... [She had "restricted" his letters to her until the year 2025.] I think he said, "Lighten up," or words to that effect. He didn't plan to be around in 2025, he said. Of course, there are more Updike letters here, in my ongoing file, which you can peruse the next time you visit.

[You've written] eight thousand words, and I'm not even born yet ... Greg, you amaze me. I would never be capable of such a feat myself. (What on earth is there to *say* about "JCO"? The subject leaves me blank.)

Our near-week in Los Angeles went very well, with the American Booksellers Assoc. convention out of the way early. I didn't find the experience nearly so much of an ordeal as everyone had warned me ... The Dutton/Penguin row was quite impressive. (Much attention given to *What I Lived For*. Poor Corky!) The Ecco Press booth, though of course much smaller, was very elegantly displayed, too ... There were three breakfast speakers at my event—E. Annie Proulx, Archbishop Desmond Tutu, and me; and two thousand people in the audience! Fortunately, we spoke in alphabetical order; it would have been extremely difficult to follow Mr. Tutu, who is a crowd-arouser, rather evangelical in his utterances ("We are all the rainbow people of God ... black and white together"), and clearly practiced at his craft. Annie Proulx was very warm, funny, intelligent, engaging—I liked her very much, especially her droll wit, in these circumstances not unlike my own. (The Archbishop, backstage, was all hammy smiles for the camera, and very commandeering. For one of the photo opportunities, when the three of us were being photographed together, someone said, "Talk to one another, please," and the Archbishop said, in the most condescending way possible, "And what kind of books do you write?" to Ms. Proulx and me; he wasn't even listening when I replied ironically, "Oh, just novels." Ms. Proulx was stony silent.) . . .

In LA, we had dinner with Ryan O'Neal (wonderful sense of humor), Farrah Fawcett, Diane Keaton, JoBeth Williams, Larry Grobel, our friend Susan Loewenberg (of L.A. Theatre Works) . . . extremely interesting people.

Joyce
(Lucy is darling!—irresistible. Those eyes . . . [I had sent her a photo.])

6 July 1994

Dear Greg,

Thanks for letting us see the enclosed poems. They're powerful, and moving! . . .

I believe the *New Yorker* is having second thoughts about my story "Zombie." It has been scrutinized by the magazine's lawyer, and has gone to an outside lawyer. Maybe it's for the best: the story isn't one I feel comfortable about my parents seeing, at least in such a public context (they subscribe to the magazine). Somehow, in hardcover, in a gathering of other stories, certain difficult stories have a way of blending in; or so I think.

"The Romance of Solitude"—what a great title! [This was a chapter title for *Invisible Writer.*]

And Ray and I are feeling it, these days. Many Princeton friends are away on vacation. Each year I want the summer to go on forever, and each year it ends in a cataclysm at the start of the fall semester.

. . . U. of Windsor was never "regal" but was, and probably still is, a very friendly place. I know this seems to contradict "feuds" of which you've heard but, oddly, even the "feuds" were fun. The one thing the university was not was cold, distant, impersonal; the English department was like a big extended family—lots of squabbling, alliances, anecdotes and (comic) grudges of long duration. (No doubt why most of us have fled our extended families.) . . .

Much affection,
Joyce

18 July 1994

Dear Greg,

Happy (belated) Birthday! (Just received your much-enjoyed letter . . . I can wait till later re. quotes, etc., in The Biography. It sounds—stupendous! Surreal!)

We just returned from our five-day trip to New York, which was a bit breathless—four nights on the road, each in a different place; many more hours of intense driving than we'd anticipated. (You would think that, by now, I'd know how dismayingly wide New York State is; and how long it takes to get out of the mountains on two-lane roads.) . . .

We stayed at the [William] Heyens', along with my parents, who journeyed to the Rochester area for the dinner, etc., in my "honor" at the library there. What a stunning/staggering display of the Heyens' collection! It was quite moving, to contemplate the display cases in chronological order; and sobering, to contemplate the "evolution" of JCO hairstyles through the decades. My parents are both surprisingly well, considering their quantity of medications and doctors' appointments.

(The Frank Aronson incident is most disturbing. He used to be—quiet! intelligent! thoughtful! Odd, that he's married . . .) [I had tried to interview Aronson over the phone but he talked nonstop for more than an hour, and would not answer the questions I wanted him to address; finally, I had to end the call.]

When we returned home, amid the alarming piles of mail was a most welcome letter—handwritten, and warmly chatty—from Gail Godwin! She has been inspired by perusing our correspondence to write, after a silence of many years. She spoke of "joy departing" from her life for these years, but didn't elaborate other than to declare she will *not* take Prozac. But she seems quite energetic now, and enthusiastic about her novel. I've only had time to dash off a card in reply to her. So, once again, The Biographer has provided a surprise . . .

I did read much of the new *Southwest Review*, and thought your story ["Uncle Vic"] one of the best . . . I liked your narrator, and his irredeemably dysfunctional family . . .

Next weekend, the Berkshire Theatre Festival in Stockbridge, Mass., is presenting an evening of dramatized stories of mine, which should be interesting. I'm not involved in any rehearsals, or in the selection. The director Elie Renfield is very good. *The Truth-Teller* will premiere at the Circle Rep in New York on or near Jan. 9, 1995. I'm very pleased about this "major" off-Broadway production, with a fine director, Gloria Muzio. Maybe you could join us . . . it *is* a comedy.

As always,
Joyce

29 July 1994

Dear Greg,

Thanks for your letter(s). By now you've returned from an alarmingly concentrated SF trip. I'm envious of you having lunch with Alice A[dams] and dinner with Billy A[brahams] in a single day. (I don't recall if you've met Alice before?—she's a wonderful, lovely woman. And Billy—Billy is inimitable. Possibly the most spirited and enthusiastic and book-loving person I have ever met, and what good fortune that he is my *editor*. I wonder if he told you that I'd dedicated *Last Days* "to William Abrahams"—without of course knowing—this lay in the future—that he would be moving to Dutton to take Henry Robbins's place. Amazing coincidence. Billy's hopes for my "career" are unflagging, too. I listen, and seem to agree, for who am I to undermine another's fantasy? Billy *always* imagines that my next novel will be the breakthrough.)

. . . I guess I will have to send *What I Lived For* to my parents. I feel reluctant, given the novel's special tone, its macho "vulgarity." My father's eyesight, too, makes reading increasingly difficult, and a novel of this length, so densely printed, will fill him with dismay. (It would fill me with dismay!)

I'd love to read Gail Godwin's new novel and hope that I receive galleys. She sounds—almost!—like her old self again. She seems to live for her work, including her "career," in a way more fiercely concentrated than I can do; no doubt because she doesn't teach, and isn't involved in literary matters much.

What an experience you had with Frank Aronson! . . . I remember him as quiet, thoughtful, articulate but never garrulous or overbearing; not shy perhaps, but reserved; very intelligent. We met in September 1957 (so long ago) in a conversational German class in the already-antique Hall of Languages at Syracuse. Our relationship was quite casual, un-passionate—this was the 1950s, please don't forget, not the 1960s, still less the "liberated" 1970s. We didn't correspond much after graduation, and when I told him about Ray, he remarked that he'd thought "we might have had a wonderful life together"—but I think this was retrospective, and not an accurate emotional judgment. You've heard of "mimetic desire"—thinking we want what someone else wants, because someone else wants it. Never was the word "love" exchanged between us in the several years we were friends. We've never corresponded since, and I have no idea where Frank works, or who his wife might be. I'm relieved he *is* married!

. . . It was an imaginative notion for Julia Roberts to latch onto your novel, which, judging by its cover, would not have a strong role for a woman. Lorraine Bracco was virtually signed up for *Because It Is Bitter* . . . when the film was scheduled for production by American Playhouse, but, according to the director Larry Schiller, didn't read the script beyond the death of her character, Persia. The production was eventually canceled for whatever reason such things are canceled—there always *is* a reason! But it does look far more definite re. *Pagan Babies*. If you are offered [the job of writing] the screenplay, you should seriously consider doing it. I've enjoyed screenwriting—it's so much easier than writing prose fiction . . .

Much affection,
Joyce (& Ray & the menagerie)

13 August 1994

Dear Greg,

Thanks for your kindness in sending me the letters to Gail Godwin; do you think I could also see copies of Gail's to me . . . ? I must say that I am appalled by the tone of the earlier letters: the rapid-fire chattiness, the (surely disingenuous) portrayal of myself as so much stupider than, surely, given the evidence of my "real" writing at that time, I was . . .

One would never get the impression of how serious I was about teaching at Windsor, and about my students, for instance; how much I thought about the texts I taught, and classroom presentation . . . And my dismissal of theater (my remark that Ray and I "loathed" it) sprang from some unfortunate productions we'd seen in Stratford, Ontario, and at local universities. Again, meaning to be "amusing," I exaggerated to an absurd degree.

It has been said of Eudora Welty that she presents to the world an unruffled persona of sweetness, Southern graciousness, and "aw-shucks" naivete, and you can't penetrate that façade. (Miss Welty was in fact rather like that during her two-day visit to Princeton a few years ago.) I certainly hope that my public "persona" of the 1970s, at least as it seems to have been constructed for Gail Godwin, was not so two-dimensional and self-betraying.

. . . Billy A. *loved* meeting you! Thought you were "about 26." All's well here, though steamy-hot.

Joyce

18 August 1994

Dear Greg,

. . . My father mentioned receiving a nice letter from you recently. (His eye is mending a bit slowly following his laser operation.) . . .

My boy cousins, and boy elementary school classmates, were jarringly profane and obscene. I think my reaction *against* their vulgarity, perceived as very male (junior-macho, but we hadn't the term "macho" then), persists still . . . I do look forward to [Gail Godwin's] *The Good Husband:* may I see your review eventually? . . . Your discovery re. Gordon Lish is fascinating; *I'd* forgotten, mercifully. [Early stories Joyce published in *Esquire*, where Lish was fiction editor, were subjected to random, egregious editing that, in some cases, nearly ruined them.] He has a reputation for having been injurious to some young writers, including my former student Walter Kirn. What handsome photos!—of you, too, I mean, as well as Freddie & Lucy. I'll be on *Good Morning America*! Oct. 4, no doubt *very* early.

Much affection,
Joyce

8 September 1994

Dear Greg,

What sad news! Ray and I are very saddened to hear that sweet Freddie has died. It must seem unreal to you . . . I have your card, and her photo, on the windowsill in front of me; her beautiful eyes . . . Please accept our condolences. I can imagine what it's been like for you; I still dream of Muffin (alive, *very* solid and affectionate) after three years. He was put to sleep by a woman vet who allowed us to hold him when he died; Tristram, his twin, actually died in our arms here at home. I hope Freddie's death was peaceful and painless, and that Lucy won't be terribly devastated. (What if Lucy wants more company than just two-legged Greg?)

. . . Another astounding bit of news from you: the discovery of Dorothea/Dottie Palmer! That is really quite amazing. How did Diane [my agent] know who Dottie is, or was? Does Dottie use her maiden name? (Amazing to hear that my old friend was married, without my knowing; and that her husband has died . . .)

As I've said several times, your next career really should be that of a private investigator. The academic life won't hold enough mystery for you. (Too bad you can't unearth some wild scandal about JCO. I'm afraid I never got around to concocting one.)

... "Zombie" is now scheduled ("tentatively") to appear Sept. 20 [in the *New Yorker*] ...

Again, please accept our heartfelt condolences.

Much affection,
Joyce

27 September 1994

Dear Greg,

... My parents just left after a brief visit, which included the opening of *The Matchmaker* at McCarter Theatre, directed by Emily Mann; a rousing production, very quick, bright, deft, "musical-comedy" in tone. Thornton Wilder is not exactly my favorite American playwright, but it was an entertaining evening, and my parents loved it. My father is in excellent spirits these days: a new hearing aid, and, at home, a new magnifying mechanism that fits onto a desk, which allows him to read despite his "macular degeneration." He's taking an advanced course in Hawthorne about which he's very enthusiastic. And my mother is well, as usual ...

Thanks for the Godwin review. It's so generous, and well-written. I'm sure Gail must be pleased with it. (Since writing a long, chatty letter to Gail some weeks ago, I haven't heard from her. Nor have I heard from Dottie P., which is unsurprising: what would she have to say to me, after all? There would be the awkwardness, too, I'm sure, of her not having read anything I've written in thirty-plus years ...)

... My story was postponed once again at [the *New Yorker*]—no particular reason given. I've given up expecting it to appear at all. I never see the magazine, in any case. The "copyediting" there is horrendous—like being picked at by a swarm of carnivorous gnats.

... Your household must be sadly quiet, with Freddie

missing. How wise you were to have acquired Lucy! When cats become old and ailing, they know they are going to die, and begin to retreat; Muffin first went to hide in closets, or beneath beds, and though he would respond with some of his usual affection, purring, etc., it was clear he preferred to be alone. Then, incredibly for one who'd been, as you might recall, a "comfortable" sort of house cat, he began going out into the woods . . . where I'd find him, just lying there, sphinx-like, not asleep, very peacefully waiting. I'd carry him back up to the house, feed him, and so forth . . . next day he'd go back out into the woods. It was . . . very unnerving. As if some force was drawing him, stronger than the bond between him and us. This went on for weeks! Finally he was just too weak, and obviously suffering, so we took him to the vet . . . It was a very sad time, as you well know. One wants to say impatiently, "Look: he was only a cat!" Which is so, he *was*. But, as Dan Halpern said, a long-term relationship is a long-term relationship, a vital part of your life . . .

As always,
Joyce

24 October 1994

Dear Greg,

Thanks so much for your superlative review of *What I Lived For*. It's really an essay-review, with much packed in, and much that is elliptical. Of the reviews I have seen so far (no doubt there are others I've been spared) Corky seems to have been surprisingly well-liked, given his "despicable" qualities. Several (male) readers have said they *are* Corky, to a degree . . . And several women have said they used to go out with a Corky or two. I had not intended him to appear to be a weakling, since he does sacrifice his life in quest of some elusive principle of truth, or justice; but in the whirli-gig of events, perhaps this was lost or obscured. In any case, I'm grateful for your review, as always. When I arrived in Chicago, I was told there was a "terrific" review in the *Chicago Tribune*; but no one seemed to have it. At my reading at Waterstone's, in the evening, a reader gave me a copy of the review, but in the confusion of book signing, etc., it somehow got lost. Very frustrating, since I knew it was yours!

Congratulations on the response to the first part of the biography [from my Dutton editor]. As I've said before, I am in awe—*how* did you make my life seem interesting? (Maybe you've extravagantly fictionalized it? That might help!) I hope, given my parents' age, that they will be able to read something of the biography fairly soon . . . I don't want to sound morbid, but—. (I know they're eagerly awaiting it, or in fact anything you've written so far.) It's the same princi-ple of their waiting dutifully, hopefully every Oct. for the non-imminent Nobel Prize, since I'd been so publicly nomi-nated for it years ago.

Enclosed is a publicity release the *New Yorker* sent out with advance copies of the issue to various media people. Do you think the editors felt they should explain the story . . . ? Its appearance in their pages? (John Updike sent a funny card, saying he wouldn't forget the story for some time, and that William Shawn must be "twirling" in his grave . . .) I'm con-tent, though, never to appear in the *New Yorker* again; once in a lifetime is probably enough . . .

I've been very busy, in the interstices of quick trips (next is to Boston, just overnight), completing projects—finishing the manuscript of the story collection [*Will You Always Love Me?*] dedicated "to Greg Johnson" (I hope you don't regret it!), and the even more bulky manuscript *American Gothic Tales*. *Will You Always Love Me?* is scheduled for next May, which seems a bit soon, and the other has not yet been scheduled. I've suggested Willem de Kooning's pastel *Seated Woman* for the dust jacket. The jacket design for *What I Lived For* is very striking, though not what I'd hoped. (I had wanted a blurred, dreamlike photograph of a cityscape seen from a moving car, blending with the night sky. Billy had wanted this image, too.)

. . . Ray and I are planning on buying a watercolor by John Marin this week, we think. His work is extraordinarily beautiful.

. . . Best wishes & affection from the gang at 9 Honey Brook. (Next letter, I'll tell you about my visit to Bennington College. I assume you know what is happening there?)

Joyce

19 November 1994

Dear Greg,

Good to hear from you; but so sorry to learn that another friend of a friend has succumbed to AIDS . . . How hurriedly people are running through their lives today, and how "precociously" others are becoming intimately acquainted with death and dying!

(How could that editor of a "porn" publication imagine that you, who have written so powerfully about AIDS, would want to write for his publication! Maybe he didn't exactly read your poems but "looked into them" as they say in Hollywood.)

This is a rapidly composed letter, as I prepare for yet another trip, to Miami (the Book Fair—where I've never been) and then back on Monday to New York where a play of mine will be given a reading, directed by Tom Palumbo . . .

Zombie, the novella, will be published in fall 1995; with

the unfortunate consequence that *Will You Always Love Me?* must be postponed a few months. Too bad! A "Rosamond Smith" novel is scheduled for March 1995: *You Can't Catch Me*. No space here to speak of Bennington College—where the manipulative president (a woman exactly my age!) fired 1/3 of the faculty, on the pretext of budget exigencies but in fact (as I gather) because of political differences. As soon as I arrived I was told "Your presence here is a political statement"! . . .

Much affection as always,
Joyce

19 December 1994

Dear Greg,

Thanks for your letter and its enclosures (a double bill with A.K., indeed!—if you will promise not to tease me about my old colleague/buddy, I will promise not to tease you about N-wt G-rich, Georgia's gift to Western civilization) and your card. Will you be "celebrating" Christmas this year?

I suppose I do enjoy visits/readings—it's so much easier than writing itself, at least the intense, nerve-racking early drafts. *Anything* is easier than the first six weeks or so of a novel! I guess I do feel, in front of an audience, at least the kinds of friendly, self-selected audiences I encounter, absolutely at ease, energetic and good-spirited. (None of this has anything to do with "JCO" of course—which is probably why it's so much fun.)

But this is hardly news to a fellow novelist!

Ray and I have been seeing the usual Princeton friends lately, yet we've had several long sunny-cold days since the semester ended; so very welcome! I've been reading Don DeLillo's *White Noise* which has many wonderful passages, a sort of lower-keyed, more protracted (and sometimes just a bit forced) D. Barthelme paranoia-fantasy. Also, Tim O'Brien's *In the Lake of the Woods*, which we'd recommend. The only movie we've seen in a year—since *The Piano* (!)—is the British *The Madness of King George*—brilliantly filmed and acted. (Though we're wondering who will buy tickets to see it, in the US?) We were, as it happened, guests of Tina Brown and Harold Evans (these diminutive—5'3" at their tallest—"Brit imports" as they self-consciously call themselves) who gave a party at the Four Seasons following a preview of the film by their friend Alan Bennett. Ray and I had seen the spectacular (literally) stage production at the Brooklyn Academy of Music last year.

(Did I mention that Tina Brown would like to send me to interview Mike Tyson in his Indiana prison, preparatory to a lengthy piece on Tyson when he's paroled next spring, and returns to boxing? I don't think I will take on this assignment, fraught with much risk. (A lawsuit, obviously.) Dan Halpern says he'd accompany me to Indiana; *he's* thrilled at the prospect. The "Talk of the Town" commission was much fun: I had an overnight deadline, thus couldn't fuss and revise much. I've been asked to do more for that department, and can see how rapidly one's time for other, presumably more enduring things would evaporate.)

Mainly I've been writing, and rewriting, short stories lately. Such pleasure! I'm in love with (relative) brevity, after The Long Novel. Poetry, too. Finite forms seem, somehow, so *sane*. Both to read and to write.

We seem not to have any summer plans for 1995 at all . . . Often we drive to upstate NY, but are gone only a few days.

Colin Wilson! An odd, opinionated, crotchety Brit, in the (self-styled) style of G.B. Shaw, whom he much admires. We have no one like this in North America except the rather Colonel Blimpish Robertson Davies in Toronto, who makes epic pronouncements of an acerbic "provocative" old-white-boy nature. He and Camille P[aglia] might be marooned together somewhere, made to endure each other's company for forty days and nights.

Fondly,
Joyce

For the next year, Joyce was occupied in writing the brief Man Crazy (1997) and her long novel We Were the Mulvaneys (1996), a book she called her "valentine to rural upstate NY." The latter would become a critical success and, thanks in part to its selection by the Oprah Book Club, it would be her most commercially successful book, selling more than three million copies worldwide. Though she continued to mention productions of her plays, her involvement in playwriting was balanced by intensive work in her usual métier, novels and short fiction.

5 January 1995

Dear Greg,

Not a very adequate reply to your wonderful letter—. We, too, had a nice Christmas; though New Year's Eve, at Emily Mann's, just Emily and her man friend and Russell and Chase and us, was especially meaningful. Please do give Dedrick our warm regards. He's such a fine person; to think that he can cook, too—!

. . . (What a good, close friend Russell has become . . . partly because we're both fairly obsessed and doggedly serious novelists, I suppose. Russell's life continues to be rockier, more troubled than my own, obviously he's more embroiled with real life than I, having been married several times and having four daughters, plus his aging mother; and many family memories, not all of them pleasant. Of my Princeton friends (but then, Russell and I are hardly "Princeton") he is the one with whom I speak most candidly . . . He called me the other day to say he'd been reading *What I Lived For* until 5:30 a.m.! (He identifies with Corky in numerous not-to-be-elucidated ways.) It's so gratifying, as you know, in the most primary of ways, to be read with such sympathy and a fellow novelist's awareness of structural, stylistic, formal aspects of a work.)

. . . Thanks for your reviews! I liked the *White Noise* particularly. The *New Stories from the South* is, as you say, an uneven volume. Shannon [Ravenel] has never chosen a story from *OR*, though we've published first-rate Southern writers . . . in my opinion, at least.

Camille Paglia!—I read with mounting horror her "Bloody Sontag" essay. I suppose, if you don't know Susan, and have never been harassed by a demented person, it *is* funny. But, Greg, how *crude*! How will you feel when, one day soon, you are tracked around Atlanta by a fierce, envious younger rival who crows to the press that he is the "new Greg Johnson"; that, if he and you meet, you'll "slap each other silly"? What can one, if sane, possibly do or say, confronted with a publicity-hungry rival? Poor Susan! I hadn't known she'd endured this . . . Paglia's superficial summation of books, people, "trends" makes her, to me, simply too "pop" to be taken seriously . . .

My new project, a "novel (of a kind) by way of short stories," is tentatively titled *Man Crazy*. *There's* pop sensibility for you!

Much affection to you & Lucy, for the New Year.
Joyce

25 January 1995

Dear Greg,

I'm enclosing the *London Review* since they've sent me several extra copies, and I thought you might find the publication attractive. It's a junior version of *New York Review*—each review much shorter, but approximately the same quality. Elaine [Showalter] often publishes here.

Yes, I did ask [my publicist] to send *You Can't Catch Me*. (Do you recognize Tristram?) Thanks for your comments! It was a fascinating puzzle, to me, to write; the appropriation of a "self" by another "self" continues to haunt . . .

. . . The Bienens are in Evanston, IL, very busy, of course, but we continue to hear from them and will see them fairly soon, back in Princeton for opening night of Emily's new play (an adaptation of the Delaney sisters' memoir). An opening night of my own is Feb. 1. (But I must attend two previews beforehand, one followed by a "panel" of Deborah Tannen and me. My play *The Truth-Teller* is about a sociolinguist—*not* Deborah!)

We had a lovely dinner and theater evening with Betsey Hansell and her husband Cliff Ridley (drama critic, *Philadelphia Inquirer*) on Sunday, before attending an excellent performance of *The Cherry Orchard* . . . Betsey said that she enjoyed her conversation with you *very* much, and asked about you. Of course, we were delighted to boast a bit about your OR book and other outstanding accomplishments. (I wonder if you know what Betsey looks like? Probably you wouldn't remember, from our photo album. She and I were extremely good friends in my Detroit/Windsor years. I feel a real sisterly affection for her, and we are both very interested in art.)

Speaking of which: I've had a truly wonderful, absorbing and fascinating few weeks, writing a monograph, *George Bellows: American Artist*, for the Ecco "writers-on-artists" series. I'd never done anything quite like this, and now I really envy art historians. Bellows's work is remarkably varied, and frequently brilliant. He'd become famous immediately for his boxing paintings, but they're a small fraction of his output; I'm most taken by his seascapes and landscapes, and some of his odd, provocative portraits.

. . . I've been asked to review, of all unlikely subjects, Jack Kerouac—*Reader, Selected Letters*—for the *New Yorker*. I have to confess I'd never read Kerouac, must simply have skimmed through *On the Road*. I hadn't known he was so self-consciously/doggedly "literary"—very much like Thomas Wolfe, upon whom he modeled himself as a young, word-infatuated writer. But what a sad end . . . dead of alcoholism, burnt out, at 47. While his fellow Beats Allen Ginsberg and sinister William Burroughs are still going strong.

. . . Did I mention that *Foxfire* is (supposedly) going to be made into a film? Production begins in March, in Portland, Oregon. I have not had anything to do with the screenplay, though I'd met the producer, or one of the producers, a literary-minded woman, a year or so ago in Los Angeles. I have the idea that not just the setting has been changed, but the era . . . which means that the very atmosphere will be different. The director is a woman of whom I've never heard—Annette Heywood Parker.

Are plans moving forward for *Pagan Babies*, and Julia Roberts? If you're invited to do the screenplay, it might be an "interesting and novel experience," as they say.

I too received the Jay Parini *Steinbeck*, and have been asked to review it (for *New Yorker*)—but declined, since I simply don't have the time. It would require rereading much of Steinbeck, which might not be a bad idea; but not right now. At the classy and expensive ($21,000 annual tuition!) Pomfret School, where I spent 2.5 hyperventilated days, every other question was about "Where Are You Going . . ." Help!

Much affection from all,
Joyce

Valentine's Day 1995

Dear Greg,

. . . I hope, as my biographer, you won't be disappointed: I declined an offer from our friend Lanny Jones, *People* editor, to write an O.J. essay for them, based upon a few days at the trial. And I'm afraid I have backed off from the Tyson piece, suggesting in my stead Thom Jones, who not only knows about boxing, but has been a boxer . . .

I'm afraid I also declined reviewing Bill Gass's *The Tunnel* for the *New Yorker*, on the grounds that Bill is a friend of mine. (That might be news to Bill.)

Pagan Babies, the script, will be so radically unlike the novel, I'm sure, that, if it is filmed (as we hope it will be!), you'll probably be in awe of such imagination. (I still haven't seen *Lies of the Twins* beyond the first ten minutes.)

The Truth-Teller received a decidedly "mixed" (and rather baffled) review in the *Times*, but has been having sell-out performances and seems to be doing very well with audiences. A gay subscribers' group had an evening, and, evidently, they loved the play. ("They are the most wonderful, sympathetic audiences you can have," the theater manager said.) Since the play is about gender-switching, among other things, this makes sense. The reviewer managed not to notice any theme of gender, nor did he speak of linguistics, which is the play's main subject. But this is more or less expected, I guess, in the theater, where one is never reviewed by a fellow playwright or writer, as in the literary world.

Ray is fine, my mother seems in good spirits, but my father is not very well, I'm afraid. Many ailments, not the least of which is his macular degeneration (gradual blindness). They weren't able to come to *Truth-Teller*, and I doubt they'll be visiting anytime soon. [Are there] "stars" in *Foxfire*? It's such a low-budget film, "asteroids" might be more appropriate. I have not heard a word. [Actually, the very young Angelina Jolie played a major role in the film, though she was not yet a "star."] . . .

Love,
Joyce

8 March 1995

Dear Greg,

What an astonishment—to open your packet and discover those letters! [The letters were to and from Carol North, a college friend.] I've been quite stunned. I read them in a virtual haze, and reread—having to see, yes, it *is* my voice, a juvenile version, embarrassingly so!—(but I suppose I was "young"—still in my teens at the time of the earliest letters). (I haven't been able to force myself, actually, to read the putatively funny [Southern] "dialect" letters—and who "Bethlehem J. Hollis" was, I don't know. A character in my fiction, I suppose.

You can't imagine how disorienting it is to confront these buried, lost "selves"; at least there is nothing scandalous or deeply upsetting involved. In fact, I'm touched that Carol North should have saved these letters for—can it be almost 40 years? Incredible. You'd think they would have been tossed away long ago, or allowed to molder quietly. (I haven't seen a letter of Carol's for decades. I doubt that I'd saved them even back in the 1950s.) It's true, I was wrong about my parents' memory of Robin and me playing chess. [Joyce had insisted to me that she and her brother Robin (a childhood nickname for Fred, Jr.) would never have played such a sophisticated game as chess; "maybe Parcheesi," she joked. Fred and Carolina had told me that Joyce, losing, would sweep all the chess pieces off the board in a fit of pique. As it happened, in a letter to Carol North, Joyce admitted that she and Robin did indeed play chess, and that Robin would usually win.] I do remember Robin's and my camaraderie (mostly during the summers); obviously we were quite fond of each other, and got along in sister/brother sitcom/bantering ways I've never experienced with anyone else. Robin was lots of fun! (Now he has matured into a soft-spoken, intelligent, and somewhat bemused "Fred Oates, Jr." in whom "Robin" still lurks, if dimly. I think we regard each other warily now as adults, each hoping the other won't reveal our utterly silly child/ teenager selves in the presence of adults!)

Isn't it odd that these early letters, in their gawky un-self-conscious "humor," including even strained dialect, are so like Flannery O'Connor's letters?—well, I mean some of her letters, if I remember correctly. Yet I would not have read these letters of O'Connor's for decades. And, evidently, I hadn't read O'Connor's fiction at this time; it seems to have been Carol North who introduced me to it.

. . . One prevailing theme of the letters, as of my life generally, is my lamenting the passage of time; my own wasting of time (which is considerable—why people imagine me "prolific," I can't guess, a morning flies by and I've accomplished virtually nothing or have in fact undone something imagined accomplished the day before) . . .

I can't imagine what Allen Tate meant by speaking of

Harvard, Princeton, Yale, et al., as "steeped in the tradition of mediocrity." (Non-slaveholding universities?)

. . . Early sightings of John Updike! Somehow, Bob [Phillips] inveigled John to give him a poem for the [Syracuse] *Review*. Amazing.

. . . The *Times* received much mail regarding my essay on so-called "victim art" (Feb. 19, Arts & Leisure); a good deal of it was said to be angry, even "vicious" . . . extremely negative. The subject has been politicized, like so much these days . . .

Much is going on here: primarily *Here She Is!*—the first preview is this evening, and a gang of us are going including Emily, Dan Halpern, Sallie Goodman. I hope it will be fun. (Sorry you can't come. Some of the plays' themes might be of interest to you. But they are available in *The Perfectionist & Other Plays*, due out soon from Ecco, with a lovely striking cover.)

. . . My favorite play of mine *Bad Girls* will be performed by a theater at, of all places, the U. of Georgia! So you'll have little excuse not to attend. The run will be brief, May 3-13, and the artistic director is someone named August Staube . . .

Again, Camille Paglia! [I had written Paglia to see if she wished to comment on Oates's work for my biography.] I read your quote from her to Elaine on the phone, and we laughed heartily at the notion that Princeton is a "hotbed" of "feminist p.c." Apart from Elaine and a few others, the English Department is quite solidly mainstream. Why anyone would "seethe" and be "driven crazy" by others' careers is a mystery to us. Camille P. obviously values the Ivy League more than its inhabitants . . .

Yes, do send my father a large-print book. His 81st birthday is March 30. I think it would cheer him, a bit. He has been—well, humbled by recent health problems. He'd had to give up—his exact words, "give up"—attending classes at Buffalo, though they've meant so much to him. (With his ailments, and his failing eyesight, he'd been waiting in freezing wind for the Greyhound bus, and just couldn't take it any longer. I feel so sorry for him! But he doesn't want sympathy, understandably.) Any note at all from you, or card, or photo of Lucy (seriously!) and you—would be appreciated. (But no suggestion of health concerns, please!)

(Ray is pioneering with a new Macintosh, and the mysteries of e-mail. Are you "on-line"? I seem to be, at least in theory . . .)

Much affection, and *many* thanks!
Joyce

25 March 1995

Dear Greg,

. . . I hope that by May 3, 4, or 5 (ideally this date) you'll be free to come to Athens, for my play [*Bad Girls*]; I must be there for a few rehearsals, and for a few performances. It's my favorite play of my own . . . I'm curious, and excited, over the prospect of seeing it, transplanted from upstate New York ("Yewville") to Georgia accents (!). Ray will also be joining me for a day or two, we hope . . .

Your new house sounds very spacious. Are you going to plant flowers, etc.? Ray is itching to get outside though the nighttime temperatures are around freezing; he isn't happy until he has planted his first crop of lettuce. We've been going out running/hiking in the very gusty winds, usually in the Hopewell area . . .

Ken Kesey!—he's very much of the '60s, still. White-haired, a bit overweight; describes himself as a "warrior";

is campaigning to have marijuana legalized in his state; a benign paternal presence onstage, though I don't think he was especially tuned into the discussion. He spoke often of the need for us all to love one another. (He dresses oddly, but only mildly oddly . . . not a disruptive "character." He carries a rubber salmon (?) under his arm, a sort of tote bag, quite realistic-looking and a conversation piece. He was friendly enough to me, if a trifle vague; I doubt he'd ever heard of me, but wasn't at all confrontational.) Tulane U. is quite attractive, and New Orleans reminded me of both Miami and Los Angeles (with the high crime rate, too) . . .

Actually, you would love e-mail. It's probably better for you that you don't explore it; you might become addicted (like Elaine, among others of my acquaintance). I certainly could be, but stay away from the computer, preferring to type out letters, as I type out prose fiction. E-mail is a sort of delicious post-literate means of communication somewhere between a letter and a telegram; or between voice mail and fax . . .

Thanks for your nice comments on my *Antaeus* story ["Mark of Satan"]. It's one of my favorites of my own, and will conclude *Will You Always Love Me?* (which as you know is dedicated to you) . . .

My father said on the phone this morning that he's feeling better, and he sounded upbeat. So I'll take him at his word. My mother is in good spirits, too. Now they're hesitant about flying—navigating airports, mainly—we won't see them until late this spring, when I give a talk at Rochester in May. I hope you sent them a photo of you with Lucy; I know they'd love it . . .

My *Mulvaneys* [*We Were the Mulvaneys*] proceeds slowly, yet richly; *too* richly—I'm already at p. 112 and have only covered about 1/10 of the story. Yet I'm not going to let the novel writing weigh so heavily upon me as *Corky* did, I swear . . .

Much affection from the gang at 9 Honey Brook . . .
Joyce

17 April 1995

Dear Greg,

We too were shocked and saddened by Diane's death. [Diane Cleaver, my agent, died suddenly in her Greenwich Village apartment at age fifty-three.] . . . It's a terrible thing, the only good aspect of which, she didn't suffer, and might not even have known what was happening.

. . . Thanks for the lovely snapshots! The house is most impressive.

. . . I'm not absolutely against a "selected journal"—only hesitant, or modest (?) about its possibilities. (Actually, Tina Brown asked me about it, and I murmured an ambiguous reply.)

My parents appreciate your recent kindnesses, and mention it each time we speak on the phone . . .

My e-mail is very, very minimal, and rare. As I'd said, I don't really care for that sort of correspondence . . .

Much affection,
Joyce

24 April 1995

Dear Greg,

. . . We'll see you on Friday (for dinner first? then the play?). I haven't heard anything from August Staube for a while, and have no idea how rehearsals are progressing. In *Bad Girls*, casting is essential . . . I'll know within minutes if it's going to be a disaster, as soon as I see the actresses. (In theater, casting is 90% of the effort. If you make a mistake at casting, there's virtually nothing you can do to rectify it, no matter how brilliantly people might work.)

. . . Yes, my father is just delighted with the books. Simply to be remembered is very nice for him. He's making an effort to keep involved at U-Buffalo though he doesn't take courses; he's going to a literary festival this weekend that includes, along with Allen Ginsberg, your friend Camille Paglia. (I hope she won't "go crazy" and denounce me on my home turf . . .)

. . . So sad: not only did the PEN/Faulkner go to another novelist (a "first novelist"), but the Pulitzer, another time. (Did I mention I'd been nominated, with four other titles, for the PEN/Faulkner? Maybe if my novel had another author's name on it, it might have fared better.) I'm looking forward to next week, though with some trepidation. (I do want to see your house, certainly—and Lucy.)

Much affection,
Joyce

20 May 1995

Dear Greg,

I certainly didn't expect the *New Yorker* to be interested in excerpts from my journal, and will be curious to see what they choose. Thanks so much for selecting and organizing. You must have a magic touch. Not only don't I reread the journal, I draw back from even thinking about it; not modesty, but a sense of *To what purpose?* I suppose it is a good idea to have a repository of memory, though. Since most things are doomed to a double oblivion—natural transience, and then being forgotten . . .

Yes, I thought the Georgia Rep did an excellent production of *Bad Girls*. I liked all the actors, and August Staube—so energetic, imaginative, and funny. Too bad the Rep does only "new" plays, which limits my connection with them, considerably. (The lengthy, large-cast Thoreau would not be appropriate there.) Where *Bad Girls* might go next, I'm unsure.

The Guthrie Theatre just called with the unexpected, good news that they will be performing *Tone Clusters*, on a bill with Albee's *Zoo Story*, July 14-Sept. 9. But I doubt we can get to Minneapolis in our already-crowded summer. I may have mentioned—I have a new play, *The Woman Who Laughed*, opening at the Sharon Stage, Conn., in August.

This Monday I'll be reading from *You Can't Catch Me* in Rochester, and we'll stay with the Heyens, and take them and my parents out to dinner. My father is in considerably better spirits than he was, fortunately. Next day, we're having lunch with Toby Wolff and some of his writer friends in Syracuse, and will spend the night in Ithaca, lovely college town.

One of the characters in my new novel [*We Were the Mulvaneys*], coincidentally, is in Ithaca at the moment, which is convenient.

My next-performed play will be a revised version of *Homesick*, at the McCarter One-Act Play Festival next month. Would you like to come up and visit? There are many more journal pages accumulated in my closet . . . I'm trying to encourage my parents to come, too. I don't have the precise schedule, but the festival runs from approximately June 9 to June 18 and there are excellent, "real" playwrights (Jane Anderson, Wendy Wasserstein) involved . . .

Good luck with choosing an agent! Ray says hello & warm regards.

As always,
Joyce

1 June 1995

Dear Greg,

. . . We aren't really planning to be away from the house more than two or at the most three nights this summer . . . If you'd like, it might be fun for you to come visit around Aug. 15, the opening of my play *The Woman Who Laughed*, in Sharon, CT. I'd guess we would drive up, stay overnight, and return . . . and you could ride with us, of course. It isn't a terribly long drive. (If you didn't mind staying at the Nassau Inn or an equivalent place. Our "guest room"—which my parents always use—doesn't really allow for much privacy.) Reynard, Christabel, and Daisy say that they miss you, and would love to see you again, with or without dachshund.

Thanks so much for sending the journal excerpts. I've read your introduction which I think is helpful. (I retain a particular fondness for the longer, more personal piece you did for your college magazine. The aptly named "The Madness of Scholarship.") . . .

Reading the ridiculous remarks I made to Bob Phillips re. *With Shuddering Fall* made me almost literally cringe . . . One ongoing feature of my letters has been, I think, an air of explicit or implicit self-disparagement, and sometimes, though not always, a well-intentioned air of wanting the letter receiver to feel good about him/herself; this is such a very "feminine" trait . . . But truly if I had hated *With Shuddering Fall*, or even had doubts about it, I would have withdrawn it or revised it. (I'm sure I did in fact revise it. I used to think of it, now please don't laugh, as my "Jamesian" novel, at least in the 1960s.)

To answer your question: *With Shuddering Fall* began as short impressionistic pieces written while I was still at college, especially in the summer of 1959. (The locale for the

novel is based in part upon some wild areas in Millersport—
and the "hermit's house" behind my parents' property, which
is still standing! . . . I imagined it as a novel in 1960-61 when
Ray was teaching at the ill-chosen Lamar College in Beau-
mont and I was a full-time housewife for the first and last
time in my life. Did I write, during those lonely months! Had
I continued in that vein, I would certainly have acquired a
reputation for being alarmingly prolific.) . . .

As always,
Joyce

15 June 1995

Dear Greg,

What a nice surprise—thanks for the birthday present!
The Love Letter [by Cathleen Schine] is definitely a novel I'd
looked forward to reading sometime soon.

. . . *Everyone* asks about The Biography. When is it due,
etc. (I wonder if they are anticipating cameo appearances?)
The journal excerpts in the *New Yorker* did make me wince
a bit, but not so much as I'd anticipated. I enjoined Alice
[Quinn] to delete some of the more complacent-sounding
entries . . .

Regarding a "lost" novel of mine: I'd wanted to use the
Oresteia legend for years before *Angel of Light*. The [dis-
carded] novel written in the '60s was an early version, apparently. (Set in Detroit. Not a very promising setting for the
mythopoetic.)

. . . Yesterday was the "Emily Dickinson" photo shoot.
The photographer Stefan Haskell seems very nice, and certainly inventive. He and his four assistants came from New
York with three "antique" costumes—I chose the oldest,
a beautiful gown made of numerous layers of (faintly yel-

lowed) lace. I was posed near our pond, on a white bench; if I look Emily Dickinson-like in the photograph, pensive and brooding, it's because I was trying not to be distracted by a bevy of gnats. The poem I am "embodying" is #903, little-known but one of my favorites. [*I hide myself within my flower, / That fading from your Vase, / You, unsuspecting, feel for me— / Almost a loneliness.*]

. . . By now, you and Dedrick have had, I hope, a wonderful vacation. He's a wonderfully charming and intelligent person . . . Again, thanks for the birthday present; you're very thoughtful!

Much affection,
Joyce

6 July 1995

Dear Greg,

It was very nice to hear from you, and to hear that you had an interesting trip. We've never been to Newport but would like to, one day. Our own brief trip, next week, is to Saratoga Springs where I'll give a reading (as I usually do, each July) for Bob Boyers's rather wonderful assemblage of writing students and fellow writers (Frank Bidart, Richard Howard, Russell [Banks] & Chase [Twichell], Marilynne Robinson, among them), then up for a quick overnight visit to the Banks's big, spacious, beautiful place in the Keene Valley. Then home again. Preceding this, arriving tomorrow, my parents will visit us for three days. We're going to attend, among other things, a performance of Britten's *The Turn of the Screw*, an eerie, powerful opera. (I just saw the dress rehearsal last night—it's wonderfully staged.) The music and poetic language are not very accessible, so I worry the NJ Opera will have a hard time selling tickets. I'm participating on a panel following the opening. My father seems optimistic about navigating the airports, so I'll keep my fingers crossed. Mom & Dad both sound cheerful on the phone.

The *Foxfire* film sounds as if it's very different from my novel; I'm sorry the title wasn't changed, as with *Smooth Talk*. None of the actresses are "known." Angelina Jolie [in one of her earliest film roles] plays Legs—to the extent that "Legs" is retained. The story has been updated to the present time and the milieu (judging from a few photos I've seen) is far, far different from upstate New York in the 1950s! . . .

How remote it seems, our concern re. the *New Yorker*! (I've received many nice remarks on the journal excerpts and the poem. Some people laugh at the "drawing," others think it's—well, nice. I keep reminding myself *It could be much worse*.) [The drawing was an unflattering caricature.] . . . Do you still want to visit here in Aug.? We'll drive up to Sharon, CT, on Aug. 14 & return on the 16th; it's a very scenic 3-hr. drive. If you want to come to Princeton earlier, to peruse journals (!) or whatever, anytime is fine . . .

As always,
Joyce

10 July 1995

Dear Greg,

. . . My parents' visit was *very* nice. *The Turn of the Screw* was a truly mesmerizing experience—it's a work I know you would find genuinely haunting. If ever you have the chance, do seek it out. We had a luncheon of distinguished elders, among them Ed & George, Sam Hynes and his wife Liz, Ted & Renee Weiss, and though my parents were typically quite quiet, they enjoyed the impressively intelligent and unfailingly interesting conversations . . . My father's hearing aid gave out just before a double bill of old Stoppard plays, so he was spared hearing perhaps 50% of some surprisingly bad, banal "comedy." Avoid *After Magritte.* (Stoppard should pull the play from public use. It was written a long, long time ago before he'd become "Stoppard.")

It doesn't look as if I can reasonably get out to Minneapolis for the open, nor even a performance of *Tone Clusters* next Friday. Too bad. There is a reading of *Bad Girls* at the Contemporary Play Festival in Shepherdstown, WV, which I'll have to miss, too. I feel panicky at the way the summer is melting away . . .

Happy birthday & pet Lucy for us.
Joyce

19 July 1995

Dear Greg,

What a brilliant "Reader's Guide" [to *What I Lived For*]—it would seem to transcend the genre, indeed. (Someone should undertake *your* biography.) How can you write literary criticism so gracefully, intelligently, yet *readably?* I've found this kind of writing, including the occasional dust jacket copy for OR Press, truly difficult. *Thanks immensely* for what you've said.

. . . Quickly to set the record straight: of course it was my grandmother Woodside, a passionate reader, who gave me my typewriter(s)—first, a toy; then, a real Smith Corona. My Grandfather Bush would perhaps not have known a typewriter from a horse collar. (He was, among other things, a blacksmith.) That old interview was riddled with errors, if I recall correctly. Frustrating! Also, I didn't destroy the letters I'd written to Kay. They're in the archive somewhere, quietly moldering away . . . We are sorry you can't join us Aug. 14

and yet more concerned about your headaches. (I hope JCO is not the source—but it wouldn't surprise me.)

Much affection,
Joyce

6 August 1995

Dear Greg,

I've been waiting for the photocopied letters from Syracuse, to send on to you, but they haven't yet arrived. Maybe everyone there is on vacation, like most of Princeton. (Which is why Princeton is so idyllic these days. Just a few friends whom we've spaced out very sparingly, as they have us. And a doe with two indescribably beautiful fawns who frequently pass by our study windows, twitching their ears and tails at us, and wondering what on earth we're doing every morning, so faithfully.)

Thanks for deleting the Dahmer reference in the "Reader's Guide." (Billy was most impressed with the "Guide," too.) There's certainly no problem about the review—in fact, the review made me want to read the novel (!); interpretations of literature do depend upon subjective readings, and it would be a bland, timid reviewer who didn't draw conclusions from certain clues. I did purposefully include the exit line, "Thanks, I've already eaten"—intending a metaphoric significance . . .

In any case, it's a vividly written review—many thanks!

. . . Our physical exercise is mainly bicycling these days—early evenings—since it's been stupefyingly hot, in the 90s, during the day. Ray sometimes stays behind to work in his garden (which is lovely, lush, bright with black-eyed Susans, cosmos, zinnias and marigolds) and I go out along country roads for as long as an hour and a half, rushing down hills, pedaling slowly up hills, trying to lose myself in the beautiful landscape and stop thinking about my obsessive novel. (The good news is it's nearly finished; the bad news, it's much longer than I'd hoped. Not so long as *Corky*, but—it was intended to be no more than 400 pp. I'll be lucky if I can bring it to a reasonable conclusion by 550 pp. . . .

I'd mentioned losing interest in e-mail—almost entirely— but our great new purchase is a fax machine, and, as Billy predicted, this *is* a worthwhile gizmo. Should you ever wish to fire off a missive circumnavigating the US postal service, our fax number is exactly the same as our family line telephone . . . I've been using the fax daily, what with play revisions sent to directors and various exchanges with *New Yorker* editors . . . We've never cultivated our brand-new Apple Mac with costly laser printer—over $2,000 worth of equipment simply sits on the Parsons table in our guest room.

The Woman Who Laughed is in rehearsal; I've only attended the first day—and came away with so many ideas, I was up until midnight revising and restructuring scenes . . .

I've just sent back the page proofs for *Will You Always Love Me?* The dust jacket design, which I haven't yet seen, is said to be striking. The stories seem to me more analytical than others of mine, at least in the aggregate; more "rendered"; perhaps less dramatic and accessible. (Code words for "fewer sales.") Still, I've arranged and rearranged the stories, selected out, selected in, and it seems to be right now. Confronted with so many short stories, as with poems, a writer could assemble a virtually infinite variety of books, assembling the individual works in different orders, with different titles and, consequently, "themes." It's an exhausting prospect—yet one arrangement always does seem better than the rest.

At a *Harper's* forum luncheon recently, where the somewhat forced topic of discussion was "gender in literature," I was most impressed with Norman Rush, whose *Whites* and *Mating* I'd admired; and quite liked Robert Olen Butler, whom many (including Russell) had warned me against, as vain and pompous—I found him friendly, unpretentious, sincere rather than articulate, engaging. Less impressive, perhaps because she chattered so nervously, was Marianne Wiggins (who could not resist criticizing her former husband Mr. Rushdie for his "moral failure" in recanting *The Satanic Verses*—which, as you probably know, he did, rather desperately hoping the Islamic death sentence might be lifted, and it wasn't) and Albert French who rambled in vague epiphanies that left the rest of us in utter baffled silence.

Everyone here says hello & much affection!
Joyce

18 August 1995

Dear Greg,

We're sorry to hear of your illness, and hope you're recovering by now. It's good you didn't plan on Sharon, CT, after all.

The carriage house turned out to be most attractive, on the estate of an 18th-century colonial New England house, beautifully furnished with antiques . . . We stayed for two nights, and our friends Mimi and Larry Danson came up for one night, to attend the opening of the play [*The Woman Who Laughed*]. Unexpectedly, the play was well received; or at least, that impression was given. Luci Arnaz was actually quite touching in the role and received enormous applause . . . We're sorry you couldn't join us but perhaps another time.

(*Bad Girls* [produced in Athens, Georgia] was, overall, a very positive experience. Except for the rather awkward post-play panel you got dragooned into joining, with our well-intentioned but alarmingly verbose friend Stan Lindberg [then editor of the *Georgia Review*] ...)

As I'd mentioned previously, there *is* a Hartland, NY, on Rt. 104. My father probably passed on to you the amazing information that his grandfather was a man named Johann (?) Morgenstern, a German Jew (?—so my father thinks) who changed his name to John Morningstar around 1894. A carpenter, then gravedigger, and eventual suicide. If so, I have "Jewish blood" in me; better yet, "German-Jewish blood." Since my mother isn't Jewish, I can't be "Jewish." But my father is—he thinks ... Yet, pressed to define "Jewish," I'd be stumped. The faces of my bright, argumentative New York Jewish friends Henry Bienen, Jerry & Alicia Ostriker, etc., rise before me, shaking their heads—"No, not likely" ...

Is your Biographical Subject—well, a bit strange? I'm engaged in not the first, nor even the second, but the third rewrite/revision of *Black*, now retitled *Double Exposure*. This play is scheduled to open in a large preview theater in Winston-Salem, NC, at a terrifyingly near date—Oct. 3. Maybe I've hallucinated it.

Both Ray and I seem to be well, but who knows?—even now some rough splay-footed creature might be dragging itself in our direction. All the domestic creatures, though, including our resident twin fawns and their mother, appear wonderfully well.

Much love,
Joyce

31 August 1995

Dear Greg,
Congratulations on the acceptance at Johns Hopkins

[I had submitted my third collection of short stories, *I Am Dangerous*, to Johns Hopkins University Press]. That's very good news.

We are trying to set back the date for *Black* (now retitled *Double Exposure*) to January . . . I hope this can be done— Oct. would be almost impossible for me. *I Am Dangerous* is an excellent title. (Is this G.J.'s secret self speaking?) Maybe *you* could do a new biography of Flannery O'C? What a pleasure to work with a finite oeuvre. Your plan to visit Princeton/NYC sounds fine. In fact, come on Oct. 20 to our party! We'd love to see both you and Dedrick here . . . Hello from all—

Joyce

12 September 1995

Dear Greg,

. . . I declined an offer from the *New Yorker* to review a batch of books on Frank Sinatra (!). And an invitation from Tina Brown to write a "major article" on "women's rage" (!). (They will have a special Women's Rage issue next February. I predict it will be a blockbuster, very controversial. But I'm not really enraged enough, at men or at life generally, to climb aboard.)

Your Gay Lit. course sounds very interesting, actually. May I see the syllabus? Michael Cadden, my colleague, has taught something similar with good results. I wonder if Mishima's *Confessions of a Mask* is still so striking as it was when I taught it, at U-W years ago. The concept of sexual identity is so central to all questions of identity. Yet, among those whose "sexual identity" is more or less defined, other questions of identity come to the fore. So, in a sense, a question of "sexual identity" particularly in a socio-cultural context that would seem to dictate "normality" is a kind of screen or buffer for the next layer of questions. Man *is* the anxiety-provoking animal! . . .

What an honor—on Sunday, Jeanne Moreau came out to visit, in the company of Ismail Merchant and an executive associated with Merchant Ivory Productions. They are "interested" in *Solstice*, with Jeanne Moreau to direct. She has directed two French films that were well received and says she's been "haunted by" *Solstice* for years. She certainly seemed to be familiar with the novel, far more than I am . . . Now in her sixties, she doesn't much resemble her haughty Parisian self but is in fact very warm, "feminine" yet intellectual—we talked a good deal about art. If I agree to do the screenplay, working with such an extraordinary woman, it would certainly be a memorable experience. I'm sure she's far closer to being Sheila Trask than I am.

I've been revising *Mulvaneys* for some time now and feel a real reluctance to detach myself from the novel. It's almost literally like leaving a family . . . leaving home. My valentine to "rural upstate NY."

. . . Ray says hello & much affection. We're both disappointed that you can't come visit Oct. 20. After that, I travel to Northwestern U. for a "Joyce Carol Oates Festival" (I cringe at the title and wish I'd been asked about it beforehand) with Ray and, if their health allows, my parents. Beyond that, I'll do some publicity traveling, possibly alone or with Ray. When do you think you'd be coming to Princeton? . . .

Much love,
Joyce

4 October 1995

Dear Greg,

. . . I've been rereading *The Scarlet Letter* which would

clearly never be published today. Far too "quiet" and inward. It seems that you had a "great hook" in *Pagan Babies* without having intended it, just as, perhaps, I have a "great hook" in *Zombie* (cannibalism) without having intended it . . . (A.K. hasn't read the novel, obviously. I don't suppose I blame him for not caring to pay a shocking $19.95 for a book, especially one so slender.) Did A.K. send the *San Francisco Chronicle* review?

(I didn't think of Quentin as "gay" in any significant sense. His psychopathic personality could as easily have resided in a "straight" man. I did intend for him to cloak himself, so to speak, in some of the platitudes of gayness, which he exploits for his own purposes, as he would exploit anything exploitable. It never occurred to me that the "P.C. police [might have] themselves a perfect target." Am I naïve? The review in next Sunday's *NY Times*, by an older academic named Stephen Marcus, more reflects the kind of hostility I had anticipated the novel might draw. I do feel that I came through with a surprising minimum of virulent attacks for *What I Lived For*, so I'm prepared for a less friendly press with this one . . . At my first reading for the novel so far, at an enormous superstore Barnes & Noble in New York, there were quite a few decidedly odd people in the audience; I mean, odder than usual. Serial-killer fans, I think. A very peculiar woman tried to engage me in conversation about "Hannibal Lecter" as if he were a real person, a "therapist" as she called him. Rosemary Ahern, Billy's assistant, tried to intercede. And there were others.)

I'll send on to Elaine Showalter your excellent, analytical review of the Heilbrun biography [*Education of a Woman: The Life of Gloria Steinem*]. It's amazing that she is, as you note, so careless a writer. Elaine and I once had an awkward lunch with Carolyn [Heilbrun}, in which she made all sorts of outrageous and/or inaccurate statements, such as "biography is always fiction." In fact, biography is not fiction, as I tried to tell her, citing such exemplary works as Ellmann's *Joyce, Yeats, Wilde*. She simply wouldn't listen. A "first-generation" academic feminist who makes the rest of us, including Elaine, cringe.

. . . I was [in the *New Yorker*'s offices] yesterday for a luncheon w/Tina Brown and others, and beforehand we were in Tina's airy, light-filled, white-walled office on the 16th floor of an attractive building, watching television as the O.J. Simpson verdict was read. Everyone—all Caucasians of course—was stunned. Somehow, we'd all expected a guilty verdict, even Tina whom one would have expected to be more knowing, or cynical. Even me . . . In retrospect, of course it was naïve to expect a just verdict. It's been such a racially divisive event, people are extremely disturbed about it here, at least those with whom I've spoken. I've assigned Ralph Ellison's "Battle Royal" and Faulkner's "That Evening Sun" to my students who all seem very eager to discuss the issue. I wonder what is being said in your circle? . . .

I think that *We Were the Mulvaneys* may appear in late 1996, instead of *Man Crazy* [which would come out in 1997]. Certainly I prefer this novel, which has taken such a chunk of my heart. Muffin is in it, and great slices of childhood scenes, and landscapes. The character of "Marianne" is very much like an aspect of myself, though probably no one would recognize this. She is an alter ego kept hidden from view most of the time even from myself. I had such an extreme emotional reaction writing about her . . . it's amazing. I suppose this is primarily what fiction writing is about, yet it's always a surprising experience. Sorry to go on at such length about a manuscript you have not read. Perhaps Billy could send a copy to you sometime, if you requested one. I haven't yet heard Billy's final response to the novel, though his initial feelings were very positive; John Hawkins and Sharon Friedman are both enthusiastic. I'll keep my fingers crossed!

Another title to appear in 1996 is *First Love*, a Gothic tale, with illustrations by wonderful Barry Moser, published by Ecco. It's a short novella, only about 50 pp.

Bob Phillips would like to read the biography, and Alicia Ostriker says she could begin by reading a chapter or two. I haven't asked Elaine (with whom, these days, I'm extremely close . . . we wrote quite a bit to each other this summer when she was in London/Paris). Should you wish to be forever in Elaine's good graces, you have only to see her son Michael perform as part of the State (sometimes replayed on MTV—a very popular comic troupe, and very talented) and pass along your praise to her. The State will be broadcast on CBS on or around Halloween—an enormous opportunity for such young people. Elaine's colleagues, who are competitive parents, are absurdly taciturn about Michael's success. For those of us who have no children, this, at least, is an area in which we aren't vulnerable.

Did you see the front-page Sept. 28 *Times* feature on opera & librettists? There I am, a tiny cameo! Johnnie Cochran at the top, & four librettists at the bottom.

Much affection,
Joyce

24 October 1995

Dear Greg—

A quick reply to your most recent letter, before we fly off to Evanston for the "Joyce Carol Oates Festival"—a title to make one cringe. (Maybe Henry [Bienen] is just teasing?) My parents, as I may have mentioned, are also flying in; and

a poet friend from Washington, Jana Harris. And others . . .
Friday evening is a staged presentation of three short stories;
Saturday evening three one-act plays; Sunday we'll go see the
enormous Monet exhibit at the Art Institute; Monday is my
marathon day—an interview at 10:30 a.m., lunch with writing students and Reg Gibbons at noon, a reading at 4 p.m.,
book signing (if there are books to be signed) and reception;
a swift trip to the U. of Chicago forty minutes away for a
second reading (!) at 7:30 p.m. followed by reception, book
signing, dinner and collapse. As my biographer you might
have a clinical interest in whether I can possibly get through
such a schedule with my 1) just diagnosed "tennis elbow" (a
mystery—the doctor thinks it must be caused by swinging
my arms when I jog—at least it's very, very minor); 2) bruised
& swollen knee (from a fall while jogging—tripping over an
invisible vine in a pastoral woodland setting of exquisite fall
beauty); 3) "cervical spine strain"—(a now fading malady
I've had since last March, essentially a virus infection [the
doctor believed it was caught on an airplane] in a neck mus-
cle, very painful initially but livable, at least) . . .

Yes, *Wuthering Heights* is simply sui generis. Remarkable
as a first, or any, novel. (And Emily B. died so young, not
knowing she'd created a masterpiece. The reviewers were so
grudging . . .)

Zombie has been quite quiet, in fact. My publishers
don't send review copies of my books to Michiko Kakutani
any longer. Nor have major reviews appeared, of which I'm
aware. Again, such a relief not to feel much pressure. It's the
sort of novel that might have been angrily attacked—but, so
far, has not been.

. . . I'm probably not going to adapt *Solstice* for Merchant Ivory—the terms are very modest, and screenwriting
is not otherwise very rewarding. I would rather write plays

of course. (*Black*, retitled, will be produced in Cambridge, MA, instead of Winston-Salem, sometime next year, with the HBO tie-in. Or so my producer, Louise Westergard, assures me.)

Thanks for your comments on the "memoir" pieces I've done recently. My parents were particularly intrigued, of course. (The drawing in the *New Yorker* is a composite based on several aged snapshots my father was able to locate, of the Windnagles' house and others. How ironic that these old, sordid, near-forgotten incidents are woven into memories that in turn wind up in a publication so utterly remote from Millersport then and now.) Another piece you no doubt missed was a brief essay on *The Scarlet Letter* . . . in the "News of the Week in Review" section of the *NY Times*, Oct. 13.

Please say hello to Dedrick for us; and pet sweet little Lucy. Much affection from the gang at 9 Honey Brook— (Christabel is dozing contentedly in my lap as I type this, and Reynard is hunting in the, to him, towering plants outside the window; Daisy is singing cheerfully, knowing that another mealtime is imminent, carrot greens his absolute favorite.)

Joyce

12 November 1995

Dear Greg,

Thanks so much for the inscribed "Reader's Guide" [to *What I Lived For*]. Rosemary had sent me a number of copies, which I've been sending out. It's so very well written, seemingly so effortless. (This kind of writing, for me, is particularly hard. Especially of books I know very well, and whose authors I know, too.) I'm sure that Billy has expressed his admiration for the work you've done here . . .

Northwestern U. was wonderful. My parents had a great time, staying with us in the Bienens' presidential house, a mansion of sorts with a very attractive indoor swimming pool. The dramatized short stories were effective, particularly "Poor Bibi"; the one-act plays were even better, with some remarkable young actors. My readings went well, I think; the schedule wasn't really tiring at all, only a bit strenuous now and then. The Bienens made us all feel so very warm and welcome, and of course, as always with Leigh and Henry, we had a lovely time. Henry is radiant as president of N.U., riding the (wholly undeserved) crest of football success, which brings all sorts of attention to the university, and to him; not to mention multimillionaire donors by the scores. Lucky Henry! . . .

[My friend Dedrick and I had suggested that her orthopedic ailments might be exacerbated by her habit of frequent jogging.] I'm sure that you and Dedrick—and Dedrick's orthopedic specialist—are right, about jogging and so forth. Actually, my ailments have mostly faded. Or, perhaps, I've ceased to notice them. The problem for me as for most runners is that there is really no substitute for running, especially in woodland scenes, or along country roads . . . these are activities that bring me so much happiness, it's difficult for me to think of giving them up. (Tantamount to giving up cats, for instance. For you, giving up dogs. Forever.) . . .

What a stimulating trip [to California] Ray and I had, overall . . . Dutton was kind enough to rent typewriters for me in San Francisco and Santa Monica, so I could continue work fairly intensely . . . I've just finished my lengthy "genre"/ Raymond Chandler review for *New York Review of Books* (do you see the publication?—I like it very much, as does Ray; there is nothing quite like it elsewhere, not even *TLS*

where reviews are sometimes rather superficial); my next review-essay is in fact for *TLS*, four books on F. Scott Fitzgerald including a new edition of *The Last Tycoon*. Fitzgerald
is not my favorite American writer, so relatively tame and
unadventurous set beside Faulkner, but rereading him should
be interesting, at least.

We spent part of an evening with Christopher Walken
(whose film, with Sean Penn, *At Close Range*, I particularly
admire), introduced by Larry Groebel (the *Playboy* interviewer), in Santa Monica. An intelligent and well-spoken
person, like virtually all of the well-known Hollywood actors
we've met. (Walken had wanted to meet me because he admires *On Boxing*. His film *Homeboy*—also *True Romance*—
are supposed to be excellent, we've been told. It's interesting
how many actors (Pacino, Hoffman, Ryan O'Neal, Walken,
Mickey Rourke, Jack Nicholson) are serious fans of boxing.
No doubt they see the boxer's performance as the real thing,
set beside which their own performances are synthetic and
without much risk. Dustin Hoffman had even wanted to be
a boxer, as a boy.) . . .

Don't apologize for liking thriller films! Chase Twichell
likes maudlin, soap-operaish films, no matter how bad;
Gordon Edelstein likes grotesque, violent films; Russell
likes to watch old movies . . . any and all old movies, if
they're late at night. Ray and I seem to spend our evenings
reading, and working, without any time for films, which
we regret. Someday, we intend to catch up. (We are the
only two people in North America not to have seen *Pulp
Fiction*.)

Bob Phillips will be visiting this Friday; we're having a
small party in his honor, and for the artist/illustrator Barry
Moser who's at Princeton briefly. You have a standing invitation to such parties, though we realize you aren't likely

to come. Warm regards to all from all at 9 Honey Brook.

Much affection,
Joyce

30 Nov. 1995

Dear Greg,

A quick response to your letter.

I'm a great admirer of Schiele, and this is a characteristically daring, dramatic image. [A reproduction of a Schiele painting would serve as the cover art for my third collection of short stories, *I Am Dangerous*.] Possibly your editor won't feel quite so sympathetic, but who knows? It is sometimes difficult, in fact impossible, to get permission to reprint "privately owned" art. A terrible irony in this, as Egon Schiele the profound ironist would agree . . .

By now perhaps your difficulties with Hopkins have been worked out? . . . Norton is not an ideal publisher, either. I'd mentioned some months ago that R.V. Cassill invited me to be co-editor of *The Norton Anthology of Short Fiction* with him, and an enthusiastic editor named Carol Hollar-Zwick worked with us. It did seem like a very attractive project and in my usual headlong way I plunged in reading stories, selecting titles, photocopying material to send to Carol; exchanging quite friendly letters with her, and Mr. Cassill, and so forth. Then, unexpectedly, Mr. Cassill decided he didn't want a co-editor after all. (He's elderly, blind, said to be infirm . . .) So, abruptly, I've been dropped. Naïvely, I'd been working without a contract, so now it appears unlikely that I'll receive much, if any, payment for my quixotic labors. Carol Hollar-Zwick has simply retreated, and John Hawkins is struggling to extract something from Norton, however token. I do confess it was my error in working without a contract; but the correspondence did seem very encouraging, and the editor was setting deadlines to be met, which I met. All this will go into a footnote in the biography, or, rather, in the index, under *Character Traits: naivete . . .*

Our Christmas will surely be quiet as our Thanksgiving. We've been invited to the Halperns' and haven't any other plans. Truly, holidays don't mean much to us; they're more significant for families with children. My Charleston visit is March 22-23, a talk and a reading at a writers' conference . . .

Your winter quarter sounds very ambitious. We have only three more flurried weeks of teaching this semester, but these weeks will be extremely condensed. Since finishing *Mulvaneys*, I've been enjoying work on short pieces, as I've probably mentioned. There is a particular intellectual pleasure in essay-reviews and the sort of cultural criticism possible in this genre. I was deeply moved by the saga of Scott Fitzgerald—what an ironic life. His last royalty check from Scribner's, in 1940, was for $13.13 . . .

Please extend my warmest regards to Dedrick. All the gang at 9 Honey Brook says hello & much affection, to you!

Joyce

16 December 1995

Dear Greg,

Thanks for your letter, filled with many fascinating items; and the long-ago Nabokov piece that must have appeared in *Saturday Review*. (Such a solid, civilized, literary publication.) My views of Nabokov haven't changed much, I suppose, in the intervening years, but I'm more sympathetic now with the artist's predicament: he, or she, has to be "interesting"; for Nabokov, that took the form of being snobbish, provocative, occasionally a bit cruel, sadistic, and something of a homophobe. The Nabokovian Bill Gass, in person a lovely man, with a truly lovely wife, has so contorted his writerly persona that his prose emerges as pitilessly bleak, hard, grudging, ironic, yet more ironic, and even misogynist—as if "real literature" has to be something like that, an imperial text. Bill has taken up color photography with much zest, and obviously it's his way of memorializing the world he can't somehow transpose into his notion of "real" art.

In fact, I didn't get very far with the collected Nabokov stories. They do seem rather filigreed, overwritten & a bit hollow at the core. Of another era, certainly. How ironic that Edmund White, profiled in the "Inside SR" feature you sent, an early disciple of Nabokov's, wrote an almost wholly negative, almost jeering review of the collected stories for the *New Republic*. How times change us all, not excluding the dead.

It's too bad that you and Jim Atlas [biographer of Saul Bellow] live so far apart, you'd have much to exchange, I think! Jim is a very nice person; very talented and hard-working; not quite so appreciated by his elusive subject Bellow as he might be. He says he understands—Bellow has secrets, or aspects of his life he doesn't want publicly discussed, and he quite rightly feels that Jim might reveal these. In fact, Jim will be discreet and gentlemanly, I'm sure. He is organizing a "memoir" issue of the *New York Times Magazine* to which I've been invited to contribute, and perhaps, in a shorter version, my "Letter to My Mother . . ." might be appropriate. Memoir writing is terribly hard, for me; I can't seem to find the right tone, lacking a fictitious persona through whom to speak. I want only to tell the truth—but the "truth" is either all-inclusive, or hyper-selective. I need to observe an objective reality partly because my parents, and others, would know if I deviated!

I've enclosed some of the correspondence pertaining to

the Norton anthology. It's ironic that John Hawkins, sometimes known to be slow about returning calls, finds his calls not returned by the Norton people. I think I was most hurt by Carol Hollar-Zwick's inexplicable behavior. So extremely friendly and appreciative of my work, so enthusiastic about the project. She even came to Philadelphia to a play of mine, where we met . . . Unless John can persevere, the situation will just fade; I can't imagine taking any sort of action myself, legally. But the experience is a valuable object lesson to us all, including you: don't work before signing a contract! *Just don't . . .*

Much love & holiday cheer—
Joyce

20 December 1995

Dear Greg:

After sending off a batch of Norton letters to you yesterday, I was informed today that, at last, after weeks of non-communication, Norton is after all willing to "compromise." I'm so pleased. Instead of working with Mr. Cassill, I will be editing an anthology of my own oriented toward writing workshops. This should be most enjoyable. (John Hawkins did a terrific job of pursuing the issue—numberless telephone calls, etc. Exactly what I could never do. And no lawyers involved in litigation.)

(We are currently snowed in, our driveway impassable!)

Joyce

23 December 1995

Dear Greg,

Thanks so much for the lovely cat tile!—it's in a prominent position in our kitchen. And the review of *Zombie* is very impressive. (I did want ambiguity, of course, about the "cannibalism"—you're quite right. A number of people have asked me re. the name "Quentin" and *The Sound and the Fury*, so from this point onward I will simply frown and look mysterious.) Did I mention—no English publisher will touch *Zombie*? Even my so-called "fans"—whoever they are—are revulsed by it, according to my [British] agent Murray Pollinger. Strangely, however, the Australians "love" it—it will be published there by Penguin, I think. It may be that Australians admire American popular culture and/or serial killers to a degree the English do not, and who can blame them?—the English, I mean.

We're shocked that someone in your department wrote an anonymous letter about your course [Modern Gay Literature], and that you've become controversial! Please do send some of these clippings. (Just wait until *I Am Dangerous* appears, with the Schiele art. The cover will be reproduced above the boldface caption *CONTROVERSIAL ATLANTA WRITER STRIKES AGAIN*. In a way it might be just as well that these issues are raised into consciousness; and that you, the very epitome of reasonableness, can articulate them for the public. At the same time, I'm sure it's very time-consuming and exasperating.)

At the moment—and these matters are so ephemeral, they are virtually of the moment—it looks as if your countryman N—t G—rich is sliding down public opinion polls. Good! . . .

I think it would be fine to discuss "After Amnesia" sometime in the future—that is, after it appears in the *New Yorker*, and anyone who happens to read it has forgotten it. The biography would not appear for a considerable amount of time afterward; my concern was that virtually everyone in my life (parents, friends, colleagues, even students) reads the *New*

Yorker . . . I don't believe I have ever quite cultivated the ideal essay voice, at least one with which I feel comfortable. The very use of "I" makes me cringe in such a context, it seems so—self-aggrandizing, self-dramatizing, and if not, implicitly coy. Almost, the very decision to write a memoirist piece is terribly egotistical unless it's in honor of someone or something else, where the focus of narration is elsewhere, not on the narrator. I still feel uneasy about it, since perhaps some people (Elaine, surely—but I'll ask her not to tell) will know who has written it, anyway . . .

We too want to see *Sense & Sensibility*—not my favorite Austen novel (*Emma* is) but everyone has said it's wonderful. We've seen a number of plays lately, in NYC & elsewhere, including a daring, brilliant fantasy on de Sade, *Quills*, by a friend, Doug Wright. The film *Foxfire* is ready to be viewed; but I don't know if I am ready to view it . . .

My mom and dad are in quite good spirits these days, despite the snow. Their new kitten, silky black with white boots and breast, has made a real difference. My father enjoyed his fall term (all Conrad!) and perhaps by the time the spring term begins Millersport will be plowed out . . .

Warm regards for 1996—
Joyce

Part Four

1996–1998

Part Four

1995–1998

The years 1996 to 1998 were typically busy ones for Joyce. We Were the Mulvaneys *appeared in the fall of 1996 to excellent reviews; its becoming a "pick" of the television book club hosted by Oprah Winfrey helped boost it into best-selling status. Joyce was also busy writing, and several times rewriting, a screenplay based on her 1985 novel* Solstice, *in collaboration with the distinguished French actress and director Jeanne Moreau, who visited Princeton several times to confer about the project. Unfortunately, the screenplay was never produced.*

Joyce also continued to be involved in playwriting, and as the letters suggest, she traveled to a number of the productions (some were produced in Princeton, with her friend Emily Mann at the helm). Countless short stories, essay-reviews, and other short projects also kept her busy, in addition to further "pseudonym novels," as she called them, such as Double Delight *(1997).*

The letters also reflect her abiding concern for her parents and their health; her father, Fred, suffered frequent maladies and could no longer attend college classes, though he could still read "the classics" with the aid of audiobooks Joyce sent him.

And Joyce and I continued to correspond about the forthcoming biography, a complex project that inspired many letters between us. I had sent her a first draft around New Year's of 1996.

7 January 1996

Dear Greg,

CONGRATULATIONS! I hope Lucy appreciates the remarkable TALENT disguised as her master.

The biography is really quite remarkable. I can't see how you have possibly made a kind of "narrative" of what has been, to me, so inchoate . . . yet there's a definite pattern; perhaps after all what Leon Edel/Henry James meant by a "pattern in the carpet." What stuns me most about the biography is its interwoven facts and details, quotes from interviews, letters, the journal, fiction, poetry, and so forth. Because the prose reads so smoothly, one might be tempted to think that this achievement is "easy"; which is very far from the truth. *I* could not have done it, certainly. Ever! . . .

I found the biography very moving. Of course, at the outset, I'd been cringing and wincing, hoping not to discover terrible things lurking within . . . writers naturally do wince at reliving bad reviews, the abrupt endings of friendships, disappointing sales, but these are inevitable and even necessary to "relive" to get a sense of what one has in fact gone through. I rarely glance through [my] journal, and in any case could not have gleaned from it the kind of unified account you have. Truly, I think you must have supernatural powers . . . and powers of patience.

If there is one (inevitable, I'm afraid) criticism that will be brought against the book, regardless of its quality, it's its quantity. Possibly your Dutton editor will suggest cuts . . . It isn't out of modesty that I think that "JCO" might not merit 700+ pages in the world's eyes. Yet you've done so much excellent research, and your critical commentary is so skillful, I can't imagine where cuts might be executed . . .

I'd been hesitant to begin reading, at all. But couldn't resist—of course. The first several pages drew me in, and the introduction is wonderful; wonderfully precise, and illuminating. Overall, I suppose Henry James *is* my spiritual mentor, though my writing doesn't much reflect his voice, subject matter, or vision.

(I'm sending off early chapters and other related pages to my parents. My crucial concern is not to upset them in any way. They're very fond of you and ask to be remembered.)

The account of the reading at Miami of Ohio [where I had first met Joyce in person, in 1976] is such a good opening. I should say that, when I first met you, shook your hand, I reported back to Ray, "Greg Johnson is *nothing* like I'd expected." "In what way?" Ray asked. "He's blond, very handsome, and *just a kid*," I said.

I found the opening chapters extremely moving. The accounts of my parents' lives actually include information I didn't know; especially my father's detailed account of his Morgenstern grandparents' household. And my mother's "sadness" regarding her having been given away had been a surprise to me, when I interviewed her for the "Letter to my Mother on her 78th Birthday" . . .

I have to confess I was often crying throughout the early sections; and the passages about my grandmother Woodside's death. My whole life and others' lives unfolding as in a movie . . .

Much love,
Joyce

24 January 1996

Dear Greg,

A quick follow-up to my letter: why don't you forget about The Biography for the time being? Your editor will probably not read it for weeks; it's out of the house; you can focus upon other, more pressing matters. I don't *at all* want you to be concerned about me . . . Just erase "JCO" from your consciousness. None of this is that important.

Ran into—of all people—Dottie Palmer last night! [Palmer was a sorority sister and close friend of Joyce's at Syracuse who had eluded being interviewed for *Invisible Writer.*] At a reading I gave in a bookstore near Verona, NJ. We embraced tearfully. She hasn't changed much . . . Amazing.

Joyce

25 January 1996

Dear Greg,

It was great to speak with you last night; and to clear up some misunderstandings. My primary purpose in writing to you originally, after reading the biography, was to congratulate you on completing such a project; that's the main thing. Then, in my usual overzealous manner (about which Ray is sometimes bemused, sometimes not so bemused) I could not resist plunging forward with more detailed responses and "suggestions." I might better have left these for another, more premeditated and less intense time.

(I've become so enamored of revision, I guess I've lost sight of the fact that not everyone might share my predilection, or monomania. I've told students enthusiastically, "This is such a good story, you should rewrite it completely, changing every word!"—(meaning, changing every word for the better, of course). There are a few students (Pinckney Benedict was one) who like very much to revise, but most simply want to move on to new work, as I did at that age.)

"After Amnesia" has been very smoothly edited at the *New Yorker*; it doesn't actually seem like my own writing, somehow, except in brief passages. A relief! I don't really care if writer friends know I've written this—it isn't a Classified Secret—but I somehow don't want my students to see it, or, I guess, Ray (it will be interesting to notice if he makes any connection—he reads the *New Yorker* fairly thoroughly; he knows I visited a prison in Trenton, but many women have visited prisons), possibly my parents, who would never make any connection . . .

Twelve deer are eating corn outside my window, including several ex-fawns. It's very distracting!

I'm having some difficulty getting into the right consciousness to write the *Solstice* screenplay, though we've enjoyed seeing Merchant Ivory films—*The Remains of the Day*, most recently. (The company sent me many videos.) Next to see is *Heat and Dust*. I would not have become involved in this project except for the honor of working with Jeanne Moreau, and hope it wasn't a mistake.

I'm amazed at the rapid response at Dutton re. The Biography. So quickly read! This augurs well—I guess—though already the attention is making me feel very self-conscious . . .

Much affection & *thanks*—
Joyce

4 February 1996

Dear Greg,

How are you? I've been thinking of you, and hope that things are not quite so tense now. I certainly didn't mean to add to your sense of being overwhelmed with my letter. [Joyce had sent me a 10-page single-spaced letter with her responses to the biography.]

I hope you're still on vacation, so to speak, from The Biography. What a massive effort . . . ! I'll enclose here my parents' comments, for you to file away for future reference when you prepare the final manuscript.

(I haven't heard anything about the biography subsequent to the immediate reports you and others had mentioned. Rosemary Ahern [then at Dutton] is a wonderful editor, in any case; if you haven't met her, I think you'd like her very much.)

Mulvaneys seems to be hurtling by: already I've received a copyedited manuscript, and dust jacket design has begun. I've expressed a mild wish that the publication be in January 1997 rather than September (!) 1996, but NAL/Dutton seems to want to bring it out in the fall. With the biography planned for early 1997 [actually it did not appear until early 1998], I feel dazed at the speed with which my "life" is moving past . . .

The film of *Foxfire* is lively and well directed and acted— several wonderful young actresses, especially those playing Legs and Maddy. In most ways it isn't my novel; set in the 1990s, with a distinctly different plot. Goldwyn, its distributor, has been sold to another company, so I'm not sure of the film's fate . . . I think that novels and films are totally autonomous creations, and shouldn't be judged in terms of one another.

Ray says hello & warmest regards. He has set out corn for our herd of deer, and a beautiful eight-point buck is among them this morning . . .

As always,
Joyce

5 March 1996

Dear Greg—
Congratulations! We're thrilled. [My first collection of short stories, *Distant Friends*, which Joyce and Ray had published with their Ontario Review Press in 1990, had been acquired for a paperback reprint by the University of Georgia Press.] I wonder if U. of GA will keep the jacket design, or come up with a new one? It's a strong, striking collection and we can supply impressive jacket quotes.

I see that Johns Hopkins Press is advertising *I Am Dan-*

gerous. (The title alone should guarantee vast sales—the same subculture that has been enthusiastic about *Zombie*.) . . .

Thanks for the review of *Will You Always Love Me?* It has not received many reviews so far. I had hoped that more reviewers would emphasize the positive elements of the collection—the conclusions of "Act of Solitude," "The Handclasp," "June Birthing," "The Girl Who Was to Die," etc.—but the usual reviewers' chords are struck, sounding so desolate and "violent." My "bleak observations in sharp . . . detail." Well.

Much affection from all—
Joyce

4 April 1996

Dear Greg,

. . . It has been a somewhat stressful spring, with too many trips (planned months ahead of time, of course) by way of Janet Cosby [Joyce's lecture agent]. I find it difficult to decline her proposals. Recently I was on ten planes in nine days—not so exhausting in fact as the ground travel surrounding such flights. Actually meeting people, giving a reading and signing a few books, is a small fraction of the time spent on such occasions. Indiana, Charleston, SC, Eureka, IL, Vassar, Fairfield, CT, and next is Lehigh U. in Pennsylvania . . .

I've been working on the screenplay for *Solstice*, after Jeanne Moreau's visit.

"Our" book—*Will You Always Love Me?*—has been well received, if quietly, in some quarters. I was recently informed that I'll be the 1996 recipient of the PEN/Malamud Award (for Lifetime Achievement in the Short Story).

Let us hear from you. Ray often asks, "How's Greg these days?" and I have to say I don't know. (All the household at 9

Joyce Carol Oates

Honey Brook is quite well, with spring flowers and a virtual waterfall of spring birdsong on all sides.)

As always,
Joyce

18 April 1996
Dear Greg,
...Thanks for your very kind remarks about *Mulvaneys*. It's my valentine to that part of the world, I suppose . . . a farm of the kind we'd never had. Oddly, I felt closest to Marianne; and if I read any sections from the novel in public, it will be Marianne and Muffin. (Unless I'd be fighting too much emotion. Somehow, emotion is taboo in "literary" novels.) . . .

I've enjoyed the collaboration with Jeanne Moreau so far; she calls frequently from Paris, and has given me not one but two surpassingly beautiful scarves, one of them a gorgeous flamey-red Yves St. Laurent which I will wear at the opera preview . . .

Again, sorry about *Pagan Babies* . . . Lucy could have had a walk-on part, at least.

Much affection,
Joyce

14 May 1996
Dear Greg,
Thanks for the letter; I'd forgotten to mention how impressed I was by your little essay in *Southern Voice* ["Teaching Gay Literature in Cobb County"], which struck just the right tone of reasonableness and feistiness. And *I Am Dangerous*—a very strong image. I've long admired Schiele.

I don't know if I mentioned that we've bought a Charles Burchfield watercolor, at least. It's very beautiful, in a softer and more poetic mode than his more characteristic paintings which are aggressively Blakean . . .

Tomorrow I fly to Dallas for a two-day event, readings and book signings. And on Saturday, I deliver a commencement address at a small college in Pennsylvania. After that—nothing for quite a while. Ray is cheerfully digging about in the soil though it's a cool, wet day; our spring is intermittent, and seems reluctant. (Though upstate NY—"Eden County," etc.—had a snowfall just yesterday.) . . .

My parents had a nice visit recently, though my father's health is not A+. It must be, for a man formerly so active, and impatient with being inactive, a strange, unreal transformation; when one malady fades, if it does, another comes forward to take its place; while his vision continues to deteriorate, and reading has been his primary happiness for decades. My mother is quite well, however. (An excerpt from my "letter" to my mother appeared in this past Sunday's *Times*, in an issue devoted to mainly confessional/dysfunctional memoirs. I thought those by Susan Cheever and Mary Gordon were particularly interesting.) "Memoir" has become very popular as a genre, for obvious reasons.

Every other person in Princeton seems to be ill! . . . Apart from the tachycardia, which hasn't struck in years, I've been very well; it makes me uneasy to think how well; for surely the odds are building up . . . But I haven't missed a single class at Princeton since coming here in 1978, and I missed very few prior to that, in Windsor and U-D [University of Detroit]. In the context of others' maladies, this seems almost unnatural . . .

I've been reading elegantly written, not very frightening "ghost stories" by Edith Wharton, many more than I'd known she had written. Now that my *American Gothic Tales* [an anthology] is finished, I find that I'm still interested in the genre; like the mystery, it almost always seems to promise more than it yields, I don't know why.

Ray joins me in sending you best wishes (and Christabel who is comfortably asleep on my lap, very warm and purring).

Much affection,
Joyce

28 May 1996

Dear Greg,

Our condolences for the loss of your friend. [A close friend, Jeff Maddox, had died unexpectedly of a heart attack while working out in the gym.]

My father asks me to say he'll be writing soon. He'd been hospitalized for pneumonia (so much ill health!) but is recovered now (at least temporarily!).

Another long-lost classmate, from high school, has begun to write to me. Bruce Burnham—possibly you have the name. Certainly, he's unusually thoughtful and intelligent; though his memories of "Joyce" don't seem wholly recognizable.

My "Letter to My Mother" has drawn an amazing response—I think because it's virtually the only memoir right now that doesn't castigate a parent.

Regarding your friend Jeff—what a shock that must be. High school athletes sometimes die unexpectedly of heart attacks. Was Jeff a fellow writer? Teacher?

Much affection & sympathy from both Joyce & Ray

22 June 1996

Dear Greg,

Thanks so much for *I Am Dangerous*. The cover is striking; very impressive. Of course, I immediately read "Hemingway's Cats"—an eerie, effective tale. I look forward to reading and rereading the stories in sequence.

I'm involved in a review-essay for *New York Review* on the fiction of John Edgar Wideman. And I've just finished a review for *TLS—The Picador Book of Sportswriting*. (Despite its perfunctory title, this is quite a solid, interesting book.) . . .

Enclosed are items of varying degrees of interest. The English reviews of *What I Lived For*, which frankly surprised me. (The English are unpredictable!) And an article from the distinguished French journal *Le Nouvel Observateur* which is supposedly a "French assessment" of my work. (I've only skimmed it, my schoolgirl French having atrophied shamefully. The headline "L'étrange dame de Princeton" seems about par for the course.) . . .

One of the great happinesses of my life (as a writer) has been preparing the play *The Passion of Henry David Thoreau*. I truly love the material, the friendship of HDT and Emerson; and something about the place—Concord, etc., the freshness and anticipation of the young Thoreau . . . as if it had been somehow my own lifetime, too. (McCarter Theatre did a wonderful reading performance of the play this past Monday, with an excellent youngish Henry David. Now I've been revising, trimming . . . the usual. I'm not sure where, if anywhere, the play might ultimately be presented.) . . .

After five years, Bob Phillips has "retired" as director of the writing program at [the University of] Houston, but will continue, of course, as a professor. The strain of working with temperamental and extremely self-willed people like Cynthia

MacDonald, Ed Hirsch, and Richard Howard was, Bob said, too much for him. How congenial our writing faculty is, by contrast. There are issues—about hiring, frequently—on which we don't all agree, but we discuss them thoroughly, and in every case we've worked things out. Russell [Banks], Toni Morrison, and I rarely disagree on anything—oddly. The poets are just slightly more contentious, but only slightly. (Why are poets obsessed with ranking? Not only the living, but the dead. If I talk about Frost, Jim Richardson and Ted Weiss debate whether he is the "greatest" American poet; whether he is "the equal of" Yeats. After seeing my play, Ted said that Thoreau is the "real thing," not Emerson; but surely both men are "great" enough? As if there's a kind of vertical paradigm of writers, a kind of stepladder of merit, when it seems so much more reasonable to imagine a horizontal plane and very different sorts of people scattered about it, more or less equal.)

The other evening in New York, we went to the annual Horror Writers of America banquet, a lively group indeed, sitting at a table with Peter Straub and Ellen Datlow, among others . . . Stephen King received a Bram Stoker award for a novella, and I received one for *Zombie*. (Though it seems unfair for a mainstream writer to be given this award, so distinguished and coveted in the genre, and so unknown outside it. You haven't seen my Stoker award of two or three years ago, I think—now I have two, on a windowsill in the kitchen. The award/thing/entity is a meticulously designed Gothic mansion with a churchy effect, about one foot high and very heavy; with all sorts of curious faces, gargoyles and baroque miniature designs, costing about $300 to manufacture.) At the banquet, it was quite an occasion to meet Harlan Ellison, surprisingly youthful, a smallish graceful attractive man who must be one of the wittiest and startlingly/corrosively funny conversationalists I've ever encountered. He is murmured to be . . . strange; but who among us (except for me) is not?

Tomorrow we are having a buffet dinner party, the first we've organized since Jeanne Moreau's initial visit. A large gathering of virtually everyone who's in town . . . In July, we'll be spending two days at the Contemporary American Play Festival . . . and in mid-July journeying north to Skidmore, the Adirondacks, Vermont (visiting Jay and Devon Parini), Maine (visiting my composer John Duffy and working a bit on *Black Water*) and Beverly Farms [MA] (visiting John Updike whom we haven't seen in years).

Please do send me your memorial article for the *Southern Voice*.

Much affection as always,
Joyce

28 June 1996

Dear Greg,

Thanks for your delightful letter! The snapshots [of my two dachshunds, Lucy and Gracie] are heartrendingly lovely. The soulful eyes of those two brunettes . . . ! It's so obvious that animals have personalities, isn't it? I'll bet that Lucy is overjoyed with a surprise puppy and feels vaguely proud of herself for having it. That's great news.

Thanks, too, for your comments on *First Love*. I do admire the Moser illustrations immensely . . .

Congratulations on the terrific review of *I Am Dangerous*. I'm enjoying the volume, but haven't seen nearly so much evidence of "influences" as this reviewer suggests. The stories sound like . . . Greg Johnson.

We had lunch with Bob Phillips today, in Princeton; tonight, dinner with Richard Ford (scheduled to give a reading locally) and Dan [Halpern]. A most unusually busy day for us, as summer days go; many days, we see no one, and the blissful high point is a long meandering bicycle ride. I'm working hard, though, perhaps even obsessively, to finish my *Story: The Art and the Craft of Narrative* for Norton. The deadline is October . . . I've been wonderfully immersed in the project and quite hopeful about the book. Jeanne Moreau returns in August for a week's intense conferring.

Much affection to *all*—
Joyce

8 July 1996

Dear Greg,

I *love* the way you've rearranged the photo sequence! I've just shown Ray, and we're both very impressed. (You are clearly moving into a new phase of your career: biographer/ graphic designer!) I love the connections between some of the photos . . . Bob P. and me with our respective cats, for instance. And other touches quite subtly achieved. I'm beginning to feel positive about the biography and not so much cringing/steeling myself for (what?—I can't imagine). *Thanks so much* . . .

I'm very pleased with this now . . . you bring together people so nicely (like Lois [Smedick, a University of Windsor colleague] and Elaine [Showalter]—both looking wonderfully youthful!). There's a wonderful compression here, a skillful employment of the tight space . . .

I'm sorry that Rosemary [Ahern] has wanted the boxing material to be cut back. Perhaps because *On Boxing* isn't a Dutton book . . . and because she isn't interested in the sport. Still, it is very central to my career . . . for many people it's the only book of mine they have heard of, still less read (!). (I do think, in terms of the biography—in terms of Other People's Opinions—it is at least something unexpected, or unusual, in a (woman) writer's life.)

About "negative" opinions: I'd suggested you query Susan Sontag, and perhaps Alfred Kazin; it's too late to try Stanley Elkin, who cordially disliked me (or what he imagined of me: he'd thought I was a best-selling writer!) . . . I don't mind, truly, "negative comments" . . . In the student evaluations I sent you, I'm sure there were some qualifications. If not, you can say that, through my teaching career, try as I have to be warm, supportive, welcoming, etc., some students invariably see me as "cold" and "aloof." Those adjectives have attached to themselves to me over the decades, like burrs.

Thanks for your comments on *Tenderness* [her new volume of poetry]. Poetry is so . . . direct, personal. Yes, it's Ray Carver about whom (Ted Solotaroff, not one of my favorite people) was speaking, at a dinner party . . . The nicest thing about the volume is the Munch cover . . . so haunting . . .

Much love to all—
Joyce

26 July 1996

Dear Greg,
. . . Though we were as usual very relieved to return home, much of our trip was lovely, and everyone we met gracious & hospitable. Including especially, yesterday, John Updike with whom we had a warm, chatty, thoroughly enjoyable lunch at an outdoor café he'd taken us to previously in charming "Manchester-by-the-Sea" north of Boston.

My reading at Skidmore seemed to go well (I dared to read parts of the chapter "Stump Creek Hill" from *Mulvaneys*) & the usual high level of literary/intellectual discussion one encounters at any gathering hosted by Bob & Peggy Boyers (of the literary magazine *Salmagundi*) was a pleasure—especially after hours of driving . . .

We met Julia Alvarez at the Parinis' in Middlebury . . . how unexpected, to meet a Dominican Republic-American writer in that rather remote New England setting. A beautiful, intelligent and charming woman, quite petite, who teaches writing at Middlebury, though not very happily (she says the English Dept. is contentious [!]). Jay Parini, droll, low-keyed and very funny, had tales of his friend Gore Vidal & his (former) friend Anthony Quinn; he's writing a biography of Robert Frost, though smarting from Jeffrey Meyers who'd visited him two years before, casually extracted from him his vision for the biography, then drove immediately to Boston to acquire a contract for the Frost biography (from Peter Davison who has made a career of publishing gossipy memoirs, a number of them by himself) which he whipped up in less than a year. (I guess no one rushed to scoop you on "JCO.") . . .

In Brent Staples's excellent memoir *Parallel Time: Growing Up Black and White in America* (which I'm reading amid much John Edgar Wideman for a *NYRB* essay-review) he makes the point that so much of one's life is sheerly chance. Yet no one seems to want to believe this fact, at least of other people. So, as Kant would say, the human mind invents "necessity"; then hunts about, to demonstrate it . . .

Joyce (& Ray)

7 August 1996

Dear Greg,

. . . I'll have to look up the Welty/Russell correspondence. (Did you know that Richard Ford is Miss Welty's literary executor?) The other evening at a dinner party . . . a woman named Ann Waldron, something of a local character, was talking of a biography of Welty she'd just finished. (She wrote one on Caroline Gordon some years ago, which I've never read.) I asked her what Eudora's manuscripts were like; if she'd revised much, etc.; and she said, somewhat defensively, "Oh, I wasn't very interested in that sort of thing, I was writing about Eudora's life." I said that a writer's writing *is* her life, and Ann Waldron said, a bit huffily, "Well, I'm a journalist, not a literary critic." I had the dismaying sense that she hadn't examined manuscripts at all. Later, she spoke of "hinting" that Eudora had had a love affair with Elizabeth Bowen. Ed [Cone] and George [Pitcher], who happened to have known Bowen, questioned if this was so; and Ann Waldron said she hadn't any evidence, that was why she was just "hinting" at the possibility. This biography is under contract from Doubleday. (It wasn't authorized; Eudora told friends and acquaintances not to speak with Ann Waldron.)

(Maybe, to liven up *Invisible Writer*, you could "hint" that your subject has had love affairs with, among others, Welty and Bowen.)

Speaking of which . . . notoriety, I mean . . . I just received a hefty sheaf of French reviews of my play *Tone Clusters*. By far the most reviews of any play of mine, ever. Evidently the production was a prominent one, in a Parisian theater, with two well-known French actors. I only skimmed the reviews—my French is as modest as Ann Waldron's critical powers—but thought you'd be interested to know that, in the words of one observer, I am "d'une notoriété considérable en Amérique." (Something for the jacket of *Invisible Writer*?)

. . . I was reading Frank O'Connor's highly regarded *The Lonely Voice*, about the short story, and quite enjoying it, until I came to his section on Katherine Mansfield. Though he had no evidence, O'Connor said that he wouldn't have been surprised if Mansfield had had "homosexual" affairs . . . her stories exhibit a kind of heartlessness, decadence and malice associated with such behavior . . .

My pseudonym novel is titled *Starr Bright Will Be with You Soon*. I think the title derived, oddly, from a dream, some years ago. It's such a relief to be writing this instead of *Mulvaneys* . . .

We missed *Lone Star*! I'd wanted to take Ray to see it. Our problem is that I usually work until about 6:30 p.m. . . . take a long bicycle ride . . . return at about 8 and make dinner . . . what remains of the evening is usually devoted to reading and note-taking for the next day. (Last night, I was eagerly looking forward to *Just an Ordinary Day*, a collection of unpublished and uncollected Shirley Jackson stories assembled by her children, but the stories are very uneven . . . somewhat disappointing at least to me.) . . .

All of the household, including Ray, a bit chagrined since his garden was virtually rained out and he has little to show for his effort (he calculates a single green bean costs about $10 calculating his time spent in growing it), and of course I, send greetings & much affection. Christabel has been sleeping on my lap for long luxuriant periods of time, allowing me to GET MUCH ACCOMPLISHED!

Joyce
(We have a doe, two spotted fawns and a feisty young buck with uneven antlers in residence this summer.)

30 August 1996

Dear Greg,

Thanks for your letter . . . "My" *Selected Emily Dickinson* is out next week. Too bad I didn't write *this* book of 100 poems.

I understand how problematic a relationship can be with an editor, any editor. I've just done a considerable revision of my Lovecraft review-essay (25 pages!) for the *New York Review of Books*; Barbara Epstein is my amazing editor, amazing in that she is continually prodding me to give more examples, explain more carefully, so that a text I'd written that seemed, to me, concise and structurally tight, is made into something richer, and far better . . . A less involved editor, or an editor at a lesser publication, would certainly have accepted the original as is; I would never have known how much more I had to say that is worthwhile.

Similarly, with plays, in which collaboration is essential, I've many times learned that what I've written, while adequate, can be enormously enriched. I've just done further (minor) revisions for *Cry Me a River* (formerly *Black*) at Gordon Edelstein's suggestion; this must be the fourth or fifth revision . . .

To reply to your questions: *Double Delight* will perhaps be published in 1997 (do you know the beautiful rose "Double Delight"?—it's Ray's and my favorite, a deep crimson shading into creamy rose; a striking image, I'd thought, for twinness; there are women twins in the novel). *Starr Bright Will Be with You Soon* was originally a play, or a very long too-novelistic attempt at a play, and is now a pseudonym novel also about women twins, though quite different from *Double Delight*. Why I'm so attracted to "twinness," I don't know. I wish that the Rosamond Smith novels could be more clearly distinct from my other novels, but they seem to be, against my intentions, coming to resemble one another; less cinematic, more "written." And I wish I'd chosen an androgynous pseudonym . . . it was a wonderful opportunity for some reason lost.

In a recent rainstorm another car struck the rear of ours

while Ray was out alone, somewhat crumpling it; so Ray decided to get a new car instead of having it repaired. (Exactly like a few years ago. It's our only way of acquiring new cars, I suppose.) We debated—"Let's get a Rolls Royce," I said, "so that Greg can add a footnote or something to the 'quiet,' 'conservative' life," and Ray said, "We could get a Ferrari Testarossa, that would be even more sensational," so we discussed the issue, but somehow, finally, ended up with virtually the same car we had before—white Honda Accord with sunroof, etc. (At least it's a new model.) I'm sorry; I can imagine Dedrick's pained smile. "Well, if they don't care what they drive . . ."

A play entitled *The Murder of Joyce Carol Oates* was recently performed in Los Angeles.

Did I mention how much I liked "Evening at Home"— one of the most meticulously, subtly *written* of your stories, I think . . .

People have been saying they've liked *Foxfire* [the movie] . . . I'm mostly at a loss for words myself. I don't want to seem critical . . . What did you think?

Much love,
Joyce

21 September 1996

Dear Greg,

. . . Last week I was in NYC for three days. Signing books at branches of Barnes & Noble, giving a reading, visiting museums and seeing a wonderfully tender, "uplifting" film in the interstices of other obligations (*Fly Away Home*); the Merchant Ivory 35th anniversary evening at Carnegie Hall was very successful, a sellout (for AIDS research); it consisted mainly of music from the films, presented by various musicians and singers. At the dinner afterward, I was seated beside James Ivory, a somewhat quiet, literary-minded and very gracious gentleman whom I'd never met before. (Ismail Merchant, wonderfully friendly and sociable, has been my contact.) . . . The *Solstice* project moves slowly along, more or less forward. Jeanne Moreau was very warmly received at the concert when she spoke onstage, like Joanne Woodward, Hugh Grant, Vanessa Redgrave and others. Christopher Reeve, Sharon Stone. (Sharon Stone? She's never done a Merchant Ivory film, of course; her price is too high. But she has involved herself in AIDS research, I hope not for PR reasons. Jeanne Moreau is a friend of Ms. Stone's and speaks of her as a possibility for Monica in our film . . . Can you imagine?)

I've been working on an essay on fairy tales for an anthology of "women writers on fairy tales." Please don't ask me why . . .

Did you note that Michael Upchurch has reviewed us both? I would like to read his fiction; he sounds very thoughtful. Enclosed are the reviews for *Mulvaneys* I've received so far. One reviewer disliked the novel for misrepresenting, in a sense, Michael Mulvaney, Sr.—no father would have behaved like that to Marianne (!). He seems not to have read the last third of the novel. All my loving effort on Muffin at the animal shelter, and Marianne is dismissed as "hunkering down on a hippie commune."

Much affection,
Joyce

17 November 1996

Dear Greg,

Thanks for your letter; and for the terrific photo of Lucy

and Gracie (they look virtually blue-eyed—and wholly innocent). Perhaps by some convolution or other they can wind up on Celestial Timepiece [this was, and is, the wonderfully thorough website on Joyce's work maintained by University of San Francisco librarian Randy Souther] . . . I noted with nostalgic interest your photo of Tonawanda Creek recently installed there. Very haunting . . .

We've had some serious upsets here. The most serious, Ray's younger brother's sudden death . . .

Also, my parents' health continues to trouble me; my father's deteriorating vision; I feel guilty, I suppose, for being relatively healthy; it's hard to feel that one should be, or even can be, happy, if one's parents are not. However, things aren't always bleak. The most recent conversation I had with them, Mom was in good spirits, and Daddy quite enthusiastic about some audiobooks I'd sent him (including fifty hours of Bob Fagles's translation of *The Odyssey*, plus an audio version of *Will You Always Love Me?* that is supposed to be quite good). He "reads" the books as he listens to the tapes, so it doesn't matter that he can't exactly see all the words, and this seems to cheer him quite a bit.

I do feel, sometimes, like a puppet on a string emotionally . . . each time I call home, which is quite often, I never know what sort of conversation I might have. A friend remarked, "It's odd that you identify with your parents so strongly, at your age." I had not thought that I identified with them particularly, but only that I feel sorry for them, as anyone might. It's the very fact of growing old, of human mortality, obviously, that disconcerts me; and obviously there's no cure for that . . .

There will be a workshop of the full two-act *Black Water* this week in NY, but I can't make it; rehearsals begin for *Cry Me a River* (formerly *Black*) soon, at about the time the end-of-semester crush & panic begin at the university.

Yesterday, I had a fascinating visit at Hofstra University—the 12th annual George Sand Conference—I gave a reading/had a conversation w/the conferees—enjoyed a quite good, rather touching play based upon the correspondence of Sand & Flaubert (who called her "Dear Master"—the play's title). I've been working on short stories/reviews/an essay on fairy tales (to appear in *Kenyon*) . . . an autobiographical piece, very short, for *Civilization* (an excellent photo-oriented new magazine published by the Library of Congress). *Mulvaneys* is selling modestly well, I gather; but Dutton seems to plan no further ads, after the very nice ad that appeared in the *NYTBR*. I was prevailed upon, after all, to review the Shirley Jackson/posthumous collection & will be extremely interested to see your review (I think you were going to review it?). What will you be doing for Thanksgiving?

Much affection from all (Daisy is singing *very* loudly)—
Joyce

10 December 1996

Dear Greg,

. . . I've been thinking about what you said in your last letter. About not having so much energy as before. But you've been working very hard on the biography; as well as turning out numerous intelligent and responsible book reviews, which certainly takes energy . . . (A few *Mulvaney* reviews have been amazing in their flippancy and inaccuracy . . . You're relatively rare in caring about a book's fate and identifying with the writer. I try to make that identification, too. It seems to me the least we owe one another, a fundamental respect.) Your current lack of interest in short stories is akin, perhaps, to my current lack of interest in poems; writing them, I mean.

Energy is a mysterious phenomenon. I feel enervated when I'm not writing, and filled with energy when I am; the writing fuels the energy, I've come to think, and not the reverse. I'd have to be terribly ill and tired not to write . . . (Of course, this has happened!)

Since *Mulvaneys*, I haven't been able to envision any long, ambitious work. I wonder if I ever will again. But I've been deeply immersed in shorter things, especially stories-in-the-shape-of-memoirs, an undefined subgenre of fiction ("memoirist fiction"? "fictional memoir"?) with experimental possibilities. A good deal of the foreground/historical texture of these stories is "real" but most of the plots and many of the characters are fictitious. Yet I doubt that I could write an entire novel, even a short novel, in this (to me) fascinating mode.

You'd asked about teaching in a previous letter . . . I've been enjoying my workshops this semester very much. I'd almost say that I love these sessions, which are two hours each, but spill over into my office afterward . . . I identify so completely with young writers, there isn't much distance between us. I have to pinch myself to realize that in their eyes I'm "Professor Oates"—as old, or older, than their parents and seemingly an "established writer." Amazing.

Thanks for your concern about Ray's brother. I think that Ray has taken this death very hard, but he doesn't seem to want to talk about it much. He has hired a lawyer to deal with the estate and is often on the phone with his sister. (Bob died without leaving a will.) . . .

My parents aren't at all bad at the moment. If my father can shift his imaginative energies from reading (which he loved) to reading (sort of) while listening to audiobooks, he'd be much happier. But he can't attend college classes any longer, or thinks he can't. (I think he can.) So a wonderful source of interest and company and newness and intellectual stimulation is gone from his life . . .

I would like to read the novels you've been reviewing. Too bad we don't live close enough to trade books. (Our house is overflowing . . . we dare not buy more.) Yes, it was Oprah Winfrey's show that catapulted the title you mention. I think that Toni Morrison is a true literary phenomenon: intransigent in her vision as a writer, decidedly not "accessible," yet wildly popular; an heir (heiress?) to Jean Toomer and William Faulkner, yet original, too. But I'm fascinated in any case by "popular writers"—storytellers—like Stephen King (whose novels I can't exactly read, but whose stories, like "The Beach," seem to me very well done.) . . .

Fondly,
Joyce

4 January 1997

Dear Greg,

Thanks so much for *The Saskiad* [by Brian Hall; I had reviewed the novel in the *New York Times Book Review*]. It's wonderfully original, very touching and convincing; the character of Jane is as vividly drawn as Saskia herself. And how heartening to learn, via the dust jacket, that so idiosyncratic a novel is a prepublication success. This is something I might well have overlooked otherwise.

Thanks, too, for the Margaret Atwood material. I'd been offered the novel to review by *TLS* but since I'd only just reviewed Margaret's *Oxford Book of Canadian Stories* . . . I thought it wouldn't be quite right to review the new novel, too. It does look wonderful. When Margaret came to Princeton, I introduced her at one of her public readings; we'd known each other, though not well, in Canada, and have always been on good terms. She's warm, funny, wholly unpretentious but capable of acerbic comments if pushed. ("Will you ever write about subjects other than Canadian?" one foolish person asked.) In Canada, in the 1960s and beyond, Margaret received a good deal of savage criticism, simply for being herself. It's amazing how much ill will a moderately successful writer (a woman?) could draw in those days, perhaps still; when she came to visit Windsor, to give a reading, before I'd met her one of my department colleagues, Peter Stevens the erstwhile poet, spoke very negatively of her; her hair "sprang out from her head" in a way that seemed to offend him. Shortly afterward, when I met her, I was astounded at how petite, attractive, gracious and wholly nonthreatening she was; her curly hair was quite contained; no more terrifyingly out-springing than my own.

Male fantasies . . . what would we do without them?

The wonderful thing about films like *The English Patient* (a lushly photographed, beautifully imagined male fantasy, indeed) and *Secrets & Lies* is that they do have the density and subtlety of good prose. Except *Secrets & Lies* is somewhat static as cinema; in fact, a filmed play. Opinion here is divided on *English Patient* with men liking it, on the whole, more than women. Still, the fact that a serious, literary novel has been successfully filmed is encouraging . . .

I had an unpleasant, though probably mildly comic, experience yesterday at the doctor's. I'd gone in for a simple office check-up and since I hadn't had a blood test in six years, I took a deep breath and decided to have one. Dr. Branon's nurse used the smallest needle they had to try to find a vein . . . to try to find a vein . . . to try to find a vein in my aching left arm while, stoic and resolute, I clenched both fists and stared into a corner of the room. In the midst of this, the door opened and Dr. Branon reappeared, bringing with him "our new associate Bill Kreiger"—a grinning young man who was introduced to "Joyce Carol Oates"—he'd gotten a BA from Princeton in 1986 but "never had the honor" of studying with me. Feebly, I shook hands with him. I murmured, "Is this a social moment?" (perspiration breaking out on my forehead as the nurse continued her futile jabbing) and Dr. Branon laughed as if I'd said something witty. Finally, the nurse gave up on that arm and wanted to try the other and I said I'd about had it for one day. As I told Elaine Showalter afterward, my next appointment, next week, is with my gynecologist and I don't want to think what will ensue in that examination room . . .

Much affection as always—
Joyce

23 January 1997
(our 36th (!!!) wedding anniversary)

Dear Greg,

Thanks for your newsy letter. I admired your review of *The Saskiad* in the *NYTBR*—though perhaps not so much as the grateful writer must have admired it. The novel does gain momentum as it progresses, and the reader is sorry when it ends . . .

The only remarks people have directed to me about "Hunters Harvest" [an anti-hunting piece published in *Playboy*] have been complimentary; but, then I'm not acquainted with feisty macho hunters (except for Richard Ford, of course). I know, I know!—I had better watch my back. (I have to confess, between you and me, I truly abhor hunting—this "sporty" American hunting at least. But there isn't much that is amusing about it.) . . .

I received a very angry, incoherent letter from someone,

perhaps an old friend of Shirley Jackson, who seemed to think that my review of Jackson's oeuvre was "negative." Yet I'd indicated that the collection was not worthy of her talent. Did you send me your review? I don't think you did . . .

I love receiving your letters; yes, I'm grateful that "Margot Peters"—whoever she is—isn't my official biographer! [Peters had published biographies of Charlotte Brontë and May Sarton.] Perhaps the only area of my life, or my thinking-about-my-life, that causes me to tense up is the imminent Biography. But . . .

(But: I have got to stop thinking about it. Especially at 4 a.m.) . . .

Outside, as I sit here at this desk, ten deer are hungrily eating the corn Ray has set out, in a long line, for them. Often there's just a doe and a fawn—an undersized fawn we call Little Fuzzy (his coat is very fuzzy). The downside of this is that we often sit and watch the deer . . . instead of working . . . for a long time . . .

Thanks for your remarks on "Faithless" (one of my favorites of my own stories) which is clearly a back-home/ Millersport tale. It's true, Lovecraft is a special taste but I think you would truly like "The Colour Out of Space" which was too long for inclusion in my anthology. [Her *Tales of H.P. Lovecraft* appeared from Ecco in 1997.] . . .

Classes start Feb. 5/6. Much busyness imminent & the usual breathlessness. All of the gang sends hello & love from our house to yours—

Joyce

7 February 1997

Dear Greg,

. . . I could not have anticipated how troubled I would

be by the prospect of *Foxfire* being banned in Toronto. (Perhaps I've mentioned this? It's been pending a while.) Not so much the novel being banned, actually in a Toronto suburb, as the accompanying media coverage which presents me, in the eyes of my critics, as a pornographer (!). *Foxfire* is said to be an "imported sex manual." Amazing—2,000 people have signed a petition to ban this book. (Which must be 200 times the number of people who've read it, let alone purchased it in Ontario.) I'm touched that any high school teacher would wish to teach the novel or recommend it to students. . . Interviewers have been calling, but I've declined being interviewed. When I was in Washington, DC, a few weeks ago for the PEN/Malamud event, I visited an "academic high school"—all black honor students—who had read *Foxfire* and *Will You Always Love Me?* and responded with the intelligence and subtlety of dream readers. Some of them very young, yet so sharp and sensitive; the boys hadn't any trouble identifying with the white girls of the novel. I do feel rather embarrassed—sullied—by the Toronto experience. The ugly publicity keeps on and on; another phone call just now . . .

I'm having a wonderful time, unusual for me at the outset of a novel (which might be an ominous sign), planning *Heart Chronicles* [later retitled *Broke Heart Blues*], set in a mythologized Willowsville (sic) in some bygone era. The theme is in fact mythologizing itself; the powerful complex of emotions to which we give the name "nostalgia." I'm afraid that, for the real Williamsville, I still feel rather little compared to the grittier, more ethnically and economically diverse Lockport. (But Williamsville was only 5,600 people! A mere suburban village-appendage of Buffalo, exclusively white, non-Jewish; mainly Protestant. I wonder if it has changed in the intervening years very much.) (The suburbs of Detroit, for instance, haven't much changed. Now they're segregated economically—which comes to the same thing.) . . .

I wrote a brief appreciation/analysis of O'Connor's "The Artificial N____r" [N-word]. You're right—it isn't one of O'Connor's best. An awkward, epiphany-driven ending. But there are some nice touches. When will the O'Connor biography be published? She remains so appealing, so tragic, dying at 39; like Sylvia Plath (at 30?) and Stephen Crane (an astonishing 29) . . .

Much affection from the gang here—
Joyce

22 February 1997

Dear Greg,

. . . The Willowsville novel *Heart Chronicles* is amazing to me, it seems to be flowing so easily. Oddly, though, there's no one remotely like me in it, and even Bruce Burnham is just a name so far—"Burnham Nurseries" in the village. (He'll be terribly disappointed since the novel is entirely fiction. The only "real" element is the powerful, heady, seductive spell of nostalgia which I see to be a truly American quality; the narcissism of perennial adolescence. Ray, however, doesn't seem at all touched by nostalgic memories of Milwaukee. So I suppose it isn't universal. What of you? I can detect in, for instance, *Pagan Babies* some memory traces . . . but not real nostalgia, I don't think. I do feel it myself, with an almost visceral power, in contemplating Lockport . . .)

I did finally agree to be interviewed re. the Canadian controversy. There have been several sympathetic interviewers. It seems, however, that *Foxfire* is doomed; it's just too much trouble, too exhausting, for the school to be dealing with these people . . . And it may be that *Foxfire* is too much for most students . . . it's written from the perspective of a woman in her fifties. (I was interviewed on the CBC national news for about six flurried minutes.) The ugly publicity does seem comical from a distance, and yet, when you're the object of such attacks, you do wind up feeling rather sullied. For of course almost no one will read the novel, only the attacks and the media coverage.

Your movie-going is daunting! I'm looking forward to—actually planning—to rent the video of the updated *Vertigo*, which I'd never seen when it first came out. This is about as close to a movie theater as I'll be able to get for a long time, I'm afraid. There are reading performances of *Bad Girls* and *The Passion of Henry David Thoreau* coming up in New York . . . The *Solstice* project, like most such projects, is drifting dangerously near the Bermuda Triangle . . .

Strange how I, too, like Randy [Souther], like [*Mysteries of*] *Winterthurn* above most other novels of mine. It's the character of Xavier, I suppose. The equation of the writer w/the detective & the evocation, so loving at the time, of an entire enclosed, dreamy & fraught-with-significance world. I wish I could duplicate the writing experience of that curious novel, now out of print and rarely, I suppose, glanced into. But the Recorded Books audio is excellent.

This semester, like last, is enormously enjoyable. I think I truly *love* the two-hour workshop sessions. There's a kind of communal/emotional intensity, though much humor, too, in our "editing" sessions. (My pretense is, we're all editors of an excellent literary magazine working on material we've accepted for publication, to improve it.) . . .

Much love,
Joyce

2 May 1997

Dear Greg,

A quick response to your very nice letter. Congratulations on the "Georgia Author of the Year Award." And on the extremely handsome paperback edition of *Distant Friends*. It's very different from our cover, and equally striking we think ...

My exact feelings about Philip Roth, too. It's true as you say that he's been doing very well lately, writing energetically and well. But I would guess, knowing what I do of Philip's personal life, from both mutual acquaintances (Philip no longer seems to have "friends"—he has either withdrawn or dropped most of them) and Claire Bloom's memoir, that Philip has immersed himself in his "art" because his "life" brings him despair. He can live in his art as he can't live in his life and he'd be the first to recognize the irony in this for it's a cosmic joke of a kind; yet, it does make for a "successful career." One of Philip's favorite Kafka stories is "The Hunger Artist" ...

What a marvelous reading/visit Stephen King made here at Princeton the other week. He came to my fiction workshop and spoke most openly, engagingly, frankly, funnily. (He's actually a big kid of about 12, as well as being wholly shrewd, intelligent, "professional.") Stephen would seem to have been the only speaker in historic McCosh auditorium to have appeared without a necktie, even a shirt—he wore a maroon T-shirt, jeans, and running shoes. The university provided security guards for him (fans had been arriving all day, from as far away as Iowa, some of them looking a bit, well, unPrinceton) and it was wonderful to see these guards, some of them black men, laughing and talking with him, telling him how much they like his writing. (Of course, no one from the English Dept. came.) We had an enormous crowd and it was one of our most successful ventures; I'll be teasing Russell Banks about this for a long time, since Russell refused to invite Stephen King (and also Walter Mosley, who came in Feb.); I waited until Russell went on leave, and promptly invited them. (Some "literary" writers, it might be said, as a kind of Wildean aphorism, try to dismiss as "popular writers" anyone whose books sell more than their own.)

Black Water opened amid a week of opera conferences/festival in Philadelphia. Several other operas opened, too, and I think we got a bit lost in the shuffle since there've been few reviews, and none that I've seen. But *Opera News*, the most important publication, at least to John Duffy, will be running a review sometime soon. Audiences have been very responsive and professionals (like Emily Mann) enthusiastic. I'd been told, however, that some music critics have faulted the music for not being "memorable" . . . or whatever . . . (Of course, I'm not a music professional. I wouldn't know if a new composition is original, derivative or what.) Certainly people have been enormously appreciative of John's music, and of the opera; Gordon did a brilliant job of directing. I'm sorry you weren't able to see it . . .

I may be working with Toni Morrison in an "atelier" seminar of hers next spring, a kind of team-teaching for about two weeks involving drama/musical composition, with student writers and performers.

We're glad you liked Hawaii. Sorry you can't come for our party.

Much love,
Joyce

                                                    17 June 1997

Dear Greg,
Thanks so much for your lovely card (dachshunds must

be the sweetest dogs of all: is it possible that, according to my dictionary, they were bred to hunt . . . badgers?) which arrived just in time for Bloomsday. It's a beautiful day here & we've already celebrated by going for an energetic hike in a nature preserve in which we saw, among other sights, a wild turkey striding just a few feet ahead of us, ostrich-like. He was in fact quite tame and reluctant to fly or flee into the tall grass.

Tonight we'll be having dinner with the Halperns & Russell & Chase, visiting Princeton for a day or two while they prepare their Princeton house for a tenant. Russell has just finished his 800-page John Brown saga [*Cloudsplitter*, 1998] at last. He was writing it concurrently with *What I Lived For* at one time, then set it aside. We were commiserating together—we will never, ever write long novels again . . . Your review of Bob Stone's book is excellent. I'd just spoken with him on the phone the other day & he's still smarting over the dismissive review in *NYTBR* so it's too bad I didn't have yours in hand to tell him about . . .

We'll be visiting my parents in early July for two days en route to Skidmore College, Bob Boyers and my usual summer reading at the writers' institute; then to the Bankses in the Adirondacks. Vaguely we're thinking of flying to LA in August . . . three of my plays (*Naked, Secret Mirror, American Holiday*) will be performed at the Attic Theatre. As a fellow reluctant traveler you'll be pleased to know that I've decided to cancel out of a nightmarishly intensive publicity trip to Germany/France in early Sept.

My *Heart Chronicles* is moving along. I'd hoped it would be about 250 pages but it's beyond 400 now. Why this invariably happens to me I don't know. Though the "Willowsville" of the setting isn't much like "Williamsville" in real life, I'm looking forward to revisiting in July; seeing my old high school, too.

Pendleton, NY, two miles from Millersport, is the home of the worst mass murderer in US history [Timothy McVeigh]. And the Good Shepherd Church which the McVeighs have always attended, & which my family & I attended while I was growing up, is still there; quite clearly exerting no true moral influence at all upon its parishioners ...

Snake Eyes was optioned for film some years ago, by Universal; I wrote a screenplay that was "promising"; nothing came of the project; about a year ago, I received a large (by my modest standards) check in the mail for its purchase; my agent called a few weeks ago to tell me that the studio rediscovered the screenplay and likes it very much; a publicity release recently noted that Robert DeNiro is starting work on a new film titled *Snake Eyes* ... But it's just a coincidence. Only the titles are identical. (Information to make a biographer sigh.)

We hope things are well with you, as, generally, they are here at 9 Honey Brook. The only additions are two water snakes who live in our pond. Ray insists they're harmless & "part of nature" ... I feel squeamish about venturing down there. Otherwise we have many bullfrogs & brightly colored carp, water iris, lily pads, rushes.

Much love,
Joyce

6 July 1997

Dear Greg,

... We're enthralled with our lovely summer life/schedule. My work on the ubiquitous novel continues more or less without cessation, like a stream, interrupted by small, containable interludes themselves quite enjoyable, or usually. (A discordant dinner party the other evening was an exception. How people *talk*, what empty rhetoric issues from their mouths, seeking to "dominate" others in social situations—why? It can be as torturous to have one's ear talked off as to have it bitten off.) Last night was the first night in a long time that I didn't work until midnight—and the letdown was considerable. Where I'd imagined I felt "anxiety" I think really I'd been feeling a meaningful urgency. Now, able to relax, or sort of, I see that relaxation is overrated!

Yes, I did complete a fairly final draft of *Heart Chronicles*. Now I'll be revising, which is always a pleasure. Like flying in a small plane over a terrain that, traversed on foot, had seemed so perilous and mysterious. What an advantage great genius would be, like Mozart's—to see the work instantly as a whole, and "get it" formally, then to take one's time executing the parts. But the "vision" I have of a work is so impressionistic, even emotional, it doesn't really correspond to what evolved, and by the end of a work, after months, might not bear much relationship to it at all. Is this your experience, too?

(It seems somehow the most "normal" writerly experience. John Updike once said in a letter—one of his wonderful longish letters, which he seems not to write now, at least to me—that he began with visual/dramatic incidents and worked outward from these. The ways in which we write are endlessly fascinating, perhaps because the "why" is unfathomable.) . . .

You must be tremendously excited about your new house. There's nothing quite so uplifting to the spirits. (Though, from our perspective, we couldn't bear to pack another box of books, ever, and move. Where we are, we *are*.) Your neighborhood seemed very affluent/suburban to me, very likely a family-oriented world like much of Princeton. Which is why our younger & more lively faculty insist upon living in NYC & commuting.

Beginning our days at 7 a.m., running (& contemplating the morning's work at leisure), & being back around 8 a.m., I have a sense of space that I didn't have previously when I wouldn't get into my study, for one reason or another, until 9 a.m. or later. I can't recall you mentioning running (?) but it's exquisitely pleasurable & I'm convinced enormously helpful to planning work, & proofreading (in one's mind, I mean); a kind of strenuous forward-motion meditation. We'll be visiting the Bankses in Keene, NY—now there's a hardy duo: they mountain climb in their area, hiking for *nine hours*. All in preparation for an October fling at Mt. Kilimanjaro, Africa.

Much affection,
Joyce

14 July 1997

Dear Greg,

Thanks for your Austen review: well done, sensible & convincing. But how does one write a biography of Jane Austen, a figure by this time shrouded in mythic luminosity? The "critical biographical" approach seems to me the only viable angle of perspective . . .

It looks as if Little, Brown will be my new publisher in England; under the imprint of Virago, the "New Virago" as they seem to be calling themselves. I haven't spoken with any editor, everything has been done through agents, and very capably . . . I'm not sure if any of this is of interest to you, re. the biography. Murray Pollinger, my elegant/eloquent [English] agent of many years, retired last year & his clients went to the Higham agency. I've never met these people but have a sense that they are excellent, and I'm certainly grateful. As you probably know, English publishing is in a terribly depressed state.

Man Crazy will be published next year, and several backlist paperback titles reprinted (possibly *Black Water*, *Foxfire*, *Because It Is Bitter* . . .). I'll be assembling a special "selected stories" for the English publishers, since story collections are even less marketable [in England], in fact far less marketable, than they are here. I only hope I won't be invited to visit for publicity purposes; I've had enough of airplane travel to last a lifetime.

I agree that the Tyson incident is grotesque & exaggerated. Primarily, I think it's because the biting—the use of teeth—has atavistic, cannibalistic overtones—violates taboo. It's symbolic & deeply distressing as a more conventional (though not less damaging) foul like eye-thumbing, headbutting, would not be. My op-ed piece [for the *New York Times*] focused upon this violation of taboo, but the editor excised most of it.

Your birthday? Congratulations! This little book can be a present, sort of. And, of course, your beautiful new house. It looks *enormous*. And wonderful. I'd been thinking of it as more casual/artsy . . . but it's actually elegant. (The chandeliers fit in.) The current owner has furnished it very well, indeed . . .

My parents are in good spirits; thanks for sending my father the large-print book. (Alas, it would take him months to read it. His eyesight is really quite deteriorated; he reads sparingly, with a magnifying glass & a special magnifying machine he can fit onto his desk. He "sees" at the periphery of what was his vision and has less trouble with short distances than the closeness of print.) We had two fine days with my parents & a warm, lively evening with my brother Fred (who tends to be quiet) & his attractive wife Nancy (who, fortunately, is quite vivacious).

Happy Birthday!

Much love,
Joyce

24 October 1997

Dear Greg,

My last card to your old address. Thanks for your Southern gallantry in offering to defend me against Mr. Conroy; but you are better out of this. [Pat Conroy had written Joyce a long letter castigating her "sorry ass" for not showing up to receive a lifetime achievement award at Birmingham-Southern College; Joyce had missed the event due to a long-delayed plane flight, but Conroy apparently had not been informed of this.] I wasn't so much appalled at his letter as by the sense it conveyed of a community in which my very name was an insult . . . but it must be exaggerated, surely I'm not so important. (Off for a vacation in Key West? Amazing!) We're flying to Seattle today, then San Francisco (will see Billy [Abrahams], among others) (Alice Adams) and Los Angeles for four days. Our fall break—I would rather spend at home revising *My Heart Laid Bare*. [A version of this long novel, one of a quintet of postmodernist Gothic novels, had been written in the 1980s; it was published in a revised form in 1998.]

Love,
Joyce

1 December 1997

Dear Greg,

By now you must be settled in your new house. I hope the move was fairly smooth and untraumatic. Your attitude has been admirable—a vacation in Key West in medias res!

Last weekend I was in Florida too, at the large, lively & on the whole enjoyable Miami Book Fair. I was there for only a brief overnight visit, reading from *Man Crazy* and signing books; and meeting friends like Maxine Kumin and Dick Bausch. I'd been at the Northwest Book Fair in Seattle a few weeks ago, and this was even larger. Suddenly book fairs, like superstores, have swept into the literary scene and seem, at least to an observer on the margins, surprisingly popular.

This is the first day—very cold, blustery & wintry—in weeks that I've had time to write an actual letter. Since early October I'd been immersed almost literally in a massive revisiting/rewriting of *My Heart Laid Bare*. The final pages went off by FedEx this morning, only a few days beyond the ideal deadline Dutton had set for me. I've never been so enthralled—sometimes exhausted—by a writing adventure . . . I grew to love *My Heart Laid Bare* as I worked on it, but I don't have any illusions that others will love it, or even in some quarters like it at all . . . Still, it's an enormous relief to be finished, and I do feel satisfied with it.

By a coincidence, your letter just arrived. It's good to hear from you. (Ray came staggering across the courtyard with an armload of mail including ominously large jiffy bags, blown by the wind. He's amazing: he still runs at 7 a.m. every morning, despite the cold. I try to get out, later in the day, but don't always succeed; if I can't run, I miss it enormously. I think my metabolism has become unhinged by the 10-12 hour writing sessions for weeks & a generally heightened/exhilarated tempo . . .)

Your Thanksgiving sounds lovely. Dedrick is a wonder. (Though in fact Ray can roast a turkey, too . . . that, and prepare eggs and toast. This is the limit of his culinary skills but he's an excellent eater.) All the movies you mention sound meritorious, & we hope to see them sometime. Of course, we've seen *The Sweet Hereafter* [based on Russell Banks's novel] which is excellent . . .

We had a lovely Thanksgiving dinner at the home of

Vivian & Harold Shapiro (president of Princeton) along w/ mostly family & two other faculty members, the dean of the Woodrow Wilson School (Henry Bienen's old post) & his wife. (My parents could not have come to visit us if they'd wanted. My father's eyesight makes traveling very difficult & my mother's health isn't stable. There's nothing "wrong" with them—so far as I know—except age. I try to keep in mind how wonderfully active & vital they've been for so many decades . . . most of my friends have lost one or both parents years ago. I try to speak with them on the phone frequently & send them cards & letters & books fairly continuously . . .)

The *New Yorker* hasn't yet run my Updike review, so perhaps they won't. I asked for "After Amnesia" back— finally—& they released it, w/apologies after more than a year. Though the magazine pays high prices for material, the editors over-buy, and it seems that a certain percentage of their material never sees print. Which is sometimes just as well . . . Everyone at 9 Honey Brook is reasonably well & sends much love—

Joyce

31 December 1997

Dear Greg,

It sounds as if you've been having a busy, enjoyable Christmas. We've had days alternating between seeing many people & seeing virtually no one. I'm in a phase of book reviewing and quite liking the short, concentrated, intense bouts of writing, most recently two books on boxing (one of them is very engaging, by an ex-South African) for the *LA Times*, for which I've never written before. Payment is as modest as the *NYTBR* but the new format is attractive, under the editorship of Steve Wasserman. What have you been reviewing lately?

Elaine S. has expressed interest, in fact rather girlish enthusiasm, for reading *Invisible Writer*, so I've asked that galleys be sent to her before she leaves for England (Jan. 5). At the MLA convention in Chicago, Elaine had to have a "bodyguard"; she'd received so many hate letters & e-mail messages, threats both veiled & unveiled. The main lobbying force is the chronic fatigue syndrome people—who have a remarkable amount of energy to expend in such campaigns . . .

We've been giving dinner parties lately—well, two. I feel positively bountiful . . . On one of our NYC days we met, at a lovely large party at Roger Berlind's penthouse apartment on East End Avenue, Whoopi Goldberg & Frank Langella who was my classmate, two years ahead of me, at Syracuse many years ago. Whoopi Goldberg is very different from her public persona, far more soft-spoken, even girlish. Very attractive . . .

Much love,
Joyce

26 January 1998

Dear Greg,

So glad you've acquired a fax. Hadn't I been urging you for months? . . .

I wish I liked traveling more. A trip to Atlanta would be attractive. On May 29, I'm supposed to be in Charleston (I believe it's the Spoleto Festival; dramatic readings of two stories of mine by actors, & I'm supposed to discuss them afterward). Possibly I could visit Atlanta first, on the 28th. *Five Points* is a very handsome magazine, and I hope to send the editors something suitable . . .

It would be great to see your beautiful dogs in person (so to speak). But I don't believe that Ray would accompany me . . .

I'm embarked upon a new Rosamond Smith novel [*The Barrens*], which moves along like a small boat in a dark, gathering current. I suppose all our writing is adventure— Adventure—of one kind or another. Sometimes it takes us where we hadn't expected to go, which makes the trip truly worthwhile.

We saw a riveting production of *Homesick*—a new more dramatic version which will appear in *New Plays* (June 1998)—in New York last week. How strange to be haunted by the contents of one's own imagination. But these were exceptionally convincing and "poetic" actors, and the use of music . . . was mesmerizing. The play received a standing ovation . . . Next week, our semester begins with much fanfare!

Much love,
Joyce

30 January 1998

Dear Greg,

. . . I'll be interested in seeing your review of *Birthday Letters*. The sole time we met Ted Hughes, in NYC perhaps twenty years ago, we found him quiet, even gentle. And I do admire much of his poetry. But this new book seems to me flat and prosy; the language isn't exciting, or even very finely honed; the poems' strategies are virtually identical throughout. What is most offensive—and you can imagine how you would feel in the "subject's" place—is how Hughes focuses obsessively upon Plath, as with a zoom lens, never allowing her any speech or intelligence, & reporting virtually every aberrant reaction of hers to anything. She's made to swing between mania & depression as if there hadn't been, for most of her life surely, a controlled & rational life in between . . .

We're having a lovely quiet weekend. It's the calm before the deluge. But a very serene & productive time . . . We laughed at your self-image of recovering from a large dinner party. The only activity in my life that exhausts me is writing, when it doesn't go well & even sometimes when it does.

Much affection,
Joyce

5 February 1998

Dear Greg,

The Hughes review is excellent. Very deft, fair-minded (at least to my somewhat feminist/American sensibility) & informative. You don't seem to have found the poems quite as morally (?) offensive as I did, which is perhaps just as well.

A starred review? Really? Your book/my life—*starred*? I would love to see this review since it must be good. (What an odd Kafkaesque situation it is, to anticipate not a book of mine but my entire life "assessed.")

My father says he can't read anything much except newspapers and magazines now, and very slowly. The last book he will probably have read is *Invisible Writer*, about which he's still talking enthusiastically. We're both—he & I—so pleased that my grandmother Woodside is represented as she is. Thank you, Greg.

(My sentimental side is emerging. Just wait till you see *Come Meet Muffin!* . . .)

Tonight we'll be seeing Russell & Chase for the second time this week. We love these two & will miss them after this semester; but they plan to buy a condominium in Princeton & return from time to time. They "love" their Princeton friends. (Russell is "all boy." He tells of climbing Mt. Kilimanjaro back in Oct., 15,000 terrifying feet, plus near gale-force winds. And this is *enjoyable*? Chase became ill, being more sensible, & had to fall by the wayside at only 10,000 feet or so. The local guides called Russell "Babu" (grandfather) & were amazed at his stamina.

Ray & I became exhausted merely listening to such macho tales. Russell, Richard Ford & Bob Fagles have all been newly elected to the American Academy; so we plan to attend the ceremony for the first time in ten years.

Love,
Joyce

13 February 1998

Dear Greg,

. . . At last after weeks of exile (in our "guest room") I've moved back to my old study, which has been extended by about ten feet outward in the direction of the street; but it's quite hidden from the street, and is partly surrounded by trees. I have windows on three sides of me and feel as if I'm in a greenhouse.

No, I don't think the two reviews [of *Invisible Writer*] were at all bad. It is good, however, that you have, or believe that you have, a thick skin regarding reviews. You may need it.

What a terrific new semester here! There's a flurry of extremely interesting "social life"—an inadequate term to suggest the range and depth of the evenings we've been having with our friends (old, like the Bankses, & newer like C.K. Williams & his wife, and Ed White who is wonderfully warm, smart, funny, charming—and an excellent cook). I feel particularly close to Russell, like a kind of sister perhaps. In most respects, Russell is "older" than I—certainly in experience, & some of it very grueling personal experience; he's a remarkably large-souled person, yet fundamentally very funny, unpretentious & in his newly burgeoning fame, which has not the slightest tincture of notoriety (so far!), he's a model of good sense & even modesty. We like Chase immensely, too— an excellent poet, a very principled & intelligent woman . . .

You might like, to a degree, P.D. James's *A Certain Justice*. But if you have a disinclination for the mystery structure, you might well feel that you're wasting your time. My approach to the genre is complicated: it's rare for me to read any mystery/suspense novel that I actually like, or can admire (as I certainly do admire James's *The Turn of the Screw*), yet for some reason I keep reading, at least the openings of these novels, as if searching for . . . precisely what, I don't know. My interest in the mystery genre must have to do with a (metaphysical?) yearning to explore Mystery itself . . . (As a biographer, you might trace this back to primary causes . . . the "mystery" of my great-grandfather's murder, for one.) . . . The novel form is the ideal way in which to explore not-otherwise-articulated obsessions.

Many spring birds are singing here; even an early robin! Happy Valentine's Day!

Much love,
Joyce

P.S. I was just now invited by *Playboy* to "have a conversation in their pages" with Donald Trump. I can't even think of a "witty rejoinder"!

25 February 1998

Dear Greg,
. . . How on earth can you have only 2.5 weeks left in your quarter? (And less, now.) It seems to me you've only just

begun. Your quarter system must be like a roller-coaster ride, breathless and blurred.

By contrast, our old-fashioned semester just rolls along . . . comes to a kind of halt at "reading week" . . . then rolls on again, to the end . . . I was struck down—almost—by bronchitis for part of last week, & though I didn't actually miss any classes, I dragged around the house & didn't accomplish much in terms of writing. (I did accomplish much in terms of very peaceful, purring cat-on-lap sessions which I recommend highly.)

I wonder if you get the *NY Times*? An op-ed piece I was invited to write is scheduled to appear tomorrow. I love these short, high-pressure assignments: the subject is suggested, the piece written & faxed & next morning galleys are faxed & there's a quick editorial consultation & the piece appears in print, almost within 24 hours. It makes writing somehow so much more immediate, & connected to a specific audience. Though one wouldn't want to do it all the time . . .

Much love,
Joyce

4 March 1998

Dear Greg,

By now you've probably heard my phone message. In any case, congratulations from both Ray and me on an excellent review. "Fascinating and well-written" are hardly innocuous adjectives. We had dinner with Ed White this evening, and again he expressed admiration for the biography. He found the early chapters particularly moving. Ed spent eight years on his Genet biography, not knowing how much work it would involve; he'd never do it again, he says. But he has written a 100-page Proust biography for James Atlas's Viking/Penguin series, and his enthusiasm for this project has led me to reconsider doing one of these myself . . . Can you guess who my subject is? (You probably know me better than anyone, or almost anyone else, so you should be able to guess who my subject is. Hint: a major American literary figure.) . . .

That's an intriguing idea—your editing some journal entries. To me, the journal is overwhelming and defies all rational thought. *At the Mountains of Madness*—a Lovecraft novella of grinding detail and obsessiveness—comes to mind as a subtitle. I couldn't begin to organize it; then again, I couldn't begin to reread it . . . [My edited volume of her journal entries eventually appeared in 2007.] . . .

Much love,
Joyce

10 March 1998
Dear Greg,

Congratulations on another excellent review! For a first-time biographer, you're certainly being appreciated & praised. If only we could quit while ahead.

The book arrived today, and looks wonderful. In every sense of the word, *weighty*. I haven't allowed myself to skim through it but have looked at the photographs, of course. These are excellent selections . . .

(I do miss the photo, embarrassing evidently to you & Rosemary, of Mike Tyson & me, both in our earlier, more innocent days.) . . .

I'd been contemplating a possible subject for a short biography for some time. Jim Atlas suggested Kafka, Nietzsche, Lewis Carroll, Faulkner, Plath . . . all of which make perfect sense. But I've chosen someone for whom I don't seem to

have much affinity, from whom I haven't learned much, &
whose later books I haven't even read. His initials are E.H.
He's no feminist ideal . . . I'm thrilled about this; & have already begun reading & thinking. (Though I'm in the midst of
a Rosamond Smith novel that is going rather slowly & is becoming too "literary" for my taste, & I doubt I'll be finished
with it for some time.) . . .

Much love,
Joyce

16 March 1998
Dear Greg,

Many thanks for the *Zabelle* review [in the *New Yorker*],
which I had not thought would be run since the novel was
published in January . . .

Too late now, but you might have included a footnote
about a benign restaurant experience last night. With Chase
Twichell & the Keeleys. In my food was what turned out to
be an inch-long nail, which I'd vaguely interpreted as (how
the mind works to rationalize!) some sort of odd shaped
spice, like a rosemary twig. But—it was an actual nail. I simply pushed it aside and continued with the meal, which was
very good; and afterward showed it to people who were hor-
rified. It occurred to me then that a "normal" response would
have been quite different . . . It was explained that the nail
"must have fallen out of the ceiling in the kitchen." I was
grateful not to have swallowed it. The headlines would have
been embarrassing:

LOCAL WRITER DIES OF NAIL IN LOCAL
RESTAURANT
Publisher "Very Annoyed"

Biography Is Already Printed
(We were not charged for the nail.)

Much love from all,
Joyce

16 March 1998

Dear Greg,

. . . I've begun *For Whom the Bell Tolls*, which I'm not sure that I'd ever read; and the Kenneth Lynn biography, which is excellent. A humane, intelligent, wonderfully detailed & researched work that reads like a novel . . .

How odd that Nona Balakian's biography of Saroyan is appearing so many years after her death. Your new identity will be that of Biography Expert. And a William Styron, too! I hadn't known one was imminent.

The fax-photo of you, Lucy & Gracie is actually kindest to you; poor Lucy & Gracie are intriguing inky blotches, while you look like a somewhat benign serial killer. I'm sure that the PR photo will be much more flattering.

Plans for the Atlanta visit sound very exciting. As the date approaches, we can confirm some details . . .

Much affection,
Joyce (& Ray)

20 March 1998

Dear Greg,

. . . I've been immersing myself in the dismal life of Hemingway & learning more than perhaps one ought to know about another human being, even a major writer. Here I sit brooding over a photo of Hemingway drinking, & the caption reads that, after receiving the Nobel Prize in 1954, Hemingway "refused to moderate his drinking & was obsessed with thoughts of failure & suicide."

(It crosses my mind that one might be obsessed with such, without winning the Nobel Prize. Or, conversely, one might not win the Nobel Prize & not be obsessed with such. All this must be my failure of imagination, I'm sure.) . . .

Edmund White returned from Atlanta & elsewhere breathless & very upbeat. He said "everybody is talking about Greg Johnson" in Atlanta, at least in the circles he frequented. (Ed seems to generate dinner parties everywhere he appears.) I asked him what people were saying about you & he said, "Well, they all know and admire Greg for his writing." That sounded encouraging! . . .

I read John Updike's story in the current *New Yorker*, & it's thematically/psychologically/stylistically identical to many others of his—nostalgia & adultery are very well done, & moving . . . Onward to April Fool's Day!

Joyce

28 March 1998

Dear Greg,

. . . I'm enclosing a paragraph from a letter from Larry Goldstein [then editor of *Michigan Quarterly Review*] about the biography. Many people are reading it! . . .

I've just finished *Nocturne*, & am in that somewhat dazed/delirious state before rewriting & rethinking. I'd wanted this novel to be about 220 pages long & it's 348 pp. which is no doubt only the most obvious of its failures. I needed that much space to fully realize the material; but a pseudonym novel should be *short*.

Everyone at the university is feeling the effect of our galloping semester. April & May are crazed here. The atelier is still very enjoyable; but most of the work is yet to come, with rehearsals, etc. Our public performances are May 7 & 8. Toni Morrison has been lovely to work with. She's visited a few classes, has asked very good, courteous questions & has, overall, let Susana & me completely alone.

We went out for supper w/Toni the other evening, after a dance recital here. We'd invited Ed White & his friend; & were amazed to hear the three of them comparing the "butts" of the boy dancers . . . Not only did Ray & I not contribute to the funny, ribald, yet somehow quite serious discussion, we hadn't noticed enough at the dance recital to have joined in. Toni is perhaps the most complex, variegated person of my acquaintance. I'm virtually always the same (sorry!) but Toni is mercurial beyond belief. Her public persona is grand & very dignified; soft-spoken, even reverential; her public speeches have a highly self-conscious, practiced air. She's as eloquent at such times as she is in her much-honed prose. Socially, she's a wild, unstoppered wit. She's vulgar, gutsy, loud-laughing & provocative. She's *theatrical*. And amazingly frank & honest (about her personal life & things that don't always go so well). I'm far more guarded, & must admit that there's no one, even in private, with whom I could be so "unstoppered." Her relations w/gay men have an ease & jocular camaraderie virtually unknown in Princeton, though I'd guess that in NYC this sort of alliance is less uncommon . . .

Much love,
Joyce

2 May 1998

Dear Greg,

Thank you for your very nice letter; & congratulations

had a terrific time. Of all the cities of the world, it's Venice and Florence our friends most praise and yearn to revisit . . .

I've just completed a pleasurable task, writing the introduction to the new Oxford U. Press edition of *Wuthering Heights*. What a wonderful novel . . . in fact, a "first novel." It's almost impossible to conceive of such genius, efflorescing so quickly and so quickly fading. And what irony for Emily Brontë not to have known that she'd created a masterpiece.

Did I mention that Lanny Jones, ex-editor of *People* and an old, close friend, is hosting a 60th birthday party for me in Princeton? He's renting an elegant restaurant and is inviting perhaps forty people! I was astounded when he first made the suggestion, and somehow didn't quite believe it, but invitations went out today to Princeton and New York-area people. (Or maybe it's Bloomsday we'll celebrate.)

The American Academy shindig is this Wednesday; we're to be seated with the Updikes & some other friends. Apparently there are considerable hard feelings over some of the awards this year. I haven't been on the committee for many years but do remember how vigorously (& shamelessly) members lobbied for their friends, not excluding little-known, very minor writer friends. The usual results are a wild admixture of deserving & perhaps less so. It's too bad that awards are always associated with hurt feelings & inevitable injustices. I wonder at the wisdom of "awards" generally. Yet we continue to give them, even at Princeton U. . . .

Much love,
Joyce

22 May 1998
Dear Greg,
. . . At the American Academy luncheon, John Updike

happened to mention that he'd looked through the biography in a bookstore and thought it seemed attractive . . . Both John and Martha looked very good, we thought. Very handsome, glowing. In fact, up close, John's skin looks rather abraded, and he'd recently had a patch of cancerous cells removed, of which he spoke in his usual droll fashion. He's become just slightly hard of hearing, kept mishearing words of mine I had to repeat over the ceaseless buzz and clatter of the luncheon. On my left sat August Wilson whose plays I've seen, and read, and who turns out to be a boxing fan, who said he'd admired my book on boxing, so I had a good deal to talk about with Mr. Wilson, too . . .

John Updike's talk was excellent, on the history of the Academy, which he managed to make both informative and funny. The shrewd organizers scheduled his talk near the end of the dull ceremony, however, knowing that the audience would drift away afterward.

Yes, I've tried to make the introduction to *Wuthering Heights* totally different from the theme-oriented article that appeared in *Critical Inquiry*. The very format of "introduction" necessitates a different sort of approach. (We saw the video of the old classic *Wuthering Heights* the other night— Laurence Olivier, Merle Oberon, David Niven. A much truncated, somewhat censored version of the darker and far more complex novel, though probably quite an achievement for its era.)

Thanks for your remarks on "The Scarf"! [I had included this story in my fiction anthology *Story and Structure*.] My mother has been giving away things for the past year or more . . . it's disconcerting. Scarves, jewelry, household items. They both seem fairly well, though, and are greatly enjoying gardening, as usual. [In Atlanta] I'll probably read the opening of *My Heart Laid Bare* and some new, short work—poems, a story. I'm looking forward to the visit very much, especially now that our dinner will be more relaxed . . .

Much love,
Joyce

P.S. Thanks for your festive Venetian postcard!

3 June 1998

Dear Greg,

Thanks so much for your kindness & cheerful hospitality last week in Atlanta. I had a great time, especially seeing your beautiful new house & sleek, fox-faced Lucy & Gracie who are models of zestfulness & curiosity (and really didn't bark overmuch, considering). It was wonderful, too, to meet Marisa Clark, Pam Durban and David Bottoms, and of course Virginia Carr . . .

My Charleston visit, too, was very enjoyable. The actors who performed my stories were extremely talented, especially Lisa Fugard who gamely—I should say very dramatically—took on "Where Are You Going . . . ?" & was able to rouse even its author to a quickened pulse. I'd been anticipating a modest audience, but the 450-seat theater (a handsome old theater, in the character of Charleston itself) was completely sold out, and people were even standing. (This left me more astounded than the performances themselves, I have to admit.)

In Chicago, I had a lovely visit with Leigh & Henry [Bienen], & have made plans to be a brief playwright-in-residence at Northwestern U. in May 1999. My Henry David Thoreau play will be produced there, with a symposium attached. The Bienens are both in excellent spirits. I signed many copies of *Come Meet Muffin!* at the ABA, and many copies of *My Heart Laid Bare* at a related bookfair . . . Then onward to St. Louis & another reading & book signing. By this time I've figured out how to present the "Little Moses" excerpt from *My Heart Laid Bare*, in an abbreviated form. It's always cheering—though it invariably seems unreal—that anyone should show up at all, & profess interest, & even buy books. (I've signed copies of *Invisible Writer* in your stead & hope you won't mind. People are always asking me what I think of it, & perhaps instead of simply saying nice things I should say evasively, "No comment." This might stir up some controversy.)

In the interstices of these events, I had many, many runs & walks in scenic areas. In the very heart of Chicago, in Grant Park, there are large wildflower fields filled with birds in the early morning . . . amazing! In St. Louis, I hit upon an attractive suburban library & spent as many hours there as the fierce air-conditioning would allow; when I was beginning to turn blue at the extremities, I'd go out running in the 90-degree heat. (I'm researching & taking notes on that odd novella I'd obliquely mentioned to you. I'm not sure that anything will come of it, but if so it will be set primarily in Los Angeles in the 1930s, '40s, & '50s.) (Don't ask me why I'm writing this, or trying to write it. *There is simply no answer.*)

Also, I've been very happily reading Jane Austen. Those novels I'd never read—*Mansfield Park* (very Jamesian, austere, not very comic & somewhat slow-moving but, overall, wonderful) & *Northanger Abbey* (in its understated way a brilliant novel). Of course, everyone loves Austen, but I've always been somewhat resistant to her charms, very much preferring the Brontës & Eliot. But why should they be compared, after all? I'm touched by what little I know of Austen's short life.

When I returned home, I received the sad news that Billy Abrahams died last night. This wasn't unexpected, but it's still a shock. Rosemary flew out to see him very suddenly & reports that he died peacefully at home, not in a hospital, with a 24-hour nurse, excellent care (including morphine), his beloved dog with him in his room; Rosemary says he was "very much Billy" to the very end, and was still working up until about two weeks ago . . . I'll miss him so much as an inimitable individual! He was warm, generous, a real lover of books (always reading classics in the background, so to speak, of his foreground professional reading) & very funny. His funeral will be small, and there will be a memorial service for him in New York in a few months. The end of an era . . .

When I came through the door of my study, there was Christabel stretched out on the rug by my desk; she rose slowly, & with much dignity ambled over to sort of greet me . . . (not quite like Lucy & Gracie would greet their master after a week's absence) & made a querulous mewing sound that might be mistaken for "hello." From a cat, believe me, this is ecstatic enthusiasm. She even made a gesture toward rubbing against my leg, more a symbolic movement than an actual touching. I'm home!

Again, thanks for driving me around, & unflagging good spirits . . . Good luck with your novel! I seem to be completely stymied, though with many scribbled notes, over mine.

Much love,
Joyce

8 August 1998

Dear Greg,

Don't miss the sure-to-be-controversial piece on Ray Carver in tomorrow's *New York Times Magazine*. (Your reference to Gordon Lish in the biography is very brief. But I did have more of a relationship with Lish than that indicated; he'd wanted to heavily edit stories of mine, too, but this didn't work out. Many writers whom he had edited, including John Gardner as well, simply reverted to their original styles when collecting stories in hardcover; but Ray couldn't do that, or thought he couldn't, since Lish was also his book editor.) . . .

Next week, I must go to Baltimore for a two-day "creative nonfiction conference." Barry Lopez will be there, too; it should be interesting. (Though I'd much rather be home of course, working on my obsessive novel.) Beyond that, England/Germany await, Aug. 25 to Sept. 11. This is so daunting a trip, I can't allow myself to think of it. *Man Crazy* is coming out in England & *What I Lived For* in Germany so a "publicity tour" has been planned. My wayward and increasingly fanatical association with "JCO" does have its sobering moments.

I try to keep John Updike's gentle admonition in mind: "For God's sake, lighten up, Joyce!"

We've been very happy leading fairly secluded and (by Princeton standards) quiet lives since returning from our last trip. Long dreamy bicycle rides, as long as one and a half hours . . .

I've just finished a piece on Marilyn Monroe for *Playboy*'s 45th-anniversary issue (January); she was their first centerfold in 1953, a fact I'm sure you didn't know. My current project is an essay on Muhammad Ali for an anthology about great athletes of the 20th century so I'm watching tapes of that bygone athlete/era.

My parents are reasonably well; but can't seem to come to terms with selling their house or even, I guess, thinking constructively about it. My father says with cheerful fatalism, "I'd like to hang on as long as I can." Their gardening means so much to them, it will be heartbreaking to give it up. Ray says hello.

Much love,
Joyce

22 August 1998

Dear Greg,

Thanks for your recent fax. We are leaving very soon for England/Germany and won't return until Sept. 11. A terribly long trip, to which I must have agreed in a sort of daze . . .

[An interviewer] came to Princeton for lunch. He arrived wearing a blazer on an extremely warm day. "It doesn't get like this where I come from," he said miserably. (Meaning the humidity.) We had an interesting conversation; he's one of those eloquent interviewers who does at least 50 percent of the talking, which is fine with me. I was inspired to be somewhat eloquent myself. But, and this didn't surprise me (you know me: the "tragic sense of life"), at the end of the two-hour talk he discovered to his horror that his taping machine wasn't operating . . .

Probably Ray Carver doesn't mean so much to you as to other people, especially of his generation. He'd achieved such renown for his early, "minimalist" short stories, it's shocking to friends/fellow writers like Richard Ford, Russell Banks, and many others to learn that the Carver style evidently wasn't his at all but that of . . . Gordon Lish (whom no one likes). Ray's later work, warm & sympathetic, is much more conventional and at times garrulous; if he'd begun his career with these, in presumably his "own" voice, he might not have had a career at all. It's like learning that Faulkner's style was created by an energetic editor . . .

(I just received a smudged fax informing me that I am the

recipient of a "lifetime achievement" award from the Balti-more Public Library. The previous recipient was Saul Bellow (!). To be in Bellow's wake seems a bit overwhelming . . . and truly verging upon the posthumous. I'll be in the odd posi-tion of being over the hill without ever having been on it.)

Everyone at 9 Honey Brook is well. Even Daisy continues to sing with unflagging spirits. Ray is, I guess, somewhat over-worked, hurrying to "get his desk cleared" before we leave . . .

I've been quite fascinated with my new novel *Gemini* [the working title for *Blonde*], and am on page 220 already, with much more than half to go. [The original manuscript would eventually run 1,400 pages, her longest novel to date.] It will give me the opportunity to explore the phenomenon of acting about which I've learned some interesting things as a play-wright and so at one remove from the life onstage. How ac-tors, often lacking coherent identities, thrive upon immersing themselves in fictitious roles and are restless if not miserable without them. (I guess this sounds familiar.) To see the world from the actor's perspective is to see it in an entirely new way. At the same time, I wish I had more genuine interest in my "career" right now. I do like meeting people, very much . . . but to represent, or to actually be, "JCO" isn't always that interesting. Maybe we could all scramble our identities & I could "be" someone else for a while. Sarah Orne Jewett?

Much love,
Joyce

29 Sept. 1998
Dear Greg,
. . . Things have been idyllic here, warm/cool sunny au-tumn days. Since we measure our happiness by *not* being on an interminable transatlantic flight, we're always in good

spirits & dare not complain about anything. (In addition to the transatlantic flight, on that last day we also had to take a four-hour train from Hamburg to Cologne, then fly to Heathrow with a long wait for our flight to JFK.) As usual we've vowed *never again*, but as usual we'll probably forget . . .

Both the English and the German trips were enjoyable on the whole, and certainly productive in a professional way. I met hundreds of people, some of them extremely nice, and interesting; and signed hundreds of books. We must have walked/hiked/trudged/limped hundreds of miles . . .

My experience in Rochester was bittersweet. Seeing my parents, and the Heyens, was wonderful, and the venue itself was ideal. My reading was well-attended and during the question-and-answer session, somehow I was able to remark that the beautiful peach-colored coat sweater I was wearing had been knitted by my mother, who was in the audience; and the audience burst into applause! (Thank God the biography is complete. I'm becoming shamelessly sentimental. During the signing, I signed quite a stack of *Muffin* books, including inscriptions like "To Mittens from Muffin & Joyce"—"to Fluffy from Muffin & Joyce.") The less happy part of the experience was that, driving back that evening in the rain, my father had a very difficult time, and he doubts he'll ever drive very far at night again. When you're old, he says, everything gets harder. (He and I talk quite frankly, it's very touching but sad . . .) Sorry to go on at such length.

Much love,
Joyce

13 October 1998

Dear Greg,

I'd prepared a package to send to you, with a card, just

before receiving your fax of the other evening, so our letters have crossed. I'd suggested that you would be an ideal reviewer for the Eudora biography. (Which I haven't yet seen. After the tribute in New York to Welty, there was a buffet dinner given by the Library of America, and everyone there was either a friend of Welty's and an ardent admirer, or just an admirer. The consensus was that the biography was very disappointing, and insulting in its emphasis upon Welty's personal appearance. In fact I've seen early photographs of Eudora Welty and she seems quite attractive.)

What a lot of traveling I've done lately . . . and even more is to come. The other Saturday, I spent 7½ hours in a limousine coming & going to Philadelphia, then to Baltimore. In that amount of time I might have flown to Frankfurt. (Of course, I don't want to fly to Frankfurt.) I gave a reading at the F. Scott Fitzgerald Society meeting in Baltimore . . . At the North Atlantic Booksellers Convention, I signed *Muffin* books galore (yes, to more cats) and at the Bouchercon World Mystery Writers Convention, I represented, or impersonated, "Rosamond Smith." I've been interviewed on CNN (TV & tonight online) re. *Muffin*. (Sample question: How old is Muffin now, and what does he think about being the hero of a book?) . . .

The Welty tribute was very well organized and interesting. (My limo, caught in rain & traffic, took 3 hours instead of the usual 1½ to get to NYC; the program had begun without me, but I dashed in.) Richard Ford, Ann Beattie (looking very different than I'd remembered her, mature/matronly, extremely nice, & with her very nice husband Lincoln, a painter), Elizabeth Spencer (who has known Eudora Welty for . . . could it be 60 years?), the black writer Randall Kenan, and Karl Kirchwey taking William Maxwell's place since Maxwell was ill. Each of us spoke briefly about Welty &

read part of a story. (In fact I read almost all of "Where Is the Voice Coming From?" which many in the audience didn't know.) . . .

My quicksand novel keeps pulling me under . . . Your Narrative course sounds so wonderful. How I'd have liked to take such a course as an undergraduate. Please send me your syllabus sometime . . .

Love,
Joyce

23 October 1998

Dear Greg,

CONGRATULATIONS on the honor of being chosen by the American Library Association. Rosemary had telephoned me with the good news, too.

(Imagine the hundreds of books that were in "competition"! I'm a judge for an award this year, and stacks of books are arising in my office at the university like shaky stalagmites.) . . .

I wasn't aware that talk of *Gemini* was on the website! I haven't been able to peruse "Celestial Timepiece" very much lately . . . Perhaps I'll see Randy when we visit SF next weekend. (It does sound as if I'm traveling constantly, doesn't it? We'll be in Phoenix, AZ, for two days, too. These are all reading-oriented visits with some book signings. I know it sounds very strange, but since I write in longhand mostly, I can work efficiently on airplanes & in hotel rooms; often, my concentration is more intense than it is at home where I am continuously interrupted by household tasks, telephone calls, cats scratching at my door to be let *in*, or to be let *out* . . . It's a lovely autumn day here, perfect weather for jogging/hiking this afternoon. Did I give the impression that Eudora Welty was at the tribute? I didn't mean to. She's far too aged or unwell to make the journey. The evening was a great success in any case. What a fantastic course in narrative! It's a brilliant grouping. In fact, enough for five or six normal courses. ("Accelerated" is an understatement.)

Much love,
Joyce

14 November 1998

Dear Greg,

. . . It was very good to hear from you. In recent weeks it seems I've been virtually everywhere, but in fact it's only been Toronto, San Francisco, Phoenix, Winston-Salem, NC, and Baltimore . . . I've become adroit at doing proofs/scribbling feverishly away/reading galleys for review in the back seats of limos & in plane terminals & on planes . . .

Things are fine here, except for the excessive traveling . . . (My last limo ride was seven hours round trip, & en route to Baltimore . . . the car broke down dramatically in the midst of rushing traffic, & the driver somehow managed to limp across three lanes to the shoulder where we waited for a half hour for a replacement; I was only twenty minutes late, not bad for the circumstances. You would have been proud of me: I continued working through the trauma, doing page proofs for *Broke Heart Blues* which I managed actually to finish before we returned home to 9 Honey Brook.) It's been a lovely mild autumn with beautiful leaves & many deer drifting by the house, only just now a handsome, mature buck with heavy antlers & a Hemingway look about the shoulders & head . . . Princeton people are generally well, & the writing program very companionable & sociable. Should you be in the vicinity, you're invited to a party on Jan. 16,

5:30 onward, in honor of Ed White's new, slim biography *Proust*.

Much love to all,
Joyce

P.S. I'm writing a 3,000-word introduction to the (English) Folio Society edition of several of Hemingway's novels, & have been rereading with admiration & some less-than-admiration (*To Have and Have Not* is a terrible novel!). I'm relieved that I decided against the Hemingway "biography" since I truly don't feel much kinship with him, and even his best writing isn't very exciting or demanding on the reader. Delving into Norma Jeane Baker/"Marilyn Monroe" is much more rewarding. I was invited by the outgoing president of the Mystery Writers of America to take over the position (!); but of course I declined. I was also invited to South Africa to take part in a celebration of Nadine Gordimer's 75th birthday, which I even more quickly declined. And another "lifetime" award from an upstate NY university I may just skip with the excuse that I am already feeling posthumous enough.

16 November 1998

Dear Greg,

I did watch John [Updike's] interview last night on CNN, and was somewhat disappointed. What did you think? So much more comes through in his writing. The questions weren't very inspired, perhaps. John came across as self-preening, rather fussy and without any "subject" apart from his own pleasure in what he does . . . John sounded like a man who has spent his lifetime constructing highly detailed miniature ships inside bottles.

I've just sent a small package off to you; our recent letters virtually crossed.

Christabel is luxuriously curled up in my lap asleep & purring. It's a lovely sunny autumn day here and I don't have to 1) fly anywhere, 2) even climb into the rear of a limo. So I am enormously happy! . . .

Yes, I did see Randy Souther briefly in SF. And I had a strange though friendly enough telephone conversation with Alice [Adams]. (Alice says she doesn't acknowledge Billy Abrahams's death. And she means it. She didn't go to his memorial service, and when she wrote about him in a recent memoir piece, she wrote as if he's still living. I was taken aback, as you might imagine. Alice knows that Billy is dead of course, yet she insists that, to her, he isn't. It's the only way she can deal with the loss of her best friend of fifty years and I can sympathize of course. "I just think of Billy as off somewhere, and I'll be talking to him on the phone soon." The memorial service in NYC for Billy was very beautiful and very moving. I'd never spoken at a memorial service before. Billy was evoked so warmly and in so much anecdotal detail, it was an extraordinary experience . . .

Much love,
Joyce

1 December 1998

Dear Greg,

Thanks for your wonderfully newsy & lively letter . . . I should have sent you a copy of *Playboy*, to spare you having to purchase one. If you'd been glimpsed, I'm afraid it would sully the reputation of "Greg Johnson" in some quarters at least. (The reputation of "JCO" is past mending, so it hardly matters with me.) [Joyce had recently published a story in *Playboy* called "The Last Man of Letters."]

Actually, I wasn't thinking of Saul Bellow, though I might have been. The story was originally dedicated "to Philip Roth." After it had been sold to *Playboy*, I decided to omit the dedication. (What could I have been thinking of? Sometimes I do seem, even to myself, terminally naïve.)

We will be attending the 45th *Playboy* anniversary party in NYC. We've been to these before & they are like no other parties, quite. (I'll be the only female in a high-necked dress.)

. . . I met Lorrie Moore & liked her enormously, at the Miami Book Fair. Where I went with a ghastly bloodied eye from a sudden hemorrhage. (Evidently these are not uncommon. It's brought on usually by stress or eyestrain and doesn't affect the vision. But it looks hideous; I was trying to hide behind dark glasses.) Stephen King was also at the book fair, surprisingly trim, though almost gaunt and graying, as if he has lost his fleshy-boyish self overnight. Still, he was very funny & appealing to a horde of fans.

Speaking of hordes of fans, I assume you didn't get to hear Tom Wolfe read? There's a remarkable review of his novel by Norman Mailer in the new *NYRB*. I have the novel but will probably not read it (unless you urge it upon me). Still, it's wonderful that so many people will buy a dense, ingeniously structured novel; a work of fiction, an actual *book*! (Even more remarkable that Norman M. would read the interminable novel, which he compares to "making love with a 300-pound woman" (how does Mailer know about such things?), and write such a thoughtful response. He makes me feel quite sluggish.)

Much love,
Joyce

Part Five

1999–2004

In 1999, Joyce was absorbed in the mammoth novel she was calling Gemini—*dealing with the life and career of Norma Jeane Baker/Marilyn Monroe—but that would ultimately be retitled* Blonde. *This novel had become the "most obsessive" writing experience of her life. Another notable occurrence of the next few years was the hubbub surrounding her 1996 novel* We Were the Mulvaneys *being chosen as a selection for Oprah Winfrey's book club. Joyce appeared on Winfrey's television program and sales of the novel skyrocketed; to date, it remains her most popular novel among general readers.*

This period was also notable for extensive traveling in both the United States and Europe. Though she enjoyed meeting interesting new people, the logistics of travel were often draining even if they did not seriously hamper her productivity.

These years likewise saw the publication of the novels Broke Heart Blues *(1999),* Middle Age: A Romance *(2001),* I'll Take You There *(2002),* The Tattooed Girl *(2003), and* The Falls *(2004), in addition to the usual innumerable short stories, essays, and essay-reviews.*

Apart from her work, another issue that continues to recur frequently in the letters of this period is the declining health of her beloved parents. Joyce produced an essay on each of them, and assisted (along with her brother, Fred. Jr.) in helping them sell their Millersport house and move to an assisted-living facility nearby.

12 January 1999

Dear Greg,

Thanks for your very welcome letter and the excellent review of the Hellman "memoir." And the recent faxed reviews. Having just returned from the Key West Literary Seminar, where we had a most enjoyable visit amid balmy sunshine and very nice people, I don't feel much like "Queen of the

Night" but it's good to know that people have such associations . . . We visited the impressive Hemingway House—and its fifty-five attendant cats! All beautiful.

At the seminar, I gave a reading from *Gemini* which was well received, and participated in two lively, quite contentious panels (on the American novel) with Bob Stone, Joe Heller, Jamaica Kincaid (who mildly insulted me), Peter Matthiessen and John Edgar Wideman. We stayed at a guest house owned by new Princeton friends Seward and Joyce Johnson overlooking the ocean . . . We returned home yesterday at 3, and at 5 attended Harold Pinter's superb reading at the university, and a stately dinner in his honor. Pinter was my nominee for this major university lecture, as Arthur Miller and Updike were in past years, and he was absolutely brilliant.

Do you have any opinions re. titles: *Gemini: An American Epic*, or *Miss Golden Dreams* (the title of Monroe's infamous nude pin-up). I rather need the "constellation" theme, but feel uneasy that Don DeLillo, in *Libra*, got there first. What do you think? . . .

How is your novel progressing? Just rejoice it isn't *long*. Yet I continue to trim & cut, like trying to reduce an elephant's weight by trimming his toenails.

Much affection,
Joyce

27 January 1999

Dear Greg,

. . . Yes, it would be a kind and much-appreciated gesture, I'm sure, if you sent something to my parents. In about two weeks might be ideal. At the present, my father is hospitalized (again!) but apparently recovering quite well from surgery; my mother is (temporarily) in a nursing home not far from Millersport where my brother visits her daily. Of course, I've been on the phone it seems continuously, & also with my brother debating what to do, since their house isn't sold and so forth, and so on. You can see why it's best not to inquire after a friend's aging parents since the problems multiply into infinity.

You would find Fred and Carolina changed from the people you knew. Not terribly, shockingly changed, at least not yet. But not the Fred and Carolina of your memory.

On another more cheerful subject: we assume you've seen *Shakespeare in Love* since you see everything; but we much enjoyed this movie, especially Ray. This evening we're seeing, with friends, *A Civil Action*. We would never be going out so frequently to movies except for our movie-going friends (Ron Levao & Susan Wolfson). I know I should be staying home and working, but . . .

A lovely novel I just read is Michael Cunningham's *The Hours*. Now I'm reading & enjoying Martha Cooley's *The Archivist*. Many cheers for the "literary" novel; the novel of "sensibility."

About Jamaica Kincaid: she didn't insult me exactly, but took offense when I seemed to be defending Tom Wolfe (while explaining that I had not read his novel) and Charles Frazier as examples of serious writers who are nonetheless best sellers. Jamaica interrupted my remarks on *Cold Mountain* to say it was a "bad novel"; when a man in the audience asked her why, she just repeated it was a "bad novel." Jamaica had been angry because her publisher, her very editor, are responsible for [Wolfe's] *A Man in Full*; or maybe jealous is more accurate. She called Wolfe a racist before an audience of perhaps 300 people which I thought was reprehensible, and said so.

My long, long novel . . . ! I do truly love writing it & immersing myself in it; but there seems no end in sight, like life stretching into thousands of pages . . . as into the farthest corners of the universe. I could not have imagined this material so richly blossoming . . . if that's the word. Already I am on about p. 900 & have much more to go. Pray you never become ensnared in anything so mammoth. It takes over your life & then you must worry: what is to be done with it? Who would want to publish it, read it? Lift it (in both hands)? After this, the "blessed novella." . . .

Much affection,
Joyce

1 February 1999

Dear Greg,

Thanks for the hilarious satire; we'll be delighted to publish it in fall 1999. I assume it will still be satire by then and not real life.

I'd promised you/myself that I wouldn't talk about my parents. But my father had an unexpectedly speedy recovery from surgery and came home a few days early. Yet more unexpectedly, my mother thrived in the nursing home environment where she was one of the younger, able-bodied women; she was helping nurses with sick patients, and seems to have enjoyed the experience . . .

I'm careening onward toward page 1,000, alternately exhausted & exhilarated. Don't ever let this happen to you! Practically speaking, such a long novel, for me at least, is a publishing nightmare.

(And I'm only in 1956 in my subject's life; she dies in Aug. 1962.)

Joyce

Valentine's Day 1999

Dear Greg,

... I'd glanced through the biography ... and came away deeply moved again by the opening chapters. I can't tell you how grateful I am that you gave a not only coherent but articulate and even eloquent shape to this material; which is to say, these people. To me, they are admirable beyond estimation. I couldn't put my feelings for my parents & grandmother into fiction because they are too genuinely "positive"; fiction requires irony & complexity, an up-close focus, and isn't adequate here ...

I feel much more encouraged about *Gemini* lately. Of course, as you say, there will be "bias" against its length. (If it's published!) This, I guess I will have to accept ... Edmund White believes that there are novels that have to be written, no matter the cost to the writer; he feels that *The Farewell Symphony* was one of these ... My mammoth novel must be one that, for me, taps into something autobiographical, though it would hardly seem so on the surface ... The novel interests me enormously, because of its language & structure, and if I'd written it in a more accessible, conventional manner, assuming I'd been able to, it would not exert such a fascination over me. I've never had such a "haunted" experience writing a novel & my fear now is that I won't be able to write after this without measuring all things against this experience, & finding them rather tame ...

(Still, I've begun to revise, & will be making my way slowly forward from the beginning even as, on p. 1100 (approximately), I'll be making my way slowly to the end. Unfortunately, as I'm revising, I seem to be inserting more material.) ...

Much love,
Joyce

2 April 1999

Dear Greg,

. . . The issue of self-confidence/ego is much on my mind these days. The experience of writing so intimately about the woman we know as Marilyn Monroe has left me infected with some of the subject's extreme self-doubt. (Monroe always suffered from stage fright, whatever that curious malady is, but it became truly crippling when she was in her early 30s. Like a stammerer, she insisted upon doing scenes over, over, over to get them "perfect." She exhausted herself and others and made an acting career virtually impossible for herself, especially onstage . . .)

I won't mind, I think, the adverse criticism for *Gemini*. It's sure to be savage. (Not just the length, which is sure to inflame many reviewers, but the portrait of JFK . . . which is rather "negative," since the novel is from Monroe's point of view, and JFK behaved cruelly to her . . . I am just so enormously *grateful* I could finish the novel as I'd wished . . . I walk around with a stunned expression like a survivor of a near air crash, and have vowed to my friends and especially to Ray that I will never, never be unhappy again! And I will never attempt anything so quixotic again. The ideal form is surely the "blessed novella" . . .

John Updike gave a characteristically eloquent if just slightly nervous talk at the book celebration. I hadn't seen the table of contents [for *The Best American Short Stories of the Century*] until that night, & am frankly a bit . . . mystified. John has omitted any number of excellent, important short-story writers (Willa Cather, William Carlos Williams, James Baldwin, Tobias Wolff, Andre Dubus, John Wideman, Richard Ford, to name just a few) & whimsically included several unknown writers, one of whom published a single story in her lifetime, in *Psychiatry*! He has two AIDS stories written not by gay men, but by women. He's included a young black woman writer but not Gloria Naylor or Toni Cade Bambara (from whom this woman surely learned a good deal). It's like including Steve Barthelme while excluding Donald Barthelme. And no Gass, no Coover, no Barth. Since he's very defensive, I don't think I will say a word of this to him. Elsewhere, the book is very good; many of the usual suspects/ classics. It should perhaps be titled *Some Fairly Good American Short Stories of the Century*. (Oddly, you might say perversely, John has included an only-average story of his own, not from the *New Yorker* that nourished his talent for four decades, but from *Playboy* which could only, because of his contract with the *New Yorker*, publish rejects. The story of mine he included is the usual ["Where Are You Going, Where Have You Been?"].) . . .

Since finishing my novel I've been reading & rereading old favorites: William Carlos Williams, Lorca's *Poet in New York,* new poets like Shahid Ali (a dashing Princeton colleague & friend), & myriad poems/short stories. It's like finding the world again . . . ! And going to readings, lectures, plays . . . I've even watched some TV (*NYPD Blue*) . . . So, you see, I am trying gamely to be, or at least to seem, "normal" . . .

Much affection,
Joyce

11 April 1999

Dear Greg,

Your NYC junket is imminent. The weather has been ideal . . . The Union Square Café is Dan Halpern's favorite restaurant; if not here in Princeton, he is invariably there. [I

had asked her for restaurant recommendations in New York.]
Another of his favorites, to which I've been taken by Elaine
Koster once or twice, is the fabled, very expensive Le Bernar-
din, where, to Dan's chagrin, he once bit into a sliver of glass
in his food. I'd once been taken to similarly fabled "44" (the
Condé Nast cafeteria) by Tina Brown upon whom all eyes
fixed, in that avid, memorizing way in which eyes once fixed
upon Mrs. Onassis; Orso's is sentimentally special to me because Marty Scorsese first took me there, & subsequently
Roger Berlind, & other theater people. To us, restaurants
are mainly social occasions since food doesn't linger in our
memories for long. NYC is a food/wine/restaurant-obsessed
culture in relationship to which we are, to put it mildly, marginal. I remember Four Seasons as opulent & pretentious &
yet, in the company of my fellow Pulitzer Prize jurors, very
enjoyable. There was a midtown French restaurant much
liked by Merchant Ivory/Jeanne Moreau. My rosy memories
of these places & others would be different, I'm sure, if I had
had to pay the bill myself, & hadn't been in such company.
Ray & I seem to do best just strolling about in places like
Little Italy & seeing what we can discover, as absolute ama-
teurs . . . The worst restaurant we've ever been taken to was
a dreadful brightly lit "authentic" Chinese restaurant in Chinatown, as guests of Susan Sontag; a passionate promoter of
the "authentic" over the comfortable, attractive, or tolerable,
Susan ordered hideous dishes like chickens' feet & thousand-
year-old birds'-nest soup . . .

I've been stunned at the early response to *Gemini*. I don't
know what I'd expected, but Rosemary Ahern's remarks, &
a call from her, have been enormously encouraging. (If only
I could have known this during the long siege . . .) Unless
John Hawkins strongly urges otherwise, I'm sure I will be
remaining at Dutton. After all, Plume is bringing out many

back titles of mine in attractive uniform editions; it would seem very odd to leave them ... Thanks again for so spontaneously volunteering to read 1,200 pp. It was characteristically generous of you, though quixotic, too, like jumping in to rescue a drowning person, with the risk of being drowned yourself!

Much love,
Joyce

23 April 1999

Dear Greg,

... I've just returned from most of this week in Evanston, IL, where my Thoreau play has begun rehearsals, & have survived a truly "turbulent" flight that arrived an hour late, but who cares? It arrived! I'm home! Christabel is even in my lap. (Oops, she jumped down.) And Ray, who'd nearly been killed yesterday when a car (driven by a distracted teenage boy) crashed into the rear of our car, is alive! ... He does feel a bit battered, but that's nothing to what might have happened ... The car was a total wreck, & now we have a new car of the same model but, shocking for us, a slightly different color, a pale champagne instead of our trademark white.

My flight from Chicago was so rocky, several people on board were nauseated. I was reading Ian McEwan's *Black Dogs*, which is ideal for a turbulent flight; its vision of life is so bleak, you feel that, just possibly, a plane crash won't matter greatly ...

I'm looking forward to hearing about your NYC trip. It's a relief to learn that it was "wonderful"; my Evanston, IL, visit was quite fine, except for astoundingly awful weather which kept me indoors mostly, in the rehearsal hall or, in a car, being squired about to bookstores. Henry Bienen gave a lovely luncheon for me; most of the guests were from the Drama Dept. The production of *Thoreau* is lavish & energetic . . .

Love,
Joyce

28 April 1999

Dear Greg,

Thanks for your solicitude about Ray. Remarkably, he is feeling very fine, with only a head laceration (partly hidden in his hair). We are *very lucky*.

Yes, the accident occurred at about the same place as the other, and in the same way. A speeding, distracted younger driver . . .

So what *is* the title of your imminent novel? *Among the Living* is a good title, I think . . . *Sticky Kisses* will be fun for the jacket designer & salesmen. My friend C.K. Williams has suggested *Blonde* for my novel, but it isn't really quite appropriate.

I forgot to thank you for the Eudora Welty material, which was very touching. How nice to be loved, & not to have sacrificed any integrity, or tried for popularity. At Princeton, Eudora simply smiled and smiled; & everyone loved her. The "artist" didn't make even a cameo appearance but must have stayed behind in Jackson, Miss. . . .

Much love,
Joyce

3 May 1999

Dear Greg,

. . . Since finishing *Gemini*, I've become virtually another person! I sleep through most nights & wake in the morning

... as I guess most normal people do ... not in the grip of tension & nervous excitement but just ... wake up to whatever the day is, or might be. It's a remarkable phenomenon. Life is so placid somehow. Though I have plenty of things to think about, & work to do ... but somehow it's nothing like those months in the Coils of The Novel; & I can't imagine why, or how, anyone chooses to live in such a manner, so obsessed & breathless, when one need not, & in any case the world doesn't care, & should not!

Everyone at 9 Honey Brook is well; Christabel has just condescended to climb into my lap & is perusing this page with her usual look of disdain ...

Much love,
Joyce

14 May 1999

Dear Greg,

... Thanks for the faxed reviews! Congratulations on the assessments of the biography. It's somewhat embarrassing to learn that I am a writer "we want to avoid" but very nice to hear that the worst to be said of my biographer is that he is "protective and loyal to his subject" ... But how sad to learn that poor Corky Corcoran [of *What I Lived For*] is, in an observer's eyes, "a middle-aged male politician on the verge of a heart attack who is obsessed with his penis." He'd imagined, like all of us, he was so special! ...

I don't want you to think that I'm dictatorial with my students ... I simply ask them if they want professional criticism/editing, and they always say yes. If things get too tense, they can always switch to another adviser, but no one has, yet. At Princeton, students have to apply to do creative theses, but departmental theses are open to anyone, and a student who isn't doing well creatively can always fall back upon a critical thesis . . .

No, I haven't completed revisions on *Gemini*, and won't for some time since, at this point, with John Hawkins in his element negotiating contractual matters, I don't even know with certainty who my editor will be . . .

Much love,
Joyce

29 May 1999

Dear Greg,

. . . Thank you for sending, most recently, the *Thoreau* review. The experience of the play was overwhelming. As you might suspect, when young actors are involved, the mood is intense and electric and so-yearning; and the young man who played Thoreau was virtually in a mystic state by the end of the opening night . . . he must have been so pumped with adrenaline, he might have levitated. The production was surprisingly lavish, with original music, very creative sets and lighting and even dancing . . . (As someone said, "We have 144 drama majors and they all want to be involved.") Several persons did MA theses on the play. The Bienens hosted a lovely, large dinner beforehand. I sat with, among others, Scott Turow, who is a friend of Leigh's, a Chicago lawyer who teaches part-time at Northwestern, a very nice, surprisingly understated youngish man you would never identify as a best-selling legal thriller writer . . .

In between flights out, I've been re-immersed in my novel, now titled *Blonde*, and shorter by perhaps 200 pages . . . (The irony: I surely agonized over each of the sentences in these pages, and at the time would have been incredulous that my effort would one day soon be extirpated from the manuscript as indifferently as one might yank out weeds from a garden. But it's always the case, there are some things we must do if only to see, in time, that they didn't need to be done, however "perfectly" executed. At least I can salvage some of this as autonomous short stories, one of which will appear as "The Photographer" in an anthology Toby Wolff is editing.) . . .

It does look as if, after so many years and so many projects, and my admiration and affection for Rosemary, I will after all be moving to Ecco/HarperCollins, as Dan Halpern's first acquisition. The reasons are complicated, but have much to do with Dan's enormous enthusiasm for the novel, and a similar enthusiasm among high-level HarperCollins executives; while, at Dutton, I am of course a very familiar name . . .

Our large party prepared by Shahid Ali was amazing. Or, rather, Shahid is amazing. If you ever have an opportunity to hear him read his poetry, I know you would be impressed & moved by him. Quite apart from his possible genius as a writer, & his charismatic personality, he's a perfectionist cook, & worked for almost two days in our kitchen preparing his lavish banquet, which people who know food claimed was "miraculous." About 30 people came, & we hope to repeat the occasion next spring. There I was at my desk pruning *Blonde*, with Christabel in my lap slumbering & purring, while across the courtyard in our kitchen Shahid was working, & singing Kashmiri/Indian songs, & Daisy the canary was excitedly singing with him . . .

Much love,
Joyce

2 June 1999

Dear Greg,

White Oleander [by Janet Fitch] does sound very intriguing. I look forward to reading it . . .

At the moment I am embarked upon Goethe's *Elective Affinities*. It's interesting perhaps more as period literature than as a compelling work of art. *The Sorrows of Young Werther* is excellent, however. Though hard to comprehend that young men were committing suicide in imitation of the rather manically romantic young hero.

If you'd read even a few pages of *Blonde*, you would not fantasize this might be a best seller. (Except by error!)

Your friend Larry Ashmead [an executive editor at Harper-Collins] sounds truly wonderful. I hadn't realized he was so involved with "women's literary fiction" . . .

My favorite Marilyn Monroe film is *Niagara*, but it must be fast-forwarded because of the sitcom subplot, forced and silly in the 1950s but intolerable in the 1990s. I suppose the filmmakers were trying for "comic relief" . . .

Our next project will perhaps be buying my parents' house & property, if it doesn't sell soon, to free them for entering a retirement village. I don't think my father wants us to do this—it would seem "charitable"—"charity"?—to him, but it may be the most practical solution to an ongoing problem. We would then sell the property at our leisure . . . (an understatement: it probably won't sell for years!)

There is a flurry of interest, unexpected to me, in *Broke Heart Blues* & I'll be giving readings, the first, unlikely enough, at a trendy "rock club" in Hoboken. (They've promised no smoking for the duration.)

As always,
Joyce

25 June 1999

Dear Greg,

Thanks so much for the birthday book; I've been reading Eudora Welty lately, in connection with the essay anthology (of course, I will be including her) & in fact have a Welty gift for you, for your upcoming birthday (I think it's July 13 ... ?) ...

I do rather miss the adrenaline high/panicky intensity of The Long Novel ... I've been rewriting pages in the manuscript here & there out of a sense of homesickness perhaps ... like revisiting a landscape in calm sunny weather where there'd been a violent storm. This comes to an end, however, since the ms. goes into production next week. Are you returned to your novel? [I was intermittently working on *Sticky Kisses*.] Or ... ? Other projects? I've been wonderfully immersed in essays [she was editing *The Best American Essays of the 20th Century*] & sidetracked by reading Welty's memoir (& talking of her with Richard Ford, whom we see often; he won't read Welty's biography [by Ann Waldron] because he's offended by its opening with the biographer's focus on Welty as unattractive ... though I did finally look into it, & thought it not bad for a biographer who so adamantly wished to ignore manuscripts & literary matters. The worst thing about the Waldron book, Richard says, is that it pushed Eudora Welty into authorizing a biography by a woman who (Richard says) will not be equal to the task) ...

Ray says hello, and warmest regards as always—
Joyce

4 July 1999

Dear Greg,

Thanks for the review from *PW*, which was very generous, and for your fax of yesterday ...

Chip McGrath [Charles McGrath was then editor of the *New York Times Book Review*] mentioned to me that there's a new biography of Carson McCullers imminent. I've ordered Virginia Carr's since I'll be writing on McCullers; I have an idea it will be a solid, reliable work. McCullers's unfinished autobiography is very touching. I hadn't realized this poor woman had to struggle with such ill health ... a stroke at the age of 29, and others to follow. She was a true prodigy; her first story, "Wunderkind," written when she was 17, is very fine. Perhaps like most prodigies she peaked almost at once. I haven't in fact read her "major work" since adolescence & am hoping it won't seem sentimental or cloying ...

You haven't recommended any movies in months! We rarely saw any, but it was good to be nudged into knowing perhaps we should have. It's so hot these days we can't venture out bicycling until evening.

Much love,
Joyce

8 July 1999

Dear Greg,

... I must not have mentioned that I'm doing a longish piece for *London Review of Books* on McCullers, the occasion being her "autobiography." I'd been quite moved by it until reading Virginia Carr's biography which presumably tells the truth about the subject's difficult, troubled, self-centered and terribly alcoholic life. In fact, I was rather stunned by the contrast between the autobiography and the biography.

Still, I much admire a few of the stories, and *The Member of the Wedding* which seems to me magical. It's so good. *The Heart Is a Lonely Hunter* is also a remarkable accomplishment for a 23-year-old, but especially McCullers's portraits of black people. These are nuanced and startling in their originality . . . The [Carr] biography is as you said competent enough, but uninspired. Dense with anecdotes, often demeaning/depressing/debunking details of the kind that find their way into biographies when the biographer might better have used a screen to keep them out. I might not have wanted to write about McCullers at all if I'd read the biography first, she's made to seem so childish & puerile. And what drinking habits: a glass of beer first thing in the morning, to get going at her work; sherry sipped *all day long* while she worked; then whiskies; then wine . . . at least two bottles of wine with & after dinner. And this is a workday, not a party day. And she chain-smoked. I'd wondered at her ill health, a stroke at 29, death at 50; now I wonder how she kept going to 29. (And here I am with my orange herbal tea in the morning . . . what a dull biographical subject.) . . .

Much love,
Joyce

24 July 1999

Dear Greg,

We've just returned from our week away, which was a wonderfully varied, quite lovely experience, though the last day's somewhat overwhelming driving has left us both drained, & I wanted to respond to your fax primarily to express relief that you are mending, & sound very much yourself. What was the experience like, in fact? [I'd had a bilateral hernia surgery.] When Elaine Showalter had major surgery some years ago, she was astonished at having "wakened" immediately after being anesthetized, or so it seemed to her. She had no sense of the duration of time at all.

I had wanted to send you a postcard from sepia-Gothic

"historic" Lockport—"historic" is a term the Chamber of Commerce gamely pushes—but couldn't find one. The downtown is more depressed than ever, & while the stagnant economy preserves the city almost exactly as it was during my girlhood, & is a powerfully nostalgic site for me to visit, it's really very sad for the inhabitants. Most of the ambitious young people must move away. There are houses in my grandmother's old neighborhood that, truly, don't seem to have changed in any detail since I'd seen them last, except to get more shabby & "historic." As I think you noted in the biography, North Park Junior High looks grim. Ray laughed sadly at the "rose garden" just minimally maintained in Outwater Park. Still, the library is very well maintained, & was a haven on a very hot day . . .

My parents are reasonably well, & ask to be remembered to you. Since they'll be moving sometime soon to an "assisted care" home, they are giving household things away to us, including many of my inscribed books & my father's old violin . . . a melancholy, symbolic object, & so strangely small. They did keep back just a few books of mine, & also the biography & *Distant Friends*. My mother looks fine & is in good spirits despite some short-term memory loss; my father does look rather aged . . . his arms bruised from chemotherapy treatments (he has to endure a drip in his arm for as long as two hours sometimes, once a week); but he's quite stubborn & courageous, & doesn't complain except of the tedium of such procedures. Their house has been sold, provisional to the buyer selling his house, in what I hope won't be an infinite regress!

The *Thoreau* opening on "historic" Martha's Vineyard (yet more historic after this past week) went very well; reviews have been excellent, & I'm particularly happy for Carol Rocamora who has worked incredibly hard. The Styrons gave a luncheon for me on opening day, & there we met among other fascinating guests the documentary filmmaker Ken Burns, whose work (*Civil War*) you probably know . . .

Love,
Joyce

31 July 1999

Dear Greg,

. . . In a few minutes, Dan Halpern will be bringing over the copyedited manuscript of *Blonde*, & my duties are set for some time. I seem to feel apprehensive about being drawn back into that whirlpool, of an urgent "voice" (I know, it's "my own"—whose else could it be?), & wish the task was behind me, & not before. I've been so happy now for months . . . & this will reawaken all sorts of emotions I would rather not experience again.

My parents' home has at last been sold, & they will be moving into their retirement condominium a few miles away, in a few weeks. What a relief for them, & yet how sad . . . I don't think it has quite sunk in upon them, especially my mother, who spends so much time happily gardening, & has lived in Millersport her entire life . . .

I was recently involved in an *Atlantic Monthly* evening honoring Hemingway, at the Algonquin Hotel in NYC, & Michael Curtis introduced me, & spoke so warmly & with much nostalgia (one of my stories ["In the Region of Ice"] was his "first" as a new editor at the magazine, & it went on to win an O. Henry Award; I hadn't realized he'd been an editor at *Epoch*, while I was sending that magazine stories under the name J.C. Oates), the audience would have thought that we two were a literary team of a kind . . .

I saw Lorrie Moore's review of *Broke Heart Blues*, &

was much moved by her fellow sister?-writerly sense of the novel's voice. Yet I was taken aback by her assumption that the novel's characters are "appalling" . . . & I surely had not meant the final lines "We love you" to be insincere. This was my valentine-novel, I'd fantasized should be my last, for its sunny/resigned ending. All of the names in the final paragraph are taken from life, & so sadly, at least two of my old friends/classmates on the list are dead . . .

I've been contentedly revising & much expanding *The Negro-Lover*, now retitled, probably tentatively, *The Idolator*. [The novel was ultimately published under the title *I'll Take You There*.] After the long novel, this is sheer happiness; almost as much as running. A minor novel no one will care much about, which perhaps won't even be published . . . ! True contentment.

Much love,
Joyce

8 August 1999

Dear Greg,

What an excellent essay-review on Emily Dickinson. I can see that you're brimming with ideas and enthusiasm about her work, after years of being intimate with it; while I feel (I think I feel) that I've said all I have to say about it. You'll be leaving soon for the Dickinson house in Amherst. (Haven't you seen it before?) When we visited, the house itself was closed, but we had a lovely long hike in the vicinity. I think of Emily D. & Emily Brontë as sisters of a kind. Both underappreciated during their lifetimes, though that's hardly the most significant fact about them . . .

Maybe I will keep the title *Negro-Lover*, since you suggest it's superior to the other. (I know it is superior to the other!) I have been having the most relaxed, convalescing/ rejuvenating summer reworking this novel & writing short, finite, sane things! . . .

We're leaving on Friday for Ireland, & though as usual I don't want to go, I suppose it will be enjoyable & worthwhile. My main dread of traveling is not knowing what to take, to wear, which is very boring; & not having enough meritorious reading material. The festival includes numerous wonderful writers like Frank McCourt, Robert Pinsky, Bill Kennedy, Eamon Grennan (an Irish poet whom we've published) & we'll be traveling to Yeats country one day with Rose Styron, a lovely woman we've come to know recently.

You've asked about the next story collection. Perhaps 2001? Next year is *Blonde* & *The Dark Century*, my horror/ suspense anthology. I doubt that HarperCollins would like a third book from me & I know I should slow my publications. (I'll be like J.D. Salinger cheerfully typing away into oblivion.) Already there are manuscripts completed & even "polished" & this new novel which I won't show anyone for a long time . . .

Edmund White is back, & we're going to the Marilyn Monroe exhibit at Christie's with him in NYC soon. Dan has seen it & says it's very moving. Few people know how avidly MM read & how through her life she looked to literature/ books for spiritual sustenance.

Our wildlife includes skunks, wild turkeys, numerous fawns & deer, foxes & even hummingbirds. A farm close by has two ostriches (!).

Love,
Joyce

13 August 1999

Dear Greg,

This will be to welcome you back from what I hope, and assume, has been a terrific New England visit.

Also to congratulate you on completing your novel. What is the title, finally?

We're leaving soon, and I've so cleared my desk of all projects . . . I seem to have a few hours to spare. Amazing! (Not only have I completed *The Negro-Lover* (back to the original title, for what it's worth . . . I doubt that this novel will ever be published) but I've written my second children's book . . . five pages long: *Who Has Seen Little Reynard?* . . .

I wonder if you will follow the advice you'd given me, to set your novel aside, write another novel, and in a year or so see what you think of it? I'm sure this is a wise, pragmatic strategy; we should keep our novels back for years, rethinking & polishing; it has certainly been a helpful practice for me, often, as with *My Heart Laid Bare* & *Broke Heart Blues* (which had been completed before Billy Abrahams's death). And preparing stories for hardcover publication, years after they've been written, is very rewarding . . .

I envy you your enthusiasm for "sacred" spaces [e.g., the Emily Dickinson house] & people. I don't think I've ever had any experience remotely approaching yours, when you first visited Amherst . . . You won't believe that people stare at me and sometimes say, "I'm so nervous! I can't believe I'm standing here talking to . . . you." The other day in NYC, at the Marilyn Monroe Christie's exhibit in fact, where we'd gone with Edmund White, a woman came up to me in such a way . . . It does have the salutary effect of making me "gracious" in public as if on display. (Poor Emily Dickinson! Imagine keeping up the "dresses-all-in-white" legend in an era before dry cleaners & washable synthetic fabrics.) The exhibit was very moving, especially the many books.

Much love,
Joyce

24 August 1999

Dear Greg,

. . . Our Irish adventures were variegated, indeed! I've sent you a card which might just arrive someday. The countryside & Galway Bay are very beautiful, & our visit to the Aran Islands was quite an experience. The festival itself was poorly organized, but other participants were wonderful, & we enjoyed the company of Michael Ondaatje & his wife, Linda Spalding, Bill Kennedy & his wife, Edna O'Brien (a lovely, gracious, friendly & funny woman), Rita Dove & Eamon Grennan & numerous others. It did feel rather more like 6 weeks than 6 days since we did so many things in so brief a space of time . . . The trek up the "hill"—in fact, a small mountain—was quite a challenge even for those of us in fairly good physical condition; it was very, very long; some 200 people, many of them . . . middle-aged & bookish, scrambling up a steep slope gasping for air in violent, chilly winds off the Atlantic. I've never given a reading in such a setting: my hair whipping, and my eyes stinging with tears . . .

Much love,
Joyce

8 October 1999

Dear Greg,

. . . What an idyllic autumn this week has been. A true

pleasure. My classes are great, and colleagues congenial as usual . . . Mark Strand gave a rather low-keyed, dispirited poetry reading, though he brightened up a bit at dinner; next Thursday is Adrienne Rich, who will be introduced not by a woman, as one might expect, but by Yusef Komunyakaa, a powerful presence. (Do you know Yusef's work? He's an excellent poet.) I'll be having both lunch and dinner with Adrienne Rich, whom I've never met . . .

Yes, I should add on Camille Paglia [to her anthology *The Best American Essays of the Century*] if only to have on board an anti-feminist. I could include the essay in which she speaks of the "erotic, fun elements of rape, including gang-rape"; include a bit of Ted Bundy on the "erotic, fun elements of rape, murder & mutilation"; follow up with Jeffrey Dahmer on the "erotic, fun elements of rape, murder, mutilation & cannibalism." Controversy! Those whose eyes glaze over at the very word "essay" will be on the alert . . .

Fred & Carolina say hello to you. They are both in reasonably good spirits, though my father is a bit tired from his chemotherapy, & it isn't clear just how much good the powerful treatment is doing him . . . I've become quite friendly with my brother Fred & sister-in-law Nancy.

Much love,
Joyce

14 October 1999

Dear Greg,

. . . Thanks for the excellent Updike review. John should appreciate such a thoughtful assessment. (You probably haven't seen the lengthy snide attack in the *New Republic* which focuses upon the book's few weaknesses.) The incidental pieces in *More Matter* are filled with fascinating insights and the collection comes to seem like the journal of an intelligence-in-process.

(As I'm writing this, a young fawn, spots just fading for the new season, has come to drink from a birdbath about ten feet from my window.)

About *Blonde* . . . I'd been intending to send you a copy of the finished book next April. The review copy has myriad little errors and flaws . . . which makes me particularly uncomfortable about your seeing it, in a sense, prematurely . . . (The HarperCollins publicist just informed me ominously that Michiko Kakutani has already requested a review copy . . . so many months before publication! Why this high-profile reviewer has a kind of vendetta against me, if a one-sided assault can be a "vendetta," I haven't a clue. It must have been *Black Water* that irrevocably offended her, & the portrait of JFK in *Blonde* is surely more "offensive" than the portrait of the Senator . . .

I am working on short, blessedly short things . . . ! Finitude is sanity, I've come to believe. Maybe I will end up writing fortunes for Chinese fortune cookies . . .

In my interminable limousine rides I've had the wonderful opportunity to read, among other provocative books, the utterly fascinating *Open Me Carefully*: Emily Dickinson's Intimate Letters to Susan Huntington Dickinson. No doubt you know this book . . . I think that Susan is the clue to ED's personal life; in the sense that the women were very, very close, & Susan's few surviving letters to ED are remarkable documents, revealing a mind & sensibility so like ED's as to seem a mirror-self/soul mate . . .

I've no doubt but that ED could have been as social as anyone in Amherst if she'd wished, but she didn't wish; she found her own company & that of books preferable to her neighbors', like Thoreau. For this, she's forever branded as the Myth. The editors of the letters hope to "debunk" the myth, but it will never be dislodged.

Much love,
Joyce

22 October 1999

Dear Greg,

A quick reply to your fax of the other day, and to respond to your excellent review-essay in *Georgia Review*. It's certainly an ambitious piece . . . Your remarks on Adrienne Rich and on Chase Twichell are especially insightful, and interesting. Ray is very happy that you took the time to so thoughtfully examine Chase's work; we'll be sending the review along to her . . .

We've had several excellent poetry readings at Princeton just this past week. Amazing. [One was] Adrienne Rich, who was at times quite thrilling, a fine reader and speaker. We'd had lunch together, with Elaine Showalter & some others, & I found Adrienne a warm, congenial, rather soft-spoken (and diminutive) person, only just slightly hobbled by arthritis (she walks with a cane) . . .

I'm still on vacation, so to speak; writing short pieces, and enjoying an idyllic autumn. Truly beautiful . . .

Joyce

7 December 1999

Dear Greg,

A quick reply to your newsy/funny letter.

By now, you're probably off your diet [the Atkins]; you will either have lost 20 lbs., or are on a respirator. A number of our friends have tried this bizarre diet & one or two have even lost weight, like Dan Halpern, but it isn't a healthy, balanced diet as you've surely discovered. (And why do you imagine you need a diet?) . . .

[We attended] a lively dinner in the Village last night hosted by Stanley Crouch, the black cultural critic of whom you may have heard. Stanley "likes" my work because, he says, I'm not afraid to deal with racial issues. He is an amazing talker, an expert on jazz & something of a formidable presence in the black cultural world, having denounced black icons in print (like Toni Morrison, about whom I think Stanley is mistaken).

Don't Bother to Knock is fascinating for Marilyn Monroe's performance, & her interplay with the difficult Richard Widmark. The awkward comedy sequences are symptomatic of the 1950s; even worse is similar material in *Niagara* (my favorite Monroe film) . . .

Your plans for the holidays sound wonderful . . . Holidays don't mean very much to Ray & me, for some reason. I guess we're not true Americans, not sentimental or especially nostalgic. I wrote an op-ed piece on the millennium which will come out later this month, & these are my truest feelings. It is all so absurdly hyped, & has no meaning at all for many, perhaps most, of the earth's population, for whom our Christian calendar has no significance. Yet some of our closest friends, like Elaine Showalter & Jeanne Halpern, indulge in a virtual frenzy of gift-giving year following year, & seem to love it . . .

My parents continue to like their "retirement village." On the phone, my father sounds exuberant often, & I think he is happy just to be alive. So many medical crises in the past decade, & yet he can still go swimming, & can read to some degree, with his magnified/illuminated mechanism. Thanks so much for having been exceptionally nice to my mother & father. I know it meant a great deal to them.

My next publication at HarperCollins after *Blonde* may be my memoir, tentatively titled *The Lost Landscape* [this book did not appear until 2015]; it will end with the selling of the old farm. So sad!

Much love,
Joyce

25 December 1999

Dear Greg,

A quick message to wish you Happy Christmas & a Merry Millennium, & to mention, if you haven't seen *American Beauty* yet, that you would like this very skillfully executed, "darkly funny" movie very much . . . We go to movies in a suburban-sprawl mall with our friends Ron Levao (the boxing amateur-expert, Renaissance scholar at Rutgers) & Susan Wolfson (Romantics, prof & scholar at Princeton). Maybe, cheered by this excursion, we will next see *Malkovich* . . .

I have been having the most idyllic time imaginable . . . for me. David Ebershoff [an editor at Random House] sent me galleys for *them*, & I have been going through the text sharp-eyed & making changes here & there; rewriting a few paragraphs to bring characters a little more into the light . . . *them* emerges as stronger than I recalled.

We're going to the Halperns later today, laden with gifts (our only gift-giving day of the holiday season) for them & other guests. I know that your family has been to visit with you, & has perhaps left by now; & Ray & I hope you've had a wonderful, not too busy/crowded Christmas . . .

Much love,
Joyce

5 January 2000

Dear Greg,

... Nothing I've ever written before received quite the attention my millennium essay did in the NY *Times*. It's amazing. (Everyone who speaks to me agrees with me. I suppose that's only logical.) Even in NYC, in the Museum of Modern Art, total strangers came up to me & spoke to me of the piece as if they knew me, which was a little disconcerting. (I think of myself as comfortably anonymous.) It didn't seem to be skeptical so much as common sense that Western-Christian calendar-reckoning is not at the center of the universe ...

Your Internet [stock] trading sounds fascinating. You have managed to combine playfulness, creativity/imagination, & practicality. When we had a computer in the house, I seem to have become somewhat addicted to it, & was experiencing mild wrist pains. (I wrote *American Appetites* with a word processor, among other things.) What condition I would be in now, I have no idea. It seemed very seductive to write for 10-12 hours ... Elaine Showalter has serious back problems, goes to a [physical] therapist three times a week, & may have to have an operation; yet, she says, she can't not continue at the computer. (What did people do before computers?) ... It's an entire new world, or cosmos, I doubt that I could enter, even if I wanted to. But, who knows? Our typewriters will soon become obsolete, & Ray & I will be forced into the New Millennium ...

Much love,
Joyce

7 January 2000

Dear Greg,

... I know it is a terribly depressed & competitive market

for literary fiction. A very few titles are acclaimed, & sell millions of copies via TV; others languish. And there is no real difference between these titles, I'm sure. When I reread *them*, I was made to realize how, if this were a first novel today, it would surely not be published; it's too obviously "noncommercial." As for my earlier Vanguard books, they would have languished in drawers like Emily Dickinson's packets of poems awaiting an improbable posterity . . .

Love,
Joyce

23 January 2000
(Ray & my wedding anniversary, but don't
calculate which one! I'm trying not to.)

Dear Greg,

. . . I am so very much enjoying these idyllic days . . . In March/April/May my life will be turned inside out like an old glove; now, in the interlude before the "spring" semester begins, I'm working on numerous enjoyable & easy things like book reviews, & the intro. to the *Best American Essays* . . . Last Sunday/Monday I was a guest of the American Library Association Convention, held in San Antonio; I gave an encouragingly well-received reading from *Blonde*, & afterward had time for several hours (!) of running/walking along the historic River Walk, in 75 F sunshine. Then an abrupt return to Newark, where the wind-chill factor made the temperature allegedly minus twenty . . .

My usual typewriter has broken down temporarily, & I am using an older one Ray keeps in his closet. It is so slow; & awkward; it feels like a manual typewriter. I could never have typed 1,400 pages, let alone the 5,000 that revisions would add up to, on this! (This is in reference to The Long Novel.) . . .

No, I haven't much to say about *Middle Age: A Romance*. Maybe even the title will be changed. I do feel reluctant to talk about any novel in progress. I think I only began speaking/complaining of *Gemini* to a few close friends (like poor Greg!) when the writing spilled over into my own emotional life, after about p. 800. (One does go rather to pieces after p. 800. If you ever have the experience of typing a 4-digit page number, that is even more . . . electrifying.)

Thank you for the information about Stanley Lindberg, whom I'd known had been ill, but hadn't known died. Poor Stanley . . . ! I suppose it was smoking-related? I'd met him originally while he was at Ohio U. in Athens, Ohio; I wrote a very strong letter in support of him as editor of *Georgia Review*, & joked afterward that it wasn't just anyone who might move from Athens, Ohio, to Athens, Georgia, with no stops in between. The magazine is certainly excellent, & very handsome to look at. *Gettysburg Review* seems clearly modeled after it . . .

Much love,
Joyce

Valentine's Day 2000

Dear Greg,

(Christabel, warmly curled up in my lap, asks to be remembered to you on this special day.) . . .

Why do you mention Bob Phillips? In fact, I don't seem to be writing to anyone lately except you. It doesn't mean anything especially, but I'm distracted by thoughts of my parents, whom I telephone very often, & whom we'll be visiting later this week. (Yes, health problems. But I won't burden you with details, I promise!) Bob teaches at U-Houston, as usual . . .

I've just finished a 58-page short story (!) for an Otto
Penzler anthology on a most specialized subject: boxing &
mystery. I had not thought I would write so passionately
about a fictionalized memory fragment. (A friend of my father's of decades ago, who'd hoped to be a boxer, but was
mismatched in a fight & injured; & years later committed
suicide, in Lockport. The only "suicide" of my childhood/
girlhood memory. Which is why boxing so naturally seems to
me symbolic of suicide, self-destruction, beneath its fleeting
excitement & glamour.) . . .

What an excellent review of [David Eborshoff's] *The
Danish Girl*! [I had reviewed the novel for the *Atlanta Journal-Constitution*.] It's better written than the *NY Times* review, though that is very positive, also . . .

Much love,
Joyce

17 February 2000

Dear Greg,

(These are among the most jangled days of my life. If I don't
seem altogether coherent to you, I hope you'll excuse me.)

In reply to your question: I think, looking back upon the
experience [of writing *Blonde*], that it is one I would not
wish to relive. In psychoanalytic terms—though we can't of
course "analyze" ourselves—I believe I was trying to give
life to Norma Jeane Baker, and to keep her living, in a very
obsessive way, because she came to represent certain "life-
elements" in my own experience and, I hope, in the life of
America. A young girl, born into poverty, cast off by her father and eventually by her mother, who, as in a fairy tale,
becomes an iconic "Fair Princess" and is posthumously celebrated as "The Sex Symbol of the 20th Century," making

millions of dollars for other people—it's just too sad, too ironic. Previous to this, the other novels that exhausted me emotionally were *What I Lived For*, *Bellefleur*, and *Wonderland*. After each, I vowed no more long novels ever again . . .

Yes, Elaine & I are very close, especially these days. She's an amazingly generous woman, & I am not exaggerating. She is *amazing* in her sympathy & solicitude. I see & speak with her often; we've become rather like sisters.

Such good news about your agent!

Love,
Greg

23 February 2000

Dear Greg,

Thanks for your very thoughtful letter.

I've been quite exhausted lately, and don't have much to say. I do hope you will continue to write to me, since I love hearing from you, but I don't feel that I can be much of a correspondent at the present time.

My father is "stabilized"—which is better news than we had expected. A doctor's glib prognosis ("he has about a month to live") upset us all terribly, but turns out not to be true. I've felt like a puppet jerked about on a string for some time now . . .

Truly, I don't want to burden you, or anyone, with this family news. The hospice people are, as you predicted, very wonderful. I've begun making donations and will be talking frequently with one of my father's nurses. (Yes, they do seem saintly. It's so very encouraging.)

Russell returned from his 23,000-foot mountain trek sunburnt, trim and lighter by fifteen pounds. Now he must make the difficult adjustment to "real" life. It was a beauti-

ful but grueling experience, he says, which he will probably
never repeat.

This evening, Galway Kinnell gave a superb reading at
the university. Rhapsodic and inspiring.

Again, thanks for your kindness and solicitude.

Much love,
Joyce

2 March 2000

Dear Greg,

As you might have anticipated, I was quite fascinated,
if finally somewhat repelled and saddened, by the [Flan-
nery] O'Connor letter snippets. [For an article in the *Atlanta
Journal-Constitution* marking the 75th anniversary of
O'Connor's birth, I had visited the O'Connor archive in
Milledgeville and read a number of the writer's unpublished
letters.] What a wicked sense of humor! The racism isn't
funny, though; I felt a stab of horror, being forced to realize
that this woman whom I had so admired, at least when I
was younger, would not have protested lynchings, and seems
utterly, mysteriously devoid of sympathy (Christian or otherwise!) for human beings with skins darker than her own. I
think I had always expected O'Connor to be "good" . . . perhaps because she died young. But clearly she's tough, cruel,
self-centered and unquestioning in her white-supremacy
delusion . . .

Of course, O'Connor probably didn't much like herself.
In a traditional Southern milieu, she'd have been without ap-
parent feminine charm, and must have been made to keenly
feel her difference . . .

As you can perhaps imagine, I've been in a state of . . . I
hesitate to say mania, that's an exaggeration, but I am very

restless & find it difficult to concentrate. I speak often with my father, with whom I've found I can speak very frankly and intimately, as I could not do when we visit; somehow, in person, in a "social" setting, & with Daddy's hearing impaired, we simply can't communicate as we have done on the phone . . . The hospice nurses are wonderful, so very caring & sympathetic. We can call them 24 hours a day if we wish. Daddy is on a partial morphine medication but is not an invalid; he & my mother continue to live in their apartment, & nurses come to him several times a week, & today they even went swimming for the first time in a while. I know, I vowed I would not speak much of their infirmities, but I do feel at least temporarily cheered by Daddy's stabilized condition. Of course, it can't last . . . Yes, I believe they would love flowers, but they won't be able to reply to thank you, so thanks ahead of time! . . .

I'm glad that your novel [*Sticky Kisses*] will appear with Alyson Books; and also that several editors are eager to read the next . . . How I wish *Blonde* might have been published under a pseudonym. That would have been so wonderful.

Much love,
Joyce

19 March 2000

Dear Greg,

We've returned, a bit dazed, from our week away; amid a small mountain of mail I was delighted to discover our interview [for the literary magazine *Prairie Schooner*], which turned out very well, I think. Thanks for your probing questions . . .

I'm looking forward—I think—to my visit at Agnes Scott

College. I remember a lovely visit there some years ago. Things are still relatively "stable" with my parents, but the situation could change at any time, and so I must be prepared to cancel plans if necessary . . .

I hope you won't be surprised that I might perhaps look a bit tired . . . I seem to have lost a bit of weight, and am very insomniac these days, or do I mean nights. No matter when I go to bed, even past 1 a.m., I wake at about 4:30 a.m. as if a switch has been pulled in my brain. There's a rush of Important/Profound Thoughts (about which one is helpless, of course) followed by an even greater rush of Secondary/Gnat Thoughts (primarily about "career" & how not to drown amidst so much busyness . . .). It's a sort of continuous video playing in the human brain, to which, at weak times in our lives, we succumb. (Except Gracie & Lucy are clearly spared such!) . . .

Trinity University in San Antonio & San Jose State U. were wonderfully enjoyable, in fact. The English Dept. chair at Trinity is from Brooklyn & an avid boxing fan dating back to the '50s when he was a boy, so we had much to reminisce about. This amazing individual had me sign 61 (!) books of mine he has collected. My next book will be *Faithless: Tales of Transgression* (Jan. 2001, in theory) . . . I will hope to see you on Thursday.

Much love,
Joyce

30 March 2000

Dear Greg,

. . . [*Blonde*] hasn't even been published yet officially, but already I have had quite enough of my new/next novel in the public sense. Help! I'd never realized how sequestered, how pleasant & sane the life of the "literary" writer whom no one much cares to read . . .

Yes, I'm working on *Middle Age: A Romance* & am somewhere beyond the halfway point. (There's a section about a woman who rescues unwanted dogs; I'm becoming very interested in dogs! Chase Twichell & Russell are going to "adopt" a border collie puppy. Can you recommend an exotic dog, somewhat large, that is generally docile but might "turn" if goaded? (Not for me personally, but for the novel.) A wolfhound? What's an Afghan—or sheepdog? (You can see how much more fun this novel is than the tragedy & anxiety of The Long Novel. Frankly, I never want to feel any emotion again, if I can avoid it.)

Much love,
Joyce

9 April 2000

Dear Greg,

. . . We woke this morning to a world transformed by big clumps of damp blossom-sized snow. And much wind. Unfortunately, Ray had to journey to NYC for a Norton sales conference. Tomorrow, I must journey in for the annual PEN banquet, a noisy "gala" you would find profoundly depressing, & seek to escape from as quickly as possible, as I do. But I'm an honorary board member this year, & must be seated at a head table with such luminaries as Henry Gates, Jr. and Stephen Sondheim . . .

The party for *Blonde*, held in an enormous, almost palatial loft in SoHo, was less crowded & noisy, & far more elegant, than I'd imagined.

I'm being interviewed almost ceaselessly, & deal with the situation by focusing exclusively upon the interviewer at hand, as if he/she were the only interviewer, ever. Most of these conversations are actually very engaging, even stimulating. And far easier than writing the novel was . . .

Much love—
Joyce (& Christabel)

16 April 2000

Dear Greg,

. . . The *CBS Early Morning Show* is already a rapidly fading memory, but I do recall quite vividly the perky interviewer asking me, just before we were on the air, "Is this your first book?" The conversation skittered downhill from there.

Another memorable question was put to me yesterday evening in Philadelphia, where I was "honored" at a dinner for well-to-do Friends of the Library. The retired gentleman beside me asked, "What led you to write a novel about Blondie?" (I should have told him I hadn't the courage to write about Dagwood.) . . .

I've been interviewed a good deal lately, & gather from interviewers' questions that *Blonde* is considered "controversial" in some quarters. Since I've been spared the details, I can be philosophical; if I'd had to confront actual hostile reviews & charges, I'm sure I would feel defensive & beleaguered. One thing I learned, among many, from being immersed in Norma Jeane's/Marilyn Monroe's life, is that we can be terribly wounded by others' judgments of us, though we may imagine we're stoic & independent. Monroe died because she'd been made to feel worthless. From now on, I hope seriously to avoid ingesting the poisonous judgments of others, even if this means not ingesting very many "positive" judgments, either . . .

A full day in NYC tomorrow, & Edmund White is hosting a dinner for me in the evening. I'm sure it will be lovely; Ed is a gracious host & excellent cook. Next morning I must be up at 5:30 a.m. to fly to Washington, DC (!) . . . (I am managing to write, in medias res. I'm in no hurry to complete *Middle Age*, & no one will be in much hurry to read it.)

Much love,
Joyce

19 May 2000

Dear Greg,

I'm home briefly, going away tomorrow briefly (a theater in Georgetown, Del., is presenting some short plays of mine & I am reading from *Blonde*) & then again next week. I am trying to catch up on meaningful correspondence & become reacquainted with Christabel. Much of my life seems to be in suspension right now. The busyness of "touring" (a misleading term, suggestive of Henry James & Edith Wharton) can actually be helpful if one hopes to keep one's mind firmly fixed on ephemeral, superficial, immediately engaging matters . . .

My two-part short story review should appear soon in *NYRB*. I seem to have missed the [Sherman] Alexie review in the *Times*, somehow. (Though my review of this writer is positive, I would not recommend him over the more literary/classic Native American writers N. Scott Momaday, Leslie Silko, Louise Erdrich. Alexie is breezy, sometimes funny, almost-profound, but rather a lightweight compared to these.) . . .

Much love,
Joyce

29 May 2000

Dear Greg,

... It's strange: I receive numerous letters, & often people come up to speak with me after readings, & the gist of these messages is that I've "inspired" someone. (Lately, I've even been assured that I've changed people's lives . . . ! Usually these are adolescent girls who love *Foxfire* but sometimes they are mature women, and even now & then a man or two.) Instead of reacting inwardly with a twinge of embarrassment or a sardonic aside, I should see these claims from a perspective not my own. They're genuine . . . I guess!

(Of course, my natural response would be a wisecrack: "Inspire *you*? I wish I could inspire myself.") . . .

We've just returned from an emotionally exhausting visit to Getzville. As you may have surmised, my father has died, & we've been with my mother, & seeing that she is comfortably situated in a wing of the Weinberg complex where her medical problems can be dealt with. My father slipped into a deep sleep that was at first considered "normal," but he didn't wake, & his ending was very merciful. As you'd said, the hospice people are truly wonderful, & we are enormously grateful to them. My mother's emotional/mental state, however, doesn't allow us to "tell" her what has happened, & sometimes she seems to know, & other times she doesn't know, or doesn't wish to know. We've been advised not to tell her anything to upset her.

I've had a very difficult time thinking about these things, let alone telling about them, so I hope you will sympathize with my situation & not allude to them; receiving a letter from you, as from anyone, I naturally hope to be nudged a bit out of myself & my haunted thoughts, & to anticipate being forced to endure condolences & to speak more of painful subjects is just too much for me right now. The only other friend I've confided in has been Elaine (whose mother died within the year, & who is absolutely understanding & respects my wishes). I have an entirely new sympathy for Alice Adams, for instance, who refused to speak of Billy Abrahams in the past tense after he died, but pretended (& acknowledged it was pretense) that he was "traveling." Much of my new novel [*Middle Age*] is about coping with the loss of a powerful masculine presence, a man much loved, not a saint, with some failings, but an exceptional person, & the aftermath of his death precipitates profound changes in people close to him . . .

You were extremely kind & made a difference in my parents' lives. They liked you enormously, & would always ask after you, until relatively recently. THANK YOU for your special sympathy in preparing the background/biographical chapters of *Invisible Writer*. This meant more to me, & to them, than can be expressed . . .

I've been in a siege mood for a very long time, dreading the telephone ringing, & speaking a good deal on it, to my father (for as long as possible) & now to my brother & mother. There has not been an hour that I haven't been thinking of my father/mother in many months & perhaps there will not be. My mother's state is "good" considering her medical problems & the primary thing is, she isn't agitated or depressed, but coping very well, & I am trying to focus upon this positive fact, & not to dwell upon what can't be changed. When/if you write, I would like to be cheered up. Dachshund news is particularly welcome. (My letters to my parents over the decades contain much, much "cat news." What a cold-eyed biographer would make of this, I don't want to think.)

Much love, and again, thanks for your myriad kindnesses on my parents' behalf—
Joyce

14 June 2000

Dear Greg,

MANY THANKS for the very beautiful candleholder. It's a work of art . . .

My birthday, such as it is, will be "celebrated" at the Bienens' presidential home in Evanston, IL, where we'll be guests at a pre-Commencement dinner. (Commencement, at which fortunately I don't have to speak but can sit back & listen to Robert Pinsky, is the following day.)

It has been a most dismal spring/early summer so far . . . rain, chill, opaque skies. At the very least it does encourage one to stay indoors & work; but then there isn't much reward for working.

You asked about my "next novel" . . . Truly, I don't know. The shorter of the two, *I'll Take You There*, is in a drawer; the longer, *Middle Age*, which I'm completing about as slowly as one can ride a bicycle without falling off, will have to be revised, which I always look forward to. At the moment I can't imagine summoning up the energy to offer either of these to John Hawkins to read after presenting him with 1,400 pages last year.

It has been so frequently drummed into my head (almost literally, it seems, with drumsticks & other weapons) that I write too much, or at least publish too much, that I can't help but feel guilty about foisting more work upon anyone. I do think it would have been a good idea years ago to have written under a pseudonym, or two. (Or three, or four . . .)

You will love Vancouver. We visited many years ago, & only regretted that we didn't explore British Columbia generally . . .

Much love, & again thanks for the beautiful birthday gift—
Joyce

5 July 2000

Dear Greg,

. . . Princeton is lovely in the summer, & we see a small circle of friends. Edmund White & his boyfriend Michael are coming out for dinner next week. (Ed has been away, I haven't heard how your dinner went. Did you attend his reading?)

I'm still revising/polishing *Middle Age*, but I'd done so many handwritten drafts while traveling last spring, I needed mainly to type out what I'd already written, with few changes. This novel has been a real balm to me. I don't know if the experience of completing it has been healing in itself, or simply that time "heals," but I am feeling much less exhausted now; my sleep is still chaotic & the dreams wearing, but consciousness is "normal"—or what passes for "normal" hereabouts . . .

Yes, Robert Pinsky & I, among others, received honorary doctorates at NU. Not related to this event—deriving more from my Syracuse U. experience—but of course hugely fictionalized—I've written a surreal tale called "Commencement" at the request of a horror/speculative fiction anthologist, who assembled the monumental *999* last year. In the story, a commencement ceremony & the ancient Aztec ceremony of (human) sacrifices are conflated. (So this passes for "normal"?) . . .

Ray is in very good spirits & says hello.

Much love,
Joyce (& Christabel)

19 August 2000

Dear Greg,

Your Vancouver visit sounds wonderful. We never got to Victoria, unfortunately . . .

Lovely quiet days here ... I am having a truly THRILL-ING experience writing my young adult novel; exactly the antithesis of *Blonde*. It's like riding a bicycle along gently sloping hills in brilliant coolish sunshine. Even if it's never published, it has been quite a vacation so far. The tentative title is *Big Mouth & Ugly Girl* ...

Your reviews are very readable. I met & liked Rose Tremain very much in England. The Denis Johnson, which I'd been sent, I didn't think very inspired or carefully written. "Minimalist" is a kind word!

Much love,
Joyce

21 December 2000

Dear Greg,

This is just to wish you a Happy Christmas ...

We're treating my brother, sister-in-law and mother to a festive Christmas dinner at an inn near my brother's home in Clarence. We are not looking forward to driving the thruway, however, especially if the weather is as treacherous as it has been. Buffalo, NY, has been snow-struck more than once this season.

(When I read your note, that Atlanta had 3" of snow, I had to look twice, thinking it must be 3'; who would take much notice of a mere 3"? Atlantans, I guess.)

I must say, I do miss my father very much in this holiday season. Ed White has told me you never get over your feel-ings of grief for a parent, and he had not greatly adored his father ... I'm not sure that I particularly want to "get over" grief, and have felt that mourning is a far more interesting, rewarding, if perhaps inevitable experience than "happiness." I've even been reading with much new admiration the poems of Wallace Stevens, which definitely belong to middle age, not youth . . .

You'd mentioned your favorite stories from *Faithless*. "The Scarf" is a fictionalized semi-autobiographical story; my mother had been giving away her things for months, including a beautiful scarf I'd given her years before. But I seem to recall that she did know I'd given it to her. I found it eerie, unsettling, when my mother began to give things away . . . Now she has relatively little, and seems perfectly content. In the nursing home, there's a resident dog she has come to love. We've bought her some things for her room including a handsome framed reproduction of a Degas painting. My own favorite story is, oddly, "Ugly" . . . and of course "Faithless."

Much affection,
Joyce

28 January 2001

Dear Greg,

We just returned from Detroit-Buffalo, very happy to be home . . .

The Oprah film crew arrives tomorrow morning [to film the segment on Oprah's "pick" for her book club, *We Were the Mulvaneys*] & the great task for the filmmaker is: how to create something remotely "interesting" out of my life . . . I have to admit, I had not seen Oprah Winfrey before. I agree with your assessment of her. She'd telephoned me to tell me of the selection, and the experience was like speaking with an old friend. I was totally unprepared, as you might imagine. Now I feel like an individual who has won a lottery she hadn't any idea she'd entered . . .

Our visit to Buffalo/Getzville went very well, but was sad, of course. My mother is fairly well physically, but has become forgetful, at least at times, in some ways. (At other times she remembers fairly clearly.) The ravages of age involve a dreamlike distortion of time & its inhabitants, I've come to see. As in our dreams we try to create narratives to explain the inexplicable . . .

As always—much affection,
Joyce

8 February 2001

Dear Greg,

. . . The jacket design for your textbook is stunning. Very beautiful. Whoever chose the Klee painting has exquisite taste.

The HarperCollins art director who did so original a job with my earlier books can't seem to come up with anything very good at all for *Middle Age: A Romance*. Dan and I have seen numerous designs he's proposed, and they seem to be getting worse. I'd have liked the Matisse dancers (late Matisse cutouts) but this is considered "too European" . . .

The [*Oprah Winfrey Show*] interview here, which was taped, to be severely edited into a film of about six minutes, leaned toward the autobiographical. I've found that it's virtually impossible to speak convincingly about the strategies of fiction; how we create a language appropriate to a subject, and don't write "from life." The interviewer kept pressing back to my personal experiences growing up on a small farm in upstate NY and I had to keep reminding him that the Mulvaneys weren't a "typical" farm family & that the Oateses were not the Mulvaneys . . . But then of course Muffin was "real," which obscures my purity as an artist, I suppose . . .

Thanks for your response to *The Barrens* . . . Your [publicity and advertising] plans for *Sticky Kisses* sound ambitious. Good for you!

As always,
Joyce

25 February 2001

Dear Greg,

... The taping for Oprah's Book Club couldn't have been more enjoyable. Oprah and her Book Club assistants made it a warm, welcoming experience, as other writers have attested, but what struck me as most valuable about Oprah and the phenomenon she represents is how a kind of community has been established throughout the country. Countless scattered, perhaps lonely people brought together by a bond of genuine feeling ...

Oprah said she'd been undecided for a while whether to choose *Mulvaneys*, or *Because It Is Bitter* . . . I think she made the right decision, absolutely ...

Tomorrow I'll be having lunch with Gloria Vanderbilt here in Princeton to discuss our project (her Dream Boxes, my text). There will be an exhibit of her work in Nov. in NYC, tied in with our OR publication ...

Much affection,
Joyce

2 March 2001

Dear Greg,

... We've found another work of art for *Middle Age* which we like even better, a pastel & charcoal drawing by R.B. Kitaj. [This jacket art, too, was ultimately rejected.] Dan & I have been going back & forth on this cover for so long, you'd think we were designing the Sistine Chapel. During the taping, Oprah commented very positively on the cover art of *Mulvaneys*, and I've noticed that the books she selects have very attractive, striking covers.

At a recent Barnes & Noble reading, the audience was enormous. The Oprah imprimatur hovered like a halo above my head. Never have I signed so many books, and so many copies of the same book for the same individual. Mainly these are women, including black women, buying three or four copies of *Mulvaneys* to give as presents. If we could have the Oprah stamp of approval on our foreheads, how warmly & enthusiastically the world would greet us.

Cynthia Ozick came to Princeton, and read light, humorous pieces (!). Instead of her tough, eloquent, hard-hitting prose. She's brilliant, but it was like hearing Horowitz play "Chopsticks" when you'd expected Beethoven.

Much affection,
Joyce

10 March 2001

Dear Greg,

. . . Your comments on the *Oprah Show* are very interesting. I've been flooded with responses since the program, which finally I did see, belatedly . . . What is Oprah like?— exactly as she seems. Every adjective you might apply to her—ebullient, smart, sassy, funny, sympathetic/empathetic, no-nonsense, warm, canny, very intelligent (without being intellectual)—is applicable . . .

Everything [in the show] was personal emotion, anguish yielding to stoicism & adjustment. In the short run, obviously this is very popular, given Oprah's viewership. In the long run, perhaps it infantilizes the viewers. Certainly, the slightest suggestion that literature is art—art is "artifice"—

met with blank stares, for no one was remotely interested in matters of form, which isn't surprising of course since most reviewers rarely comment on such things, and give plot summaries primarily. What was engaging about the Oprah experience was, first of all, Oprah herself, an "original," and the seriousness with which a book, any book, might be taken if (but only if) it mirrors an individual's personal experience . . .

I would love to immerse myself in *The Falls* [her new novel-in-progress], but it's virtually impossible these days. Tomorrow I leave early for Seattle & three days away . . .

Your new story sounds very interesting. Your intercalating of an individual not well-known with famous individuals reminds me of a Woody Allen film, *Zelig*. (I was seated beside Woody Allen at a lovely dinner at Gloria Vanderbilt's last week. A very appealing man, soft-spoken & unassuming, both like & unlike his familiar screen persona.)

As always,
Joyce

6 April 2001

Dear Greg,

. . . Robert Pinsky gave our Tanner lectures this year, very capably. He dislikes the lecture format and would have preferred to speak spontaneously, as he does so brilliantly. Still, Robert was very good. Less good were his respondents John Hollander (a dull, pompous man who, while scolding the younger generation for not speaking or writing clearly, mumbled) and Jonathan Galassi, a very nice person but ill at ease in a large lecture hall. Antonia Byatt and Marianna Torgovnick were much more lively and engaging . . .

Mulvaneys is winding down, and will seem to me, in retrospect, an utterly unexpected, serendipitous experience in a career of wholly "other" experiences. Toni Morrison, with whom I had dinner last night, says she felt the same way. The astronomical sales allow one to reflect, soberly, how little difference there is, from that perspective, between sales of 10,000 copies & 100,000; that modest range in which most of us live out our publishing lives . . .

Joyce

23 April 2001

Dear Greg,

. . . I'm having a difficult time with *The Falls* though I've made myself vow that, after *Blonde*, I would never complain (even to myself) again. Never.

At a reading in LA, during the question & answer period, a well-intentioned woman asked me how I felt about having been one of the nominees for the Pulitzer Prize, which, I had to confess, I hadn't known I had been, until that moment. So though it's disappointing to lose (again, the fourth time!), still it's encouraging to think that, though we have miserable experiences sometimes in bringing a novel to some sort of fruition, still it can work out, and someone can even admire it. Well, sometimes . . .

I wish I felt as if I had an "ideal" subject at the moment. My original plan for this novel doesn't seem to be quite right, any longer. I feel like a traveler who has come to the end of a trail, can see the trail (or something resembling it) resuming some miles away, on the far side of an abyss. Though I've been racking my brains almost literally (well, perhaps not "almost") for weeks, especially during my lonely hours in Los Angeles, I can't figure out how to resume that trail . . .

Joyce

27 June 2001

Dear Greg,

I've been meaning to write to you since we returned from Venice, but I've been swamped with less engaging responsibilities. Of course, we loved Venice, as everyone does, and my involvement in the conference was stimulating and rewarding. (Though addressing a large audience of mostly Italians, wearing earphones to listen to a not-very-fluent translator, is an arduous task! The audience stares keenly at you, but isn't listening to you; any feeble attempt at wit or irony is met with silence.) . . .

Gloria Vanderbilt has become a close, supportive friend, and she and a (male) friend will be flying out to Seattle for the opening of my play *Miss Golden Dreams* at the beginning of August. Plans for the new production are quite exciting. (Though I haven't written a play in a long time, seemingly focused upon prose fiction almost exclusively.) . . .

It's such a pleasure to be home, it does seem like madness to travel long distances. You expressed surprise that I can write while I travel, but you should remember that my traveling is very different from yours. Mostly it's for "business" purposes, not sightseeing. Since I can't sleep well on the road, I have a room service dinner, often in quite elegant quarters, then write (in long hand) from perhaps 10 p.m. till 3 a.m. You'd be surprised at all that you can accomplish in these absolutely quiet hours . . . Ray says hello.

Joyce

10 September 2001

Dear Greg,

. . . Things are somewhat sad in our household: Christabel, 15 years old and quite feisty until perhaps a week ago, is becoming enfeebled, and is obviously withdrawing in the unmistakable way of a dying animal. As Muffin had done, she wants to go outside more and more frequently, and to stay away in the woods. It's a strange, obviously powerful instinct that seems to erase the "domestic" overlay of house pet and companion, and is very sad to experience. We're not letting her outside, because she's too feeble to protect herself against marauders like other cats or raccoons. Several times I've gone looking for her, some distance from the house, and there she is—still responding to her name with a querulous "mew?" but less and less readily. She has virtually stopped eating, and weighs very little now. Still, fifteen is a good age for a cat, and Christabel has had a very good, somewhat spoiled & pampered life . . .

Since finishing *The Falls*, and putting it away in a drawer for a year, I've been writing wonderfully short things like stories & reviews for *TLS*, & once again *New York Review: The Collected Stories of Muriel Spark* and *The Selected Stories of Patricia Highsmith* respectively. Neither would interest you greatly, I think, though there are two or three Spark stories, set in Africa, that are very well done. Otherwise, both are lightweight writers in that breezy arch-Brit way that quickly wears the patience; especially compared to William Trevor, for instance.

I've just begun my second "young adult" novel, which must be restricted to about 200 pages. It's a pleasure to write things that won't attract much, perhaps any, attention. This week my novel *Middle Age* will be reviewed in various places, I suppose, but I hope not to be distracted by bad reviews especially, anticipating them beforehand. It's almost literally like running a gauntlet past stones, sticks, bricks, dead cats (not a very appropriate image!), rotten tomatoes. If one can just get past this onslaught, things are fine. We have to accept being "punished" as, perhaps, what we deserve for being writers when no one has asked us to be . . .

As always,
Joyce

11 September 2001
Dear Greg,
This has been such a devastating day . . . When Ray and I first saw the television images, we were struck speechless. I guess "speechless" is the only profound response . . .

And it had begun with Christabel dying, lapsing into unconsciousness by degrees and simply . . . ceasing to breathe. We were sitting outside in the sunshine with her, petting her and comforting her. And it was quite emotional, especially for me, but (we tell ourselves at such times) she was an elderly cat, and certainly had had a good life.

I thought that would be the emotion for the day, but when we went inside the house there was a phone message from a friend, alerting us to the catastrophe. And after that, the very thought of emotion for an elderly cat has seemed absurd. Or any kind of emotion, nearly . . .

I can't imagine teaching tomorrow, or having taught today. But by Thursday, when I meet my first workshop, life should be shifting back into normalcy, or nearly. I wonder how your teaching day has gone!

Joyce

25 September 2001
Dear Greg,
. . . At the moment, a demonically spirited gray tiger kit-

ten, Cherie, is bounding about my desk. We adopted her a few days ago from the Hopewell animal shelter where she was desperately lonely in a cage, having been abandoned. She's a slightly older kitten, about six months, with mink characteristics. She spends time absorbed in staring at the three-by-three reproduction of the cover of *Come Meet Muffin*! that leans against the wall in my study, as if she can actually see that these painted images are "cats." (Is this possible?)

I was advised to cancel my trip to England in October since war might be "declared." It isn't a good time to be out of the country, of course. I wish the Lincoln, Nebraska, conference would be canceled . . . I certainly feel that I must attend, even if no one else does.

My first class, two days after the terrorist attack, was rather shell-shocked, but subsequent classes have been nearly normal. I think our students are in a state of denial . . . I hope the semester is going as well as possible for you. Ray says hello . . .

Much affection,
Joyce

7 October 2001

Dear Greg,

Thanks so much for sending us "Double Exposure" [a short story dealing with Sylvia Plath]; we would love to publish it in *OR*, and hope that fall 2002 won't be too long for you to wait. It's a thoughtful, most original story, quite different in tone from others in the "series." How many do you have, and what is the general title? Congratulations on such excellent work . . .

Isn't Gloria Vanderbilt amazing? Her energy, her enthusiasm, her intelligence? As she responded to your Virginia

Woolf story, so she responds to numerous other things: novels, poetry, a Laurie Anderson CD, works of art, people. Yet she's quite quiet, soft-spoken . . . I haven't turned on my computer since May, & wonder how Celestial Timepiece is faring in this transformed US . . .

Joyce

3 November 2001

Dear Greg,

Thursday evening we journeyed to NYC (via train: the Lincoln Tunnel is 1.5 hours now, with terrorist-alert security plus ordinary traffic) to Gloria's opening at the K.S. Gallery. A lovely white-walled setting for the jewel-like Dream Boxes floating on pedestals. It was a very fine opening and I think Gloria is enormously pleased . . . We own two of the Boxes in the exhibit and consider ourselves fortunate . . .

Little Cherie, silky & sweet & sometimes demonically naughty, is peering up at me quizzically. "Scribble, scribble, scribble! Eh?" . . .

Much affection,
Joyce

10 December 2001

Dear Greg,

Did you see the very attractive full-page ad for your novel in *Ploughshares*? (It's a good issue of the magazine, also.)

My most extraordinary experience recently was attending an immense beautiful party at which perhaps half the 150-200 guests, strangers & friends alike, came up to me to stare & to stroke the long silky minuscule-pleated sleeves of my dress, murmuring, "How beautiful!" . . . meaning not me, nor even my oeuvre, but the dress, a sea-green Fortuny gown which Gloria Vanderbilt gave me as a present, "from her collection." There was something dreamlike about the evening, as if I'd drifted into someone else's fantasy . . .

I've completed my second, and final, "young adult" novel, *Freaky Green Eyes*, which won't appear until 2003. The genre is challenging, but rather more in the way that a screenplay is challenging. The slow/expository/descriptive passages that must be excised from YA fiction seem to me the very soul of writing . . .

Happy Holidays from Joyce & Ray, Cherie & Reynard

23 January 2002
(41st wedding anniversary!)

Dear Greg,

(Yes, it does seem like science fiction, our anniversary. Ray & I are quite baffled how time has passed so swiftly, & we have not learned a thing.) . . .

I've been asked to participate in the next Ken Burns documentary, on Jack Johnson (the first black heavyweight). I'm undecided: I don't much care for myself on screen, and the Burns documentaries have tended to be rather slow & ponderous. (Ken sent us the Mark Twain, which is generally good, but might well have been shortened.) We'd met & liked Ken very much at the Styrons' home on Martha's Vineyard two summers ago . . .

Jean Windnagle, with whom I've been corresponding, surprised me by sending photocopies of old snapshots . . . Some of these photos look like Tobacco Road, yet they've evoked much emotion for Jean & for me.

You probably didn't see the list of the 100 "great minds" in the *NY Times* on Jan. 19. People have been talking about it, mostly grumbling. It's supremely silly, but you'll be pleased to learn that your biographical subject ranked #42, just ahead of Bertolt Brecht (!) & Ayn Rand (!!). (Poor W.B. Yeats was only #97.) People are saying, however, that any listing that excludes those masters of bloviation Harold Bloom & Cornel West can't be all bad . . .

Much affection,
Joyce

15 March 2002

Dear Greg,

. . . Thanks for your commentary on "Upholstery" [a story published in the *New Yorker*]. I only just today received my contributor's copies of the magazine, which I opened with some dread, and was at once overcome by a sensation of . . . can such trivia really be published/packaged/marketed/purchased? I don't mean the "arts" content so much as the dreadful/contemptible advertising and the fashion writing. People have said that the illustration for my story is, well—"striking." (Even upstate New York males don't look quite this bad.) I did enjoy working with the youngish editor Meghan O'Rourke, however, who is far less fluttery & fussy than Alice Quinn. In fact, she seems quite delightful . . .

You mention *Marya: A Life*, & I can't help but wonder if that novel is still in print.

(I expect to glance into a mirror one day & see a blank space with the notice *OUT OF PRINT* across it.) . . .

I've thought of you & your elusive Zelda [I was currently working on a novel focused upon Zelda Fitzgerald], having just read *The Beautiful and Damned*. There are excellent passages in this rather unfocused novel. Fitzgerald seemed not to know whether his protagonist was a satiric object, as he emerges at the end, or whether he's of more merit. The ominous & terrifying rise of what Fitzgerald can't bring himself to call Semites in NYC is fascinating to note in passing.

Much affection,
Joyce

30 April 2002

Dear Greg,

Thanks for the *PW* review. The young adult/children's division of HarperCollins is very enthusiastic about *Big Mouth*, and has all sorts of plans for me that I'm afraid I won't be able to fulfill. (You would not believe: a "satellite" interview, in which the author, like the subject in a torture experiment, is interviewed by numerous parties via telephone—"with some breaks, of course"—from 6 a.m. to early afternoon . . .)

I thought that the film of *Mulvaneys* was quite well done, especially Blythe Danner and the young actor who played Patrick. The film received excellent reviews nationwide, I've been told. And thanks for your comments on "The Skull," which I'm impressed that you discovered, in *Harper's*. (Do you subscribe?) Everyone will remark on a story or prose piece in the *New Yorker*, but rarely in *Harper's*, unfortunately. (There was a nice piece on David Remnick in yesterday's *Times* . . . The magazine has more readers than during Tina Brown's final days, & is considered successful, though in the next paragraph it's noted that the magazine loses about $8 million a year . . . An odd sort of "success.") . . .

Much affection,
Joyce

3 July 2002

Dear Greg,

With Cherie on my lap, very affectionate & purring, and the air conditioner operating, I feel immune (at least for now) from the alleged 115-degree "heat index" blazing outside.

(Some of us had vaguely thought "global warming" would emerge after our lifetimes . . .)

Otherwise, things are lovely here; quiet days, with trips to NYC & elsewhere, and seeing some of the usual friends. I'm glad that you had a good visit in Greece though I'm sympathetic with your dislike of long plane rides, & am not looking forward to my trip to the UK in August . . .

In my alarmingly stylish Issey Miyake clothes, a birthday gift from Gloria, I'll be going to a party & lavish dinner for Otto Penzler's 60th birthday next week. "From Millersport to Miyake"—"From Sears to Fortuny." No one would believe it.

I'm feeling unusually past-haunted right now because I am rereading & will be revising parts of *A Garden of Earthly Delights*, which David Ebershoff will reprint as a "20th century classic." Nothing more mesmerizing than returning to an old novel. (Imagine, 1966! It hardly seems possible.) . . .

I'm just completing a Rosamond Smith/"psychological suspense" novel titled *Take Me, Take Me with You*. I had hoped for a novella like *Beasts* for Otto Penzler's series, but it has turned out over 200 pages, unfortunately . . .

Much affection—Ray says hello—
Joyce

23 July 2002

Dear Greg,

. . . It's so interesting that you should feel a connection/

identification (?) with *I'll Take You There*. I guess it must be the most from-the-heart of my novels, in a voice so like my own I suppose I should simply say it is my own. So I could hardly give the protagonist a name. She feels, as I do, that her life is transparent to her as a glass of water and of about as much interest . . .

My visit with my mother in the Beechwood home was a bittersweet experience. She is physically quite well, and very content with her surroundings which are pleasant and peaceful. Fred and I went together. (We are closer now that we see each other only a few times a year, than we were when we lived in the same house.) . . .

I followed Gloria Vanderbilt by a week at the Southern Vermont Arts Center, where her Dream Boxes are being exhibited, and I read several of my Dream Box poems, which worked out quite well. People were still talking about Gloria's appearance and presentation. (Evidently, she was somewhat controversial. Elderly trustees muttered about her "negative themes"!)

I did get an enormous amount of work done, planning the rewriting of *A Garden of Earthly Delights*. It's utterly mesmerizing to return to this novel that's like an old house I know by heart, one room leading to another, everything so familiar if at the same time distant. I'd always felt that I "knew" the characters, but in the mid-1960s I didn't have the technique to allow their voices to modulate the prose . . .

So thrilled to be home, and back at my desk! Reimagining Carleton, Clara, and Swan/Steven Revere [of *Garden*] is utterly irresistible to me; though I would guess it might seem a very strange activity to someone else.

Much affection,
Joyce

6 September 2002

Dear Greg,

. . . My play *Homesick* was well performed by the Provincetown Theatre Company, and the audience seemed enthusiastic. It was lovely of Norman & Norris Mailer to attend. We spent some time with the Mailers in Provincetown, and Norman seems scarcely changed though he complained good-naturedly of "falling apart"—losing his eyesight, losing his hearing, losing his ability to walk without two canes. He will be 80 in January . . . He was enormously sweet about my writing, which he seems to like; perhaps because we share an interest in boxing. Quite sincerely, if a bit naïvely, Norman told me he'd like some time to talk with me in private about the ways in which I could become a "major playwright." ("What am I now, a minor playwright?" I asked him. Norman seems to think that I am.) . . .

Much affection,
Joyce

26 December 2002

Dear Greg,

. . . This is my "holiday break": I've taken two or three days off from my mesmerizing but exhausting *Gravedigger's Daughter* [her new novel-in-progress] . . . to work on a much easier project, and to reply to letters. What a relief!

I look forward to *Last Encounter with the Enemy* [my new collection of short stories]. It's always exciting to be choosing cover art . . .

Yes, I do have difficulties with HarperCollins; ludicrous ones, I'm sure they would seem to other people. For instance, though I have written my last young adult/children's book, the publisher has scheduled *three* of these publications (one YA novel, one YA short story collection, one children's book) for 2003. I have tried to reason with them, to alter this, but no. *The Tattooed Girl* [formerly *The Beneficiary*] has at least been pushed back to June. (Since a May publication, I pleaded, would coincide with *A Garden of Earthly Delights*.) . . .

Much affection,
Joyce

1 February 2003

Dear Greg,
. . . Philip Roth took Ray & me to dinner the other evening at the very festive/ethnic Russian Samovar in Manhattan, where Philip is "known" and celebrated. It was years since we'd seen him, of course he is somewhat changed. As funny, smart, wonderfully conversational as always, and dauntingly well read. I know, however, from other sources that Philip has more or less broken with virtually all of his old friends, as well as former lovers of whom there were many. He spoke with scorn of newspapers, TV, the Internet, none of which (even the *New York Times*!) he now reads. So amazing, in the man who was so utterly captivated by politics in past decades. (He has also broken with John Updike, absolutely. He won't read a word John writes any longer. My rather more mild disillusion with John doesn't extend that far, and never would.)

Last night was to be Norman Mailer's 80th birthday celebration, at his beautiful East River-fronting home in Brooklyn Heights (with a dramatic view of the World Trade towers destruction), but abruptly and so far without explanation it was canceled just yesterday.

Edmund White just called, back from Key West. He is very upset about the world/political situation as I guess most clear-thinking people would be. It does make our literary/ intellectual anxieties seem so very inconsequential & especially our small pleasures in what we imagine we have accomplished.

I've thought of you often, & have been meaning to write, beginning numerous letters in my head that have grown longer & longer with the passing days . . .

Much affection,
Joyce

8 March 2003

Dear Greg,
. . . I've more or less ceased corresponding with John Updike. He seems to have grown strangely curmudgeon-like in his older/much revered age. I often teach early stories of his which are wonderfully spare and deft, and students respond immediately to them. The older Updike has become obsessed with his childhood in a way that somehow lacks drama and relevance for others. We are on very cordial terms, though, and should we ever meet (not likely, since I don't go to American Academy ceremonies) I'm sure we will be quite friendly . . .

This evening we are giving one of our large dinner parties. Edmund White & his friend Michael will be coming, as well as many of the usual Princeton crowd. Do you know Elaine Pagels's work? She is the author of *The Gnostic Gospels*, quite a renowned religious/cultural critic, and a good friend . . .

Much affection,
Joyce

24 March 2003

Dear Greg,

Thanks so much for your recent letter. Enclosed is the "young adult" collection. [*Small Avalanches.*] (I'd written two new stories for it, "Capricorn" and "The Visit," which are more explicitly young adult, I think.) . . .

Isn't Key West a lovely place? Perhaps a little insular if one lives there for half the year, like many of our friends . . . but ideal for a shorter visit. I hope that you had a chance to visit Hemingway's old house, and see the numerous beautiful cats.

Thanks so much for your comments on *The Tattooed Girl*. Somehow, I feel that people will not "like" this novel, overall . . . the subject is so relatively grim. (Though we live in grim times.) . . .

The Gravedigger's Daughter is nowhere near finished. I think of a remark Philip Roth made about the new novel he's writing, which is one of his longest novels already, and nowhere near finished—"I would like to work on this the rest of my life" . . .

Much affection,
Joyce

3 May 2003

Dear Greg,

. . . *The Gravedigger's Daughter* is moving with frustrating slowness, already at page 520 and the end quite a few chapters away. My grandmother Blanche Woodside gazes upon me at this desk, in that lovely, somehow melancholy photograph which you reprinted in the biography, which is propped up nearby. By this time in the novel, the protagonist has grown far from what my grandmother might ever have been, or would have wished to be. I have not written a short story in a very long time, so absorbed in this quixotic project. You asked about *The Falls*. I did put it away for over a year, revised it and sent it out; now Dan Halpern is reading it. More recently, I wrote a novella set also in Niagara Falls titled *Rape: A Love Story*, which Otto Penzler will publish under his imprint at Carrol & Graff. (Niagara Falls seems to have displaced Lockport . . .)

Much affection as always,
Joyce

23 May 2003

Dear Greg,

Your very welcome letter and the novel about Sylvia Plath just arrived. A coincidence, I'd been intending to write to you this morning.

My mother died last night, in the Beechwood Nursing Home in Getzville, at about 8 p.m. Evidently she died in her sleep, it's believed of a stroke. My brother called this morning. There was no anticipation that this would occur though my mother had been, as I have probably told you, or suggested to you, no longer herself for some time. She did not recognize my brother Fred when he visited about once a week. The last time I saw her, some months ago, she seemed vaguely to recognize me and to remember my name . . . I recall my father saying how, beyond age 80, everything seemed to begin to go, and that was true for both my parents. Through their 70s, they were so remarkably vigorous and optimistic! We have to be grateful for that, I know. Many of my friends lost their parents years, even decades ago.

I've been spending the morning looking through snapshots of younger, happier times, and want to thank you again for bringing a good deal of interest and vitality into my parents' lives. You wrote with such understanding and compassion of their early lives . . .

There will be no funeral, since my mother's body, like my father's, was to be sent immediately to the University of Buffalo Medical School. This had been their wish, years ago. Such an abrupt ending!

I do feel stunned. Yet I suppose I will carry on with my more-or-less usual day today, returning to *The Gravedigger's Daughter*, another coincidence since it is of that "lost world" much of the novel revolves upon. Without *Invisible Writer*, those few pages devoted to my grandmother Blanche's early life, I doubt that I would have been galvanized to write this novel, so I must thank you . . .

Much affection,
Joyce

5 June 2003

Dear Greg,

Thanks so much for the elegantly written review. I had wanted to respond before now . . .

It has been a difficult time . . . Lucinda Franks/(Mrs. Bob Morgenthau) is arranging a small dinner for my birthday, in New York City, and Gloria Vanderbilt and a few others will be attending, so I look forward to that if not to the birthday per se. Gloria has been so very thoughtful, writing to me often since my mother's death, in a way that is altogether natural and sympathetic and yet "wise" in the deepest sense of the word. Edmund White has also been very thoughtful. And I'm grateful for your sympathy. When a person dies, it suddenly seems that the person's entire life becomes somehow "simultaneous": I don't so much think of the nursing home patient my mother had become since May 2000 (when my father died, and my mother immediately began to decline) so much as the vital, lively, warm and generous and unfailingly good-natured person she had always been prior to that.

More and more, my mother had lapsed into an inner world. I think it must have been very like the "twilight" that precedes sleep, or the semi-waking state as we rise toward consciousness. In that state, my mother's emotions were calm, on the whole benign; unlike my father, who was deeply unhappy, and angry, as a consequence of aging and illness. My father's consciousness was acute to nearly the very end of his life, before he had morphine injections (at the hospice); my mother's consciousness simply faded by degrees until finally she was rarely "awake" and one evening simply died in her sleep of a stroke. I keep thinking of them almost continuously . . .

Much affection,
Joyce

3 July 2003

Dear Greg,

Thanks so much for your last letter. It's very touching of you to be concerned. We continue to make discoveries about ourselves through our lives, but the discoveries that follow a parent's death are probably the most unexpected . . .

The other evening we had dinner with Steve Martin in his elegant but not pretentious large light-filled apartment overlooking Central Park West. He's a lovely person, oddly quiet in social situations, or at least not nearly so vocal as others. He showed us through the apartment to see his art: a large, immediately recognizable Hopper just inside the front door, another Hopper in the living room, a Francis Bacon on a nearby wall, and, facing the dining room table, the very same

Eric Fischl painting I'd chosen for the cover of the *Norton Book of Modern Fiction*. Eric Fischl & his wife April Gornik were both guests at the dinner, very interesting people . . .

I've been in a state of vast relief after completing *Gravedigger's Daughter*, an unexpected 650 pages (!). (Still, it isn't 1,400, like *Blonde*. That was true madness.) My reward now is a vacation of sorts: writing short stories, reviews, starting a new young adult novel, etc. As soon as I finished the novel my head was flooded with ideas & energy . . . As soon as I finished the revisions I put the manuscript away in a drawer to look at if I, and the world, are still here next summer.

(I kept thinking how I would love to share this novel with you & get your early opinion. You will recognize so many small "real" details amid so much that is invented. I would guess that this is the first time in the history of humankind that a novelist has been inspired by a page or two in her own biography to write a novel. The vision of my grandmother working in a factory was somehow captivating to me. So strange!)

Yes, I did take *The Falls* out of our fireproof drawer, at last. Dan seems to be enthusiastic about it so it will appear in Oct. 2004, which seems a very comfortable distance away.

Thanks for the comments on [the newly revised] *Garden of Earthly Delights*. That was the single most pleasurable writing experience I've ever had, & really much of the inspiration, too, for starting *Gravedigger's Daughter* since I found the revising so enthralling . . .

What an excellent review-essay of yours in *Georgia Review*! I note your rueful/comic remarks on the masochism of writing biographies . . .

Much affection,
Joyce

19 October 2003

Dear Greg,

I've been meaning to write to you for a long time, but as I accumulate more things to say, the task becomes ever more daunting! So I think I will simply plunge in if only briefly . . .

The young adult novel I'd been speaking of has been altered considerably, and is now quite short, 160 pages, titled *Sexy* and about a 16-year-old boy. It's amazing that, though my young adult books surely sell modestly compared to best sellers in the field, they do seem to outsell my so-called adult novels, when I give readings at least. The one book that will outsell everything, when I appear in bookstores, is *Where Is Little Reynard?* (If you want to know, Big Reynard is sleeping at this moment, purring contentedly without the slightest awareness that he has a somewhat false kitten image floating about in the world.) . . . My next children's book is the enigmatically titled *Naughty Cherie!* It is quite a pleasure to begin a novel at 10 a.m. & finish it by 6 p.m., with a long afternoon break, too . . .

Much love,
Joyce

10 January 2004

Dear Greg,

Happy New Year! It's good to hear from you, I've missed your newsy letters . . .

How was your holiday break? Ours was extremely enjoyable. We went to only a few parties, probably not more than five, but each was a special occasion (Christmas Day dinner with the Halperns, dinner at Ed White's before he & his partner left for Key West, New Year's Eve at Steve Martin's lovely art-filled apartment on Central Park West) and the rest of the time was spent in extreme quiet, revising my new novel, & finishing it at last. (In actual time, *Blood at the Root* didn't take quite four months; in the time I seem to have experienced, it took years. I wonder why this is????)

I seem to want to write novels now, despite the exhaustion. I wish that I could swerve into a short story mode, better yet a "miniature narrative" mode, but somehow I can't.

Your letter is so very brief. What are you working on? Stories? When is the story collection out from Johns Hopkins? I wonder what the cover art is . . .

Blood at the Root (title from the song "Strange Fruit") is a short novel of about 300 pages, to come before *The Grave-digger's Daughter* which is somehow too overwhelming to me, to publish next. I haven't even shown it to anyone. I think, superstitiously, that *The Gravedigger's Daughter* will be my final novel, at least my final ambitious novel . . .

At Steve Martin's, I had especially interesting conversations with Mike Nichols (who turns out to be surprisingly literary-minded, quite intellectual), my old friend Mary Karr (the quintessential bad girl, from Port Arthur, TX), the veteran *New Yorker* cartoonist Bruce McCall, who'd lived in Windsor as a youth, & other *New Yorker* writers & editors. I've probably told you that Steve is bookish & art-oriented, rather than theatrical in the usual sense; he majored in philosophy at UCLA (!) & one never gets over a philosophy major, I think. (Or a minor, either.) [Joyce had minored in philosophy at Syracuse University.] His abiding passion is collecting art, mostly of the 20th century.

I am very happy not to fly until Feb. 20 when I give a reading at Duke. Such a lovely reprieve! But the so-called spring semester will be daunting.

Ray, Reynard, Cherie & I wish you a warm & cozy New Year.

(Good news: *Naughty Cherie!* will appear as a Harper-

Collins children's book sometime in the probably-distant future. Now the cat books will be a trilogy, & all romans à clef.)

Much affection,
Joyce

28 February 2004

Dear Greg,

. . . I hope that things are well there in Atlanta, and that you're having a good semester, as I am, for the most part. After weeks of idyllic quiet, I am back to traveling again: next week to Buffalo, where I will be a "writer in residence" for a very full day, and have time for a quiet meal with my brother Fred and sister-in-law Nancy. Though we have not really that much in common, especially since our parents have died, I feel very close to my brother, who seems to me one of the most admirable, if reticent, people I know. I can't recall if you met Fred, perhaps not. I hope you didn't try to "interview" him, it would have been inordinately frustrating!

Blood at the Root . . . is about two college freshmen, a white girl and a black girl who room together in the early 1970s . . .

I've been in a strange ferocity of novel-writing since finishing *The Gravedigger's Daughter*. You will shake your head in disbelief if I mention that I've embarked upon yet another novel . . . titled *Missing Mom*. Frankly emotional, sentimental, an unapologetic "women's novel" about a woman missing her lately deceased mother, in various senses of the word "missing." (Yes, the mother is not unlike Carolina Oates. Though there is an almost wholly fictional plot.) . . .

I have not shown *The Gravedigger's Daughter* to anyone yet. A kind of coda or epilogue, a self-contained short story that brings the action of the novel to a conclusion some years later, will appear in *Harper's* under the title "The Cousins."

(The name "Hazel Kelly" appears in my novel, but now, Gloria Vanderbilt will be using that name in a novel she's writing, so I must change my character's name to something else.) (I don't mind, at all.) Gloria's memoir *It Seemed Important at the Time* will cause quite a stir, I think . . .

I'll be in your fabled city on June 4-5. Seems distant.

Edmund White is very well, concluding his tell-all memoir, a chapter of which appears in *OR*. Ray, noisily ripping open his daily stack of mail (ever more fiction submissions, as many as 12-15 a day now) in the other room, says hello & warm regards.

Though I'm not a dog owner, I have become quite a dog fancier, via Animal Planet. (Do you watch this cable channel?) Dachshunds are certainly very nice, & I think I would like fox terriers also. All the dog breeds seem to fascinate me, I don't know why.

Much affection,
Joyce

4 May 2004

Dear Greg,

You'd mentioned that you were sending your book of stories, but I have not yet received it; I've been waiting for it, before replying to your two very welcome letters. Sorry to be so belated. I really have no excuse since I am forever starting letters in my head, "Dear Greg . . ." at inopportune times like running outdoors or preparing dinner! . . .

I'm afraid that I haven't been writing to many people lately at all. Only just Gloria Vanderbilt who has become a kind of unexpected pen pal. Gloria is very literary, in the way that Jeanne Moreau is literary; though the world sees these fascinating women in very different guises . . .

I'm deeply immersed in the perhaps-misbegotten *Missing Mom*. I'd hoped that it would be relatively short but already it is moving toward p. 300 & no end in sight . . .

Will you be in NYC this month? . . . Ray won't be coming with me to Atlanta, but I'm sure that I would be free to see you. I don't have my schedule yet but the evening of June 5 looks open. "Mythic Journeys" is the somewhat quixotic subject. My last conference was the recent "Faith and Writing" at Calvin College which was very interesting. Surprising to meet a graduate student of yours, so far from Georgia. She says you are "terrific" as a teacher which we always knew . . .

Much affection,
Joyce

16 May 2004

Dear Greg,

I've just returned from a trip, and had the pleasure of reading *Last Encounter with the Enemy* nonstop. Congratulations on a beautifully crafted, imaginative, and moving collection of stories. I'd read quite a few of these, and quite enjoyed rereading such idiosyncratic achievements as "Double Exposure," "First Surmise," and the tour de force title story. (Flannery O'Connor would have been impressed with this if not quite dumfounded.) . . .

Two days' rest, then I fly off to Minnesota for two days, & then return to Princeton & to Washington, DC, for a play reading (*The Tattooed Girl,* which will be performed in January . . .). I look forward to seeing you in early June though I've heard horror stories of the Atlanta airport . . .

Much affection,
Joyce

6 June 2004

Dear Greg,

It was lovely to see you two days in a row in Atlanta. Our evening at N'an [a Thai restaurant] with Dedrick was terrific. Again, thanks so much. You are a most thoughtful friend, and it was a pleasure to get together after some time. (Sorry to have not met your dogs.)

Amidst esoteric yoga practitioners, New Age therapists and artists, devotees of Joseph Campbell, musicians and drummers, Galway Kinnell and I did feel somewhat isolated, like specimens of a near-to-extinct species. Only Robert Bly seems to have bridged the gap between the literary and the "esoteric," mostly by way of having joined up with some musicians . . .

It's thrilling to be back home, with a prospect of no airplane travel until mid-October. Amazing! . . .

Much love,
Joyce

10 July 2004

Dear Greg,

I hope that you'll be having a most enjoyable birthday . . .

It isn't exactly true that I am "between novels." Now that I have finished *Missing Mom*, I've gone back to revise sections of *Blood at the Root*, which will probably be published in fall 2005. I haven't been able to allow myself quite yet to miss *Missing Mom* and hope to stay busy for as long as possible in this other, very practical & intensely engaging task . . .

Each time the HarperCollins publicist calls with exciting new ideas & invitations, my heart sinks at the prospect of the summer coming to an end. (I'm sure that I have said this

1,500 times. It occurs to me that every schoolchild feels exactly the same way.)

Did I mention how much I've admired Colm Tóibín's *The Master*? Perhaps you have to take Henry James very seriously & to be thrilled by incursions of the "real world" into his imagination, ghostly foreshadowings of certain of his novels into his life. Tóibín doesn't imitate James's language but has found a convincingly dreamlike & meditative voice for him . . .

Much affection—
Joyce

4 August 2004

Dear Greg,

We had dinner with Gloria Vanderbilt and other friends last night in NYC, and Gloria expressed another time admiration for your "Virginia Woolf" story and hopes that someday she can meet you. I'm wondering if you might wish to send her your short story collection . . .

Next time you visit NYC, I will be sure to arrange for a visit to Gloria's studio, which you'll very much enjoy, I think. We were there yesterday evening looking at her new collages, quite different in technique from her Dream Boxes . . .

(Did you receive the special dog treats I'd sent for your birthday? I hope that your little dachshunds enjoyed them.)

Another highlight of our recent trip was a visit to East Boothbay, ME, to the gorgeous Oceanside home of Richard & Kristina Ford where we spent one night. If you read last week's *New Yorker* story by Richard, you were actually reading an excerpt from his novel-in-progress, the last of the Frank Bascomb trilogy. Richard's fictional character Frank—affable, garrulous, unexcitable, forgiving—is the very antithesis of Richard himself, in a startling variant of the more familiar phenomenon of meek writer/"dark" protagonist.

Much affection,
Joyce

14 September 2004

Dear Greg,

Just a quick note to thank you, as usual, for your thoughtfulness. I am about to be whisked away to NYC for a day of . . . well, impersonating "JCO." (Edmund White & I are considering swapping literary identities, for a change of pace.) Classes have begun at Princeton with the usual hectic concentration of activities. My Washington, DC, play reading of *The Tattooed Girl* went exceptionally well. If only DC weren't so far away from Atlanta, I would love for you & Dedrick to be guests at the opening in January.

Dan Halpern is hurt & angry that the upcoming review in the *New York Times* of *The Falls* was assigned to a film critic. He is friendly with the new editor at the *Review*, Sam Tanenhaus, & feels betrayed. Ugly caricature of me.

(If only I'd begun writing under a pseudonym, or pseudonyms, decades ago! And now it is too late.)

Let me know how you are, I miss hearing from you. Still recall our Atlanta dinner with much pleasure. What fun you & Dedrick are together!

Much affection,
Joyce

6 October 2004

Dear Greg,

Thanks for the letter . . . "What am I working on these

days?"—a painful question. I am trying almost desperately to work on *The Stolen Heart*, a Lauren Kelly novella, but it isn't going very well at all. My life seems to be coming apart. [Joyce was in the midst of a grueling publicity tour for *The Falls*, while teaching and writing, as usual.] I feel like an animal with a leg in a trap, who has the option of gnawing off the leg and hobbling away to survive, or not. I am thinking that if I can just get through the next six weeks or so, I will be all right. (After years of relative quiet, the Nobel Prize rumors and buzzing are very distracting this year, with foreign journalists calling already (!), and my sense of déjà vu/irony rising up in waves to further distract me from whatever it is I am trying to do . . .) I know, these problems are hardly fatal, or even serious, more like large flies buzzing about one's head, very distracting in a seriocomic way. By Thursday, the Nobel rumors at least will have blown past. I am sure that whoever receives the award will be very worthy, and probably a name of which I have never heard . . .

Many thanks for the commentary on *Uncensored* [her forthcoming book of essays and reviews], and your plans for the Gender Studies course which sounds intriguing. *Blonde* is the novel people often ask me about, overall.

Much affection,
Joyce

15 October 2004
Dear Greg,

Thanks so much for the corrections and suggestions [for the *Uncensored* galley, which had been riddled with errors], which are much appreciated . . . I don't seem able to calibrate at what point I should simply give up and become resigned, rather than continue to struggle with these matters . . . Sometimes it does seem totally quixotic, futile.

Of course you're right, a sane person would cancel out on some of these commitments. Maybe, if I become really exhausted, and if the dreaded flu overtakes me, I will . . .

My problem is that my editor Dan Halpern is a friend of mine, and I'm reluctant to let him down, as I feel very reluctant to disappoint my lecture agent Janet Cosby. If I had a purely businesslike relationship with these people I would not do 1/10th of what I've agreed to do, especially this fall when everything seems to be caving in.

But these are trivial concerns, certainly! Nothing that has to do with books and the literary life is really of much significance, a fact we should keep in mind . . .

You're certainly a wonderful friend, to have gone to so much trouble for me. Thanks enormously . . .

The most surprising development of recent months is that Dan Halpern wants to publish *Missing Mom*, which I had not even wanted him to see since it's a "woman's novel" and not what Ecco Press usually publishes. I had anticipated publishing it under a pseudonym with a woman editor at another publisher. I had not thought that Dan would be able to read through the first chapter. The novel is a sort of genre experiment in short, simple sentences, a restricted vocabulary and a tone of forthright, sometimes comic directness with NOT A TRACE OF IRONY.

Much affection, and, again—*thanks!*
Joyce

29 November 2004

Dear Greg,

. . . I hope that you had a very nice Thanksgiving and are beginning to recover from the disappointment of election day (though the country, and the world, aren't likely to recover for a long time). Our Thanksgiving was with friends whom you don't know, mostly, a very fine evening except there was the usual talk of politics, at least two people drank too much and were annoyingly garrulous and belligerent, which is really not at all typical of Princeton in my experience at least.

So interesting that you've come to like Ruth Rendell! I have never met this amazing woman/writer, but much of her writing is very, very good. She was generous in giving Rosamond Smith a wonderful quote some years ago. Her Barbara Vine novels in particular are richly atmospheric.

By now you're nearly finished with your fall term. Since I will be on sabbatical, too, next semester, I can appreciate your sense of closure about now . . . Since the start of the "book tour" for *The Falls*, to my last engagement in 2004 on Dec. 6, I will have done twenty-seven talks, readings, visits in various parts of the country, most recently in Boston . . . Not all of these involved airplane flights, fortunately . . .

Finally, after what seemed like a very long time, I completed *The Stolen Heart*. A kind of mosaic, or crazy quilt, written piecemeal in desperate lunges in the rears of cars headed to & from airports, in airports & in airplanes, in hotel rooms while awaiting late-evening room service dinners, and stitched together when I arrived home to a typewriter . . . (Still, there is the admirable precedent of Emily Dickinson, who allegedly jotted down poetry fragments on scraps of paper to stick into her apron pockets and put together later in the privacy of her room.) . . .

Much affection,
Joyce

Part Six

2005–2006

In 2005 and after, Joyce was occupied in a wide range of projects, as usual. Several novels, a book of short stories that did surprising "takes" on major writers such as Emily Dickinson, Henry James, and Ernest Hemingway—later collected under the title Wild Nights!*—and the usual complement of essays and reviews took up most of her time. Added to these projects was a considerable amount of travel.*

Around this time, our correspondence changed from letters and faxes to that now-universal form of communication, email. As a result, our "letters" became more frequent but also much briefer and probably, to an outside reader, less engaging than the long letters we exchanged in the 1980s and 1990s. Thus this selection of our correspondence, for the purposes of this book, ends with this section.

22 January 2005

Dear Greg,

Yesterday I returned from Columbia, South Carolina, in just the nick of time, for today there is a virtual white-out in our part of the country. Fine-sifting snow that has accelerated to a blizzard and will continue for hours . . .

In Columbia, at the university, I was the 2005 recipient of the Thomas Cooper Award (for literature) and the first woman in the history of this venerable honor. I'm mentioning this because, as the citation was read, and some remarks made about my writing, the speaker drew upon Greg Johnson at considerable length. It wasn't just a brief passage, it went on and on (from *Understanding JCO* [my 1987 critical study]). When I received the medallion (so heavy, it couldn't be lowered over my head as they'd done with previous (male) recipients) I remarked what an honor it was to be named "one of the boys at last." This was greeted with genial laughter all around.

(Next day, returning through airport security, I was stopped and examined on account of the suspicious "round object" that showed up on the X-ray machine, the truculent likeness of Mr. Cooper.) . . .

Warm regards & much affection to Dedrick, also. Hope you both are well.

Joyce

2 April 2005

Dear Greg,

. . . Wonderful that your textbooks are so successful! G, G, & L [i.e., Greg, Gracie & Lucy] would be a logical name for your corporation, don't you think?

Yesterday at the university Joan Didion gave an excellent talk: "The Personal and the Political." I had not seen Joan in several years, and was shaken by how she has aged, and how frail she is; though of course Joan has always been extremely petite, probably weighing about 85 pounds. Yet, when she began to speak, barely visible behind the podium, she was sharp, acerbic, fact-filled, ironic and even tough-talking in the way (as a colleague commented) of a newspaper reporter in a 1940s film. I was touched that Joan spoke of my writing admiringly, as concerned with politics, particularly "class" in America which of course is probably my most obsessive theme.

A misadventure the other day, in NYC where I was one of twenty-two (22!) hapless readers who'd agreed, in moments of ill-conceived altruism, or lapses of common sense, to give a public reading for the Guggenheim Foundation. The idea would have been fine except the new executive director Ed Hirsch . . . seemed to have lost control and not only invited too many of us, but several of us (notoriously, Shirley Hazzard, an older woman whose gracious, patrician manner masks a raging egotism and indifference to others' suffering) who, known never to read within time constraints, shouldn't have been invited at all. (We were each to read for no more than five minutes but Shirley Hazzard, amazingly, read for about twenty minutes, at a time when the program was already very behind schedule.) I don't know why I do these things, and Ray certainly doesn't know why, either. To paraphrase Gloria Vanderbilt's title, "It seemed like a good idea at the time" . . .

Of the literary prose forms, the "blessed novella" (James's famous definition) is the most difficult, at least for me. I seem to have an imagination bent upon enhancing, "developing," investigating alternate points of view, not ideal for novellas which should move through choppy water like sailboats, not ships or barges. The novella requires a sleight-of-hand technique, to suggest more than the writer is going to spell out clearly, while the novel is such a large, loose form, it can accommodate any number of approaches. I am trying to work out a novella now, and have enough notes already for a novel, which is discouraging . . .

Much affection,
Joyce

13 July 2005
Dear Greg,
. . . I finally finished my lengthy Cormac McCarthy review for *New York Review* and have told Barbara Epstein that I am now going on a small sabbatical. It was an exasperating experience to be taking so much time for what is, in essence, just a review at which most readers will only glance, if they don't simply turn the page. And I'm sure that McCarthy doesn't read his reviews. (Dan Halpern, who'd been his

editor some years ago, says that Cormac will not change even a punctuation mark in his manuscripts. He takes no editorial suggestions whatever, and it shows.)

However, McCarthy is undeniably a "major" writer. He has written some truly remarkable things . . .

The interim between emotionally draining novels seems to be taken up now, in my writing life, by young adult fiction, Lauren Kelly pseudonym novels, and lengthy review-essays for *New York Review*. A few years ago, I tended to write poetry at such times, and plays; for some reason, I seem to have shifted interests, at least temporarily. The response is so much more evident, the entire writing experience so much more engaging, I'm afraid, than the writing of poetry is.

Ecco has scheduled *Blood Mask* [a Lauren Kelly novel] for summer 2006. In fall 2006, the novel formerly titled *Blood at the Root*, now titled *Black Girl/White Girl*, will probably appear. In the spring, *High Lonesome: Selected Stories, 1966–2006*. At some point, *Naughty Cherie!* is supposed to appear, but I don't have any date and have become resigned to the astonishing slowness of children's book publication . . .

Happy birthday! And give Dedrick my warmest regards.

(I'm sure I don't know, either, what any of us would do without our closest friends and companions, both two- and four-footed.) . . .

Much love,
Joyce

14 November 2005

Dear Greg,

. . . Paris was exquisite, though our days were extremely crowded. [Joyce had recently won the Prix Femina for her novel *The Falls*.] (Two days in Paris! Of which only about three hours one afternoon were free for me to walk along the Seine, to visit the Musée d'Orsay, and other famous sights. Otherwise, I was involved in ceremonial matters, like the presentation of the Prix Femina at the fabled Hotel Crillon, being photographed & interviewed (it's something of a shock, that French journalists take literary matters so very seriously, flattering but perhaps also somewhat overwhelming) . . . I would not have made such a sudden trip, in the midst of so much else, except Dan Halpern suggested that it would be "insulting" if I didn't appear for the award, and Ray was wonderfully supportive and enthusiastic . . .

Gloria Vanderbilt, always unpredictable, has embarked upon a new project: painting small, impressionistic "portraits" of me. I'm sure that the more impressionistic, least realistic, will be the most attractive. The two I have seen so far are fascinating . . .

Gloria has recently acquired an exquisitely beautiful, magically charming Russian blue kitten, named Sasha Blue. You would swear that this cobalt-blue-eyed kitten is some emanation of Gloria's soul.

Much love,
Joyce

17 December 2005

Dear Greg,

. . . You've asked what I am working on, and I guess it's a novel though I had wished for a long time that it might be a novella, for Otto Penzler's novella series. But already the material has grown to beyond 150 pages, and the end is distant. I wish that I could somehow program myself to write what Henry James aptly called the "blessed novella." Probably it will be a Lauren Kelly novel, titled *Suspects*.

Also, I am beginning to revisit *The Gravedigger's Daughter*, and to do some revisions. It has been a lengthy cooling-off period for this novel that was, at one time, utterly gripping and exhausting, and seemed to crowd out everything else from my brain like a very large package stuffed into a small space. I will probably deliver the manuscript to John Hawkins in the spring. I'm sure that this will be my last "ambitious"—or, anyway, "long"—novel, but by the time it appears, perhaps fall 2007, I will be emotionally removed from it, I hope.

I hope that your Christmas will be delightful and that you'll manage to avoid holiday stress.

Much affection—
Joyce

23 December 2005
Dear Greg,

. . . By now, maybe you've heard from John Hawkins? John wants to oversee the journal project himself, rather than assign it to Warren Frazier. I hadn't realized that you have the journals photocopied. [I was beginning work on a selected edition of Joyce's journals.] . . .

Your reviews are very engaging. It's certainly true that Harold Bloom "hyperventilates." (Have you ever seen him? He is massive, perspiring, a living caricature of pedantic self-absorption.) . . .

These lovely mostly quiet days! We are seeing friends every two or three evenings but the rest of the time is given over to work and reading. It's been very sunny—and cold—and so our house is flooded with light through the day. I've been working on a suspense novel (I think) and going through *The Gravedigger's Daughter* and doing some revisions. A long novel is a massive chunk of granite to be chiseled into some sort of shape! You can say that the effort requires inspiration, or audacity, or talent, but what it mainly requires is time . . .

Much affection,
Joyce

5 January 2006

Dear Greg,

Happy New Year, belatedly. Perhaps 2006 will be an improvement over 2005, politically and morally. (How could it be otherwise?) . . .

We did have a lovely time at Steve Martin's New Year's Eve party which was somewhat larger and more gregarious than usual. Steve played banjo with an old high school friend . . . the high point of the evening . . . The occasion ended on a jarring note, however, when it was discovered that a woman guest's full-length mink coat had been stolen, plus another guest's fur hat, and a handbag. There were numerous caterer's assistants and servers at the party, much movement in and out of the hall, two entrances to Steve's apartment since he had acquired a second, adjacent apartment on the 11th floor of the [apartment building].

(I don't want to sound like a prudish, punitive Animal Rights sort of person, but the first thought that came to me, unuttered, was that it's hard to sympathize with someone's "loss" of a full-length mink coat.)

We did see *Brokeback Mountain* and thought that it was unusually "writerly": unhurried, thoughtful, beautifully nuanced, powerful and moving without being sentimental. Extraordinary performances by both male actors . . .

Thanks for your advance reports on *High Lonesome*! You are the first to read these stories as a collection. I guess now that I am not so dubious about the publication, though still there is something about its very heft that causes me to shrink and cringe . . .

Much affection,
Joyce

1 February 2006

Dear Greg,

Thanks for the packet of material! Your "proposal" is wonderfully well written and decisive. I think my problem with presenting myself as a journal writer is simply that I don't have the first coherent or faintly interesting thing to say about myself. Yet, you say these things with such confidence!

I took a deep breath and glanced through, skimmed through, many of the journal entries. I guess it isn't so bad as I had anticipated . . . I do remember, quite vividly, many of these passages. (Stanley Elkin mimicking riding back and forth over the grave of his dear friend Bob Coover in his wheelchair, for instance, I can see clearly; I must remember that Stanley's priority was, like Lenny Bruce, to shock and to amuse, and not to be "nice," which somewhat alienated him from me, as from others.) . . .

I've written a story in which Emily Dickinson appears in a transmogrified state as a computer-generated manikin to be manufactured and sold to consumers for household use . . . which will appear in a special issue of *Virginia Quarterly Review* devoted to fiction that involves "real, historic" writers in some way. Michael Chabon is the guest editor . . .

Many thanks!
Joyce

Valentine's Day 2006

Dear Greg,

This is only just a quick note. I've been on the phone with Dan Halpern and he has been saying the most unexpected, extraordinary things about the journal, and about you. He is extremely enthusiastic about the project, saying "I'm blown away." (Not likely, considering Dan's size & density.) Unusual for Dan to go on at such length about a manuscript, yet he did, & I listened in astonishment. He thinks that you have written a first-rate preface and is very impressed with your work. (I'm always impressed with your intelligence and prose, but not so surprised by now.) Neither Dan nor I thinks that 600 pages will work, though; perhaps more like 300.

Did I tell you about my experience at the Connecticut Forum two Saturdays ago, on a panel with Kurt Vonnegut? Kurt is so very droll, with heavy-lidded eyes like a turtle's, and something of a turtle's impassivity. There were 2,700 people in the audience, who'd bought tickets . . . Kurt would say, as he's surely said many times before, intoning like a Buddha/tortoise, "Humankind is a disease. We're like syphilis, we should be stamped out." The high school students stared & took notes. No one seemed to think that Vonnegut might not be entirely serious . . . At the evening's event in an enormous theater in Hartford, he continued in this vein, oracular even when silly. Asked what was the meaning of the universe, Kurt said, "The meaning of the universe? Why ask me? I'm full of baloney." It was a very enjoyable/comical evening overall . . .

Thanks for such good work with the journals, and of course the *Conversations with Joyce Carol Oates*.

Much affection,
Joyce

17 February 2006

Dear Greg,

. . . Dan is reading *The Gravedigger's Daughter* more or less at the present time. I did complete *Sparta*, a fairly short novel, in a burst of "addictive" energy; now I am immersed in a not-very-pleasant descent into the last days of Ernest Hemingway's life in Ketchum, Idaho, in July 1961 . . .

Ray loved the "Preface" [to *Conversations with Joyce Carol Oates*]. I thought perhaps he'd told you.

Very cold here, despite global warming. So you Southerners love your rare "snow days." Oh, my . . .

Much affection,
Joyce

14 March 2006

Dear Greg,

Thanks for your birthday greeting for Ray. We had a lovely day—absolutely quiet. (Except for the frogs, newly awakened, who are singing robustly down at our pond, and numerous spring birds. Today is sunny and gusty with near gale-force winds.) . . .

Yes, "Papa at Ketchum, 1961" is almost entirely fictional, though laced with facts from Hemingway's life. It is far too long at 40 pages, unfortunately.

Now I am working on the last months of Henry James's life, a much more magnanimous and exhilarating life, surprisingly: "The Master at St. Bartholomew's Hospital, 1914–1916." What will come of these experimental ventures, I have no idea. [They would be collected in a volume entitled *Wild Nights!*] . . .

Gloria is in deep mourning for her old, very old and very devoted friend/lover/confidant Gordon Parks who died last week at 92. What a striking couple they must have been, for decades! ...

Much affection,
Joyce

27 March 2006

Dear Greg,

   ... Thanks for editing these journals so very well! One thing that I have actually learned from reading them is a remark somewhere that I'd told my students to keep journals, to record details, and out of details some sort of "meaning" will emerge. This is not bad advice which I can use at the present time, researching the emotionally tumultuous but disjointed years of Samuel Clemens/Mark Twain ...

   The final years of Clemens's life are sad, poignant. As perhaps you know, Clemens became quite obsessed with young girls—"I collect young girls," he reputedly said—of his granddaughters' age, had he had granddaughters. Some of the photos of Clemens with these girls show quite mature-looking girls, indeed! His own daughter Clara was very embarrassed & annoyed, as one might expect. All of his emotional life seemed to be channeled into his "angelfish" & yet he was capable of simply dropping a girl when she turned 16. What to make of this! All my ideas are scattered across this desktop ...

Much affection,
Joyce

21 April 2006

Dear Greg,

   It will be exciting planning *Women I've Known* [my collection of "new and selected" stories which Joyce and Ray would publish in 2007]. I have already begun casting about for a possible cover. Klimt is wonderful of course, but some of the images, like the one used for *Solstice* in hardcover, have been used frequently. We will be seeing Gloria on Sunday and will tell her about the project. Her new series of paintings is astonishing: rich, vivid colors, dreamlike shapes and an unfailing painterly touch. There are several impressionistic portraits of me of which you've seen one. Another, "Joyce at Work," has a snarled face which is certainly appropriate . . .

This journal has left me quite nostalgic for the days in which Susan Sontag and I had actually, almost, been friends; though for a long time friendly, our relationship never went beyond that. Perhaps because I'd never been with Susan alone; nor did I confide in her in any intimate way, which Susan seemed to have invited, as evidently she did with others. And we rarely, in fact never, see the Updikes any longer, though John has casually invited us to visit them in Beverly Farms, on our summer trips. (When we might have visited the Updikes, we visited the Fords instead, in Boothbay, Maine.) . . .

I've completed the far-too-long story titled "Grandpa Clemens & Angelfish 1906," which is the last in the deranged series of stories about writers. The strain of condensing so much biographical material into so relatively small a space is considerable; I don't intend to write any more of these.

Yesterday & today Dave Eggers was visiting us, gave an excellent—and jammed—public reading & spent an hour in my workshop this afternoon answering students' questions in the warmest, least pretentious ways. *A Heartbreaking Work of Staggering Genius* is the youth title to end all youth titles.

Much affection,
Joyce

25 July 2006

Dear Greg,

. . . My lengthy (50-page) story "Grandpa Clemens & Angelfish" will be published in this fall's *McSweeney's*. I can't recall if you have ever seen this quirky, very original "magazine" that sometimes appears in hardcover and has an amazingly high circulation for a literary publication, something like 30,000 copies per issue.

Will write again when we return from upstate NY. We'll be going to Niagara-on-the-Lake with my brother Fred and sister-in-law Nancy on Saturday, to see two Chekhov plays. Our Saratoga Springs visit should be enjoyable as usual . . .

I'm reading & rereading much of Margaret Atwood, as probably I have mentioned. Did you ever read *Oryx & Crake*? Very ambitious, very well done though "postapocalyptic" science fiction, which is difficult to make original.

Much affection,
Joyce

7 August 2006

Dear Greg,

Our upstate New York visit went, on the whole, very well, though we did drive considerable distances and, as usual, crammed too much driving into the final day, more than eight hours (!).

My 50th high school anniversary reunion was surprisingly enjoyable, rather like a Princeton-type gathering of older individuals . . . Among the admirable individuals in the 1956 Williamsville High senior class is Stephen Lewis, a respected long-term president of Carleton College. I was touched when one of the class bad-boys, who'd stayed in the area to live, came up to me to say how he'd swum at the same health club pool that my parents had swum at for many years: "I loved your mom and dad, Joyce. I miss them" . . .

Both Fred & Nancy are in very good spirits. Fred is doing very well as a draughtsman—mechanical engineering via the computer. Yet he says that he has only a fraction of our father's "talent" for tool design. In that instant I felt that I scarcely knew my father at all, I mean in his professional work . . .

At the NY State Writers Institute, Russell Banks read one evening & I read the next, to quite enthusiastic audiences. Do you know the work of Amy Hempel?—a lovely woman, and a brilliant miniaturist in prose. Henri Cole is an excellent poet, also on the faculty. On our way up, we took Gail Godwin to lunch, & had a lovely visit with Gail as well. If only Gail lived closer to us, we would see her often . . .

I've recently begun, with excruciating slowness, a new novel, a first-person "confession" with the tabloid title *My Sister, My Love: The Intimate Story of Skyler Rampike*. It is intended to be less intense/exhausting than previous novels, but so far hasn't been. The usual story! . . .

(Gloria Vanderbilt recently returned from a Capri vacation. Imagine watching your son Anderson Cooper on CNN, in a flak jacket & helmet, practically dodging Hezbollah rockets.)

Much affection,
Joyce

November 21, 2006
Dear Greg,

How wonderful to see you and Dedrick looking so well. [We had met Joyce and Ray at Gloria Vanderbilt's art exhibit opening in New York.] (How was *Grey Gardens*?)

I'm glad that I could introduce you to a few NYC people like Ben Brantley (so very nice in person, so terrifying as a reviewer), soft-spoken/diminutive Anderson Cooper, Amy Hempel and others. As I'd mentioned, it was somewhat comical to those of us who'd seen *The Sopranos* for several seasons to observe the menacing Michael Imperioli—that's to say, Christopher Moltisanti—mingling so readily with Gloria's genteel guests. Evidently not many of them watch HBO, and in fact Ray & I no longer do, having lost interest in *The Sopranos* two years ago . . .

Thanks for the drinks in that cozy yet elegant New York steakhouse setting. I hope that 46th St. after the (very long) play worked out well . . .

Much affection,
Joyce

26 December 2006

Dear Greg,

. . . No, I am nowhere near finishing my novel! It was only begun in late August, with many interruptions. It has been evolving in an entirely different direction, as usual becoming longer (!—the bane of my existence) & more complicated/paradoxical. I've been impatient with its progress, or lack of, but have tried to console myself: no one is eagerly awaiting this!

We'll be going to Steve Martin's small (about 30 people) elegant New Year's Eve party in NYC and a New Year's Day brunch here in Princeton but will otherwise be fairly quiet over the long holiday. On Jan. 10, we fly to Key West for five days which will surely seem a day or two too long by the time we leave . . .

Much affection,
Joyce

It should be added here that some dramatic life events, both positive and negative, would occur in the coming years. Joyce's beloved husband Raymond J. Smith passed away after a brief, sudden illness in February 2008; the couple had been married for forty-seven years. But in August of that same year, Joyce met a distinguished Princeton professor of neuroscience, Charlie Gross, who would soon become her second husband. I attended Joyce and Charlie's "wedding celebration" at their newly purchased home in Princeton; the guests included her longtime colleague Elaine Showalter, the novelist Richard Ford, and actor Steve Martin, among dozens of others.

While Ray, an editor and scholar, had been relatively quiet and book-oriented, Charlie became a dynamic presence in Joyce's life, encouraging her to accompany him on his worldwide travels. Later, in a typical email, Joyce reported to me that "Charlie is very very busy—he's a neuroscientist who often gives talks & papers at conferences—some of them far-flung in China, India, Africa—he would like me to accompany him & I have been doing so, in a limited—i.e., European—way" (August 20, 2010).

But after a protracted battle with cancer, Charlie too passed away, and Joyce's work of the ensuing years not only included reminiscences of her life with Charlie but also a good deal of fiction that dramatized themes of illness and mortality. More recently, Joyce's good friends Gloria Vanderbilt and Bob Phillips also died, so it's not surprising that Joyce's later emails took on a tone of sadness and resignation.

Through the vicissitudes of her life, however, she never flagged in her dedication to her work, and her emails continued to inform me of her current projects. During this period *she began sending me new stories and novels as soon as they were completed, and I would provide her with detailed commentary. This kind of exchange became, in fact, from the late 2000s to the present day, a staple of our ongoing correspondence.*

What remains consistent in her letters and emails is her generosity of spirit, her astonishing energy, and her never-flagging eloquence in whatever form of correspondence she undertakes, from the briefest emails to the longest letters. Not only in her correspondence addressed to me, but in that sent to people like John Updike, Gail Godwin, Bob Phillips, Gloria Vanderbilt, and countless others, she has certainly become one of the great letter writers of our time.

Also available from Akashic Books, edited by Joyce Carol Oates

A DARKER SHADE OF NOIR
NEW STORIES OF BODY HORROR BY WOMEN WRITERS
EDITED BY JOYCE CAROL OATES
FEATURING STORIES BY: Margaret Atwood, Tananarive Due, Joyce Carol Oates, Megan Abbott, Raven Leilani, Aimee Bender, Lisa Lim, Cassandra Khaw, Elizabeth Hand, Valerie Martin, Sheila Kohler, Joanna Margaret, Lisa Tuttle, Aimee LaBrie, and Yumi Dineen Shiroma.

"Cloaked in these stories are themes of powerlessness and loss of identity . . . *A Darker Shade of Noir* will appeal to a variety of readers, especially fans of gothic horror and supernatural authors like Brian Evenson and Shirley Jackson." —*Washington City Paper*

"From Tananarive Due's unnerving tale of a grieving granddaughter who can't stop dancing to Margaret Atwood's amusing story of a snail reincarnated into the adult body of a bank service representative . . . [T]hese fifteen stories evoke all the weird ways in which strange bodies can make us shiver and heave." —*Bust*

CUTTING EDGE
NEW STORIES OF MYSTERY AND CRIME BY WOMEN WRITERS
EDITED BY JOYCE CAROL OATES

Includes the Edgar Award–winning story
"One of These Nights" by Livia Llewellyn

FEATURING ORIGINAL WORK BY: Joyce Carol Oates, Margaret Atwood (poems), Valerie Martin, Aimee Bender, Edwidge Danticat, Sheila Kohler, S.A. Solomon, S.J. Rozan, Lucy Taylor, Cassandra Khaw, Bernice L. McFadden, Jennifer Morales, Elizabeth McCracken, Livia Llewellyn, Lisa Lim, and Steph Cha.

"Oates's stellar anthology of female noir . . . is an inclusive homage to the female/feminist perspective . . . Taken as a whole, the collection is a surreal yet satisfying journey into the darker side of the female consciousness, a book that, for all its murk and mayhem, celebrates feminine strength, cunning, and determination." —*Booklist*

PRISON NOIR
EDITED BY JOYCE CAROL OATES
FEATURING BRAND-NEW STORIES BY: Christopher M. Stephen, Sin Soracco, Scott Gutches, Eric Boyd, Ali F. Sareini, Stephen Geez, B.M. Dolarman, Zeke Caligiuri, Marco Verdoni, Kenneth R. Brydon, Linda Michelle Marquardt, Andre White, Timothy Pauley, Bryan K. Palmer, and William Van Poyck.

"Reading the fifteen stories in *Prison Noir* is a sobering experience. Unlike most claimants to that much-abused term, this is the real thing . . . The power of this collection comes from the voices of these authors, voices suffused with rage, despair, and madness."
—*New York Times Book Review*

"These are stories that resonate with authenticity and verve and pain and truth. Any collection edited by the National Book Award–winning author Oates deserves attention, but the contributors are deft and confident, and great writers without her imprimatur. . . . Authentic, powerful, visceral, moving, great writing."
—*Library Journal,* starred review

NEW JERSEY NOIR
EDITED BY JOYCE CAROL OATES
FEATURING BRAND-NEW WORK BY: Joyce Carol Oates, Jonathan Safran Foer, Robert Pinsky, Edmund White & Michael Carroll, Richard Burgin, Paul Muldoon, Sheila Kohler, C.K. Williams, Gerald Stern, Lou Manfredo, S.A. Solomon, Bradford Morrow, Jonathan Santlofer, Jeffrey Ford, S.J. Rozan, Barry N. Malzberg & Bill Pronzini, Hirsh Sawhney, and Robert Arellano.

"It was inevitable that this fine noir series would reach New Jersey. It took longer than some readers might have wanted, but, oh boy, was it worth the wait."
—*Booklist,* starred review